Non dilexerunt animam suam usque ad mortem.

The Latin, *Non dilexerunt animam suam usque ad mortem*,
translates, "... they loved not their lives unto the death." Revelation 12:11

On The Cover: *Massacres at Salzburg* took place in 1528 when
Prince-Archbishop Cardinal Matthaus Lang of Salzburg issued
mandates sending police in search of Anabaptists. Many were
captured and killed. This engraving illustrates the sufferings and
sacrifices these Dissenters endured when their government, in
conjunction with established religion, attempted to coerce and
impose uniformity of religious belief. Hence, this picture is a
reminder of the cost of religious liberty and the ever-present need
to maintain the separation of church and state. We use this art to
represent our Dissent and Nonconformity Series.

THE REFORMERS

and Their

STEPCHILDREN

LEONARD VERDUIN
1897-1999

THE REFORMERS

and Their

STEPCHILDREN

---

by

LEONARD VERDUIN

Grand Rapids
Wm. B. Eerdmans Pub. Co.
1964

he Baptist Standard Bearer, Inc.

NUMBER ONE IRON OAKS DRIVE • PARIS, ARKANSAS 72855

Thou hast given a *standard* to them that fear thee;
that it may be displayed because of the truth.
-- *Psalm 60:4*

*Reprinted
by*

THE BAPTIST STANDARD BEARER, INC.

No. 1 Iron Oaks Drive
Paris, Arkansas 72855
(501) 963-3831

THE WALDENSIAN EMBLEM
lux lucet in tenebris
"The Light Shineth in the Darkness"

ISBN #1-57978-935-8

To my wife
Hattie
without whom this book
could not have happened.

Foreword

With the popularization of the distinction between "church" and "sect" — two misunderstandings of the Church derived from Ernst Troeltsch's *The Social Teaching of the Christian Churches* (American edition, 1931) — many Americans have fallen victim to the Constantinian view of the role of religion in human society. Any individual or group which raises the Biblical question of the integrity of the Gospel and the discipline of the community which confesses its power is here, as in old Christendom, immediately charged with "enthusiasm" (*Schwärmerei*) and "sectarianism." Nothing has contributed more to the failure of American Protestantism to achieve and maintain a sound self-understanding in recent years than fear of that fatal charge.

In this brilliant and extremely well-documented book, Mr. Verduin shows that there exists a permanent tension in sound Christian faith between the strengthening of the community of the elect unto holiness and the work of the Christian movement in baptizing and christianizing society. If this tension is broken in either direction, the proclamation is corrupted and the Church laid captive to unbaptized ends or to pride. The tragedy of the "magisterial Reformation" was that it continued a "sacralist" understanding of the relationship of Christ and culture. The tragedy of the "radical Reformation" was that, in good part as a result of savage persecution, it withdrew from the world for which Christ died.

This tension between two misunderstandings — of the Church as continuum and the Church as fortress — has continued to corrupt society, state, education, and sound religion in Europe. In America, however, the Constitutional achievement of religious liberty and voluntaryism makes possible a sounder view and practice of high religion and a healthier politics. Our problem is that we have for so long continued to draw our supplies

5

through a tunnel reaching back through four hundred years, without facing the fact that the situation of composite loyalties within which Christians here preach and work is utterly different from the entire Constantinian settlement.

To restate the problem involves in part a rehabilitation of the views of the radical Reformation, a rehabilitation now possible through the editing and publishing of long-suppressed documents. The pioneers of the Free Church are quite differently judged if we value compositism and voluntary church membership. To compel men by law to support and participate in religious exercises in which they have no faith is unworthy of Christians who put their trust in the Sword of the Spirit. Ultimately, of course, Truth is one. But the triumph of Truth, and the Lord of Truth, comes about through sound preaching, right practice of the sacramental life, and a sound exercise of voluntary discipline, *not* through coerced outward display of public piety.

Careful study of this book by pastors and in lay study groups will contribute greatly to sounder preaching, more loyal churchmanship, and a purer witness to the honor of the Name of Jesus Christ.

FRANKLIN H. LITTELL

Chicago Theological Seminary
September 1, 1964

Preface

In the Fall of 1963 the Calvin Foundation, with headquarters in Grand Rapids, Michigan, sponsored a series of lectures on the subject "The Reformers and Their Stepchildren." The contents of these lectures, somewhat amplified and reinforced with documentation, are herewith presented in printed form. It is the hope of the Calvin Foundation, of the publishers, and of the author, that in this way the lectures may serve a wider public and further that cause for which the Calvin Foundation exists.

It was the privilege of the author of these pages to spend the greater part of 1950 in Europe, under the terms of a Research Grant in the Fulbright Program, examining the record of the medieval dissent against the order of "Christendom." What is offered here is largely the fruit of that year of study.

Since this work would have been impossible without the benefits of said Grant we wish to express our appreciation for it here. We must thank also the curators of Campus Chapel at the University of Michigan, an institution which we were privileged to serve for over two decades, for granting leave of absence. A word of thanks to the Calvin Foundation is in order. Most of all do we thank Him whose good hand has been upon us.

Footnotes have been supplied. They are of two kinds. Those that provide additional information, and which the reader will therefore want to consult as he reads, are indicated by small letters and are printed at the foot of the page. Those that supply merely bibliographical data are referred to with numerals and have been printed at the end of the book. No attempt has been made to make this bibliographical data complete or exhaustive; enough has been given, we trust, to supply the more ambitious reader with the necessary leads.

Translations are by the author, unless credit is given. The policy has been to keep out of the general text, as much as possible, expressions in languages other than English; in the footnotes, however, passages in foreign languages are freely quoted, a policy that we trust the reader will approve.

—LEONARD VERDUIN

Ann Arbor, Michigan, 1964

Contents

Preface	7
List of Abbreviations	10
Introduction	11
1 Donatisten	21
2 Stäbler	63
3 Catharer	95
4 Sacramentschwärmer	132
5 Winckler	160
6 Wiedertäufer	189
7 Kommunisten	221
8 Rottengeister	243
Postscript	276
Bibliographical Footnotes	282
Index	289

List of Abbreviations

B.R.N.	=	*Bibliotheca Reformatoria Neerlandica* ('s-Gravenhage, 1903-14)
Cornelius	=	C. A. Cornelius, *Geschichte des Münsterischen Aufruhrs* (Leipzig, 1855)
Corpus	=	*Corpus Documentorum Inquisitionis Neerlandicae,* ed. Paul Fredericq ('s-Gravenhage, 1889-1903), in five volumes
C.R.	=	*Corpus Reformatorum*
M.Q.R.	=	*Mennonite Quarterly Review* (Goshen, Indiana, since 1927)
Quellen I	=	*Quellen zur Geschichte der Wiedertäufer, I Band, Herzogtum Württemberg, von Gustav Bossert* (Zürich, 1952)
Quellen II	=	*Quellen zur Geschichte der Wiedertäufer, II Band, Markgraftum Brandenberg* (Bayern I), *von Karl Schornbaum* (Leipzig, 1934)
Quellen III	=	*Quellen zur Geschichte der Täufer, III Band, Glaubenszeugnisse oberdeutschen Taufgesinnter, von Lydia Müller* (Leipzig, 1938)
Quellen IV	=	*Quellen zur Geschichte der Täufer, IV Band, Baden und Pfaltz, von Manfred Krebs* (Gütersloh, 1951)
Quellen V	=	*Quellen zur Geschichte der Täufer, V Band, Bayern, II Abtheilung, von Karl Schornbaum* (Gütersloh, 1951)
Quellen VI	=	*Quellen zur Geschichte der Täufer in der Schweiz, I Band, Zürich, von Leonhard von Muralt und Walter Schmid* (Zürich, 1952)
Quellen VII	=	*Quellen zur Geschichte der Täufer, VII Band, Elsas, Theil I* (*Stadt Strassburg, 1522-32*), *von Manfred Krebs und Jean Rott* (Gütersloh, 1959)
Quellen VIII	=	*Quellen zur Geschichte der Täufer, VIII Band, Elsas, Theil 2* (*Stadt Strassburg, 1533-35*), *von Manfred Krebs und Jean Rott* (Gütersloh, 1960)
Quellen IX	=	*Quellen zur Geschichte der Täufer, IX Band, Balthasar Hubmaiers Schriften, von Westin-Bergsten* (Gütersloh, 1962)

Note: These *Quellen* have been printed by the *Verein für Reformationsgeschichte* and have been given *other* serial numbers in the *Quellen und Forschungen zur Reformationsgeschichte* put out by this *Verein*.

Quellen Hesse	=	*Urkundliche Quellen zur hessischen Reformationsgeschichte, 4 Band* (*Wiedertäuferakten, 1527-1626*), *von Günther Franz* (*nach Walter Köhler, Walter Sohm, Theodor Sippell bearbeitet*) (Marburg, 1951)
Recovery	=	*The Recovery of the Anabaptist Vision,* ed. Hershberger (Scottdale, 1957)

Introduction

Before the Reformation was ten years along it had become evident that not all who were rebelling against the medieval order were of one mind and heart. It had become apparent that within the camp of the dissenters there were deep-seated differences, tensions of such dimensions that a parting of the ways was in the making. It had become plain that the Reformers would as a result be obliged to deploy some of their forces to a second front; they would have to divide their energies between two opponents, Rome and the Radicals.

From the outset the Reformers realized that the opposition that was shaping up on the Second Front was going to be formidable — at least as formidable as the opposition from the side of the Catholics. As early as May 28, 1525, Zwingli, in a letter to Vadian, expressed the opinion that the struggle with the Catholic party was "but child's play" when compared with the struggle that was erupting at the Second Front.

The opening of the Second Front affected the course of the Reformation very significantly. By way of reaction to it the Reformers backed into a corner where they would not otherwise have retreated. The opening of the Second Front caused the Reformers to go back on their own former selves; it made them swing to the right. This bending to the right, occasioned by the emergence of the Second Front, caused much that was latent in the earliest rustlings of the Reform to go underground, as it were, not to emerge again until much later times.

No suitable name has been found for the Second Front. A name that has gained rather wide usage is "The Left-wing of the Reformation." This name, however, is less than wholly satisfactory. The term "Left-wing" is borrowed from the parliamentary scene and stands for the faction that wishes to go faster and farther than the center, and much faster and farther than the right. We would therefore expect a "Left-wing of the Reformation" to out-Luther Luther. But an examination of

11

the record shows that the men of the "Left-wing" did not do this; in fact, we find them going against Luther, and at very crucial points.

Let us take for example that very central doctrine of the Reformation, the doctrine of justification by faith and its bearing on the place of good works in the scheme of salvation. In his haste to establish the doctrine of justification by faith rather than by works Luther down-graded good works; the only place he had left for good works was at the very end, as a sort of postscript or appendage, something that needed attention after salvation was an accomplished fact. We meet in Luther, to put it theologically, a very heavy emphasis on the forensic aspect of salvation and a correspondingly light emphasis on the moral aspect. Luther was primarily interested in pardon, rather than in renewal. His theology was a theology that addresses itself to the problem of guilt, rather than to the problem of pollution. There is an imbalance in this theology between what God does *for man* and what He does *in man*. It was this imbalance that caused Luther to collide with the Epistle of James.

The people of the Second Front showed from the very first a critical attitude toward Luther's disparagement of good works. They did not go along with his one-sidedly forensic theology. They complained that "Luther throws works without faith so far to one side that all he has left is a faith without works." They suggested that Luther's *sola fide* was heresy — if taken, as it was taken by some, to mean *faith unaccompanied.* In this matter, which takes us to the very heart of the Lutheran vision, the men of the Second Front stood to the *right* of Luther, so much so that their enemies accused them of being "heaven-stormers" and "work-saints," people who think to earn salvation by their good works. Surely this is not left-wing; one could with greater propriety consider it, at this vital point, to be right-wing. These men stood closer to Rome than to Luther in this matter. We do well, therefore, to avoid the expression "Left-wing of the Reformation."

Another name that has come into quite common use is "The Radicals of the Reformation." This name is similarly inadequate, for it likewise implies that the people of the Second Front were quite similar to the Reformers, only more headlong.

But the difference between the Reformers and the men of the Second Front was not simply a quantitative one; the difference was qualitative. Although we shall be using the term "Radicals" occasionally, we do so with this reservation. They were radicals, it is true; but they differed from the Reformers in kind, not simply in degree.

The men of the Second Front have also been referred to as "The Stepchildren of the Reformation." This is a much better term, and we shall be using it freely. This name is appropriate for two reasons; first, because the men of the Second Front were indeed treated as stepchildren allegedly are wont to be treated; second, because they were the victims of a second marriage. Later we shall point out what this second marriage was. We shall also, likewise in its proper place, suggest still another name as a useful designation of these Stepchildren.

Contemporaries called the Stepchildren by all sorts of derogatory names, each of which calls special attention to an aspect of the disagreement that had developed. These names were not intended to convey information; they were intended to convey opprobrium. They were one and all hateful to the persons to whom they were affixed.

The Stepchildren wanted to be known as "evangelicals," as "brethren," or simply as "Christians" or "believers." On their part they called the Reformers "Scribes" or "the learned ones"; those who followed these were called "name-Christians" or "heathen."

Not one of the ugly names used by contemporaries to designate the Stepchildren was new; not one of them was coined in the sixteenth century. All were old terms of opprobrium, most of them were very old. Nor were the ideas that are characteristic of the Stepchildren's vision new; these too were old, very old. Not one of them was invented in Reformation times. When we examine the thinking of the Stepchildren in its several items, whether it be the rejection of "christening" or the refusal to swear an oath, or certain convictions in the matter of economics, or an apparent toning down of the sacrament, etc., we find that it was not in any sense new when the Second Front rallied to it. This explains why no new names were invented. Men have need of new names only if and when they encounter new commodities; there were no new commodities; hence there was no need for the coining of any new names.

It must also be pointed out in this connection that the record does not credit the vision that prevailed at the Second Front to any person alive in those times. Who it was that broached the idea, so central in the vision of the Stepchildren, that the Church of Christ must consist of believing people and of them exclusively, the sources say not a word. Nor do the sources say who it may have been that first challenged the propriety of "christening." The same situation confronts us when we examine the rest of the vision of the Stepchildren. This is passing strange, if it is assumed, as has become the vogue, that the Stepchildren were simply the fruitage of the Reformation. Imagine the story of the rise of Communism without the mention of its Karl Marx!

How is all this to be explained? The answer can be quite simple. We do not read of any new commodities or new names, or of any father of it all, for the simple reason that what erupted at the Second Front was a resurgence, a reiteration, a restatement, precipitated in a way by what began with the posting of the now famous Theses, but essentially older than 1517. What erupted at the Second Front was a resurgence of those tendencies and opinions that had for centuries already existed over against the medieval order; it was connected with ancient circles in which, in spite of the persecutions, a body of ancient opinions and convictions was still alive. It was not a thing arising without deeper root out of the events that began in 1517. To ignore this fact is to fall into error, an error the more serious since even the experts have strayed into it.[a]

---

[a]To quote but one example: When Josef Beck set himself to edit a volume of original source materials, *Die Geschichts-Bücher der Wiedertäufer in Österreich-Ungarn* (an in-group account of the rise of the Anabaptists of Austria-Hungary) he deftly exscinded "a piece of Church History extending from the year 344 to 1519" for the reason that "it has nothing at all, or very little, to do with the matter in hand." Surely this is arbitrary procedure. The people who wrote this early account — their own biography — were of the conviction that one must pay considerable attention to the events that lie between 344 and 1519 if one is to understand the origin and history of the people described. Surely it is to beg the question to wave this testimony to one side, just because it does not fit into a preconceived historical construction!

The dissent against the medieval order was in 1517 already a millenium old and extremely widespread. Because it had been obliged to carry on under cover, so that conference between the dissidents was quite out of the question, it had gone in all directions. The "medieval underground," as it has been called, was unable to have its "town meetings" to discuss and then come to consensus; hence the endless variety. The Church called all its foes by one and the same name, "heretics," who "like the foxes of Samson, have diverse faces but are all tied together at the tail." The Church had no desire to differentiate between group and group; they were all guilty of one and the same sin, that of challenging her monopoly; and she vented her spleen on them indiscriminately.

This will go far to explain why the "Left-wing of the Reformation" or the "Radical Reformation," or whatever one wishes to call the camp that developed the Second Front, shows such bewildering diversity.[b] The Church had long had a sort of catch-all, a kind of wastebasket into which she thrust everything she didn't want; when the Reformation failed to satisfy there was again and at once the same multifariousness; Menno and Müntzer, Schwenkfeld and Servetus, and many more, all clubbed together under a single label.

Fortunately for us, the record shows that there were great polarities right within the camp of the "heretics," in medieval times and also in the days of the Reformation. We find Menno Simons, for example, aiming his criticism quite as much at fellow "heretics" as at the Catholics and the Reformers. If we allow ourselves to be taught by these built-in polarities we can narrow down the area of our investigation; we can then perhaps arrive at some such thing as the "typical Anabaptist" or the typical "Stepchild of the Reformers." If we allow ourselves to be guided by the recorded antagonisms we will be able, it is hoped, to arrive at a kind of standard, the typical man of the Second Front.

[b]Even a cursory examination of "The Radical Reformation," as discussed by George H. Williams in his recent and monumental book by that title, will show what a motley crowd is covered by that name. Elements are included that have literally nothing in common except the fact that they were neither Catholics nor followers of the Reformers.

Until comparatively recent times men were obliged to speak of the Stepchildren in the idioms of their foes. Men could do little but repeat the ancient vilifications that had been part of the psychological warfare raging at the Second Front.[c] By and large the primary sources in the matter, consisting of court records, correspondence, confessions, testimonials, etc., were tucked away in ancient archives. There was not much historians could do but repeat the old legends.

All this has changed. During the past thirty years a vast array of the primary sources has been made available in print, accessible to all who have an interest in the matter. Enough is on hand now, in fact, to warrant the assumption that further bringing to light will not alter appreciably the outlines now already wholly clear.[d]

One of the things that has become apparent is that near the heart of the conflict that raged at the Second Front lay two irreconcilable and mutually exclusive concepts of the delineation of the Church of Christ. Modern investigators have, one by one, singly and in combination, come to see that this was the heart of the matter, two diverse and disparate conceptions as to what the Church of Christ is and what its relation is to that which lies around it. All the several features of the struggle are so many implications of this master struggle. It is very nearly correct to say that there is consensus at this point.

The Stepchildren believed that the Church of Christ is by definition an element in society, not society as such. Their opponents, the Reformers as well as the Catholics, were un-

[c]Mörikhofer, in his biography of Zwingli, asserts that "Zwingli presents in lurid colors as facts that which came to his ears as rumor." But one does not have to ascribe to outright falsification the many misrepresentations that the Reformers committed in their polemics against the Stepchildren. Much of it was due to failures in communication. The two groups proceeded from such radically different presuppositions that they were unable to do each other justice. In all events, as we shall have occasion to point out often enough, there was plenty of reporting that must be taken with the proverbial grain of salt.

[d]George H. Williams, in the first sentences of the Preface to *The Radical Reformation,* asserts that the bringing to light of the source materials concerning the Stepchildren has much the same significance for the interpretation of the whole of modern Church history that the discovery of the Dead Sea Scrolls has for the study of the New Testament and Church history.

willing to go along with this; they continued to look upon the Church as coextensive with society.

It has been said of late that Luther was faced with a dilemma, the dilemma of wanting both a confessional Church based on personal faith and a regional Church including all in a given locality. It was this dilemma that gave rise to the Second Front.

This dilemma was a cruel one. He who thinks of the Church as a community of experiential believers is bound to oppose him who thinks of it as a fellowship embracing all in a given territory; he who operates with the concept of the Church as a society embracing all in a given geographic area must of necessity look askance at him who restricts the Church to the believing ones. The two views cannot be combined; one cancels out the other. In the one view the Church is *Corpus Christi*, the body of Christ, which consists of believing folk and of them solely; in the other view the Church is *Corpus Christianum*, the body of a "christened" society. As we shall see, attempts have been made to combine these two, but without success.

Upon the horns of this dilemma Luther was impaled. And not only Luther — all the rest of the Reformers were torn between the same two alternatives. They one and all halted between two opinions. They one and all tried to avoid an outright choice. All tried to ride the fence.

It was this fence-riding that was the immediate occasion for the exodus of the people who thereupon came to be known as the Stepchildren and treated as such. When the Reformers gave evidence that they were not minded to let go of "Christendom," that is, of the Church embracing a whole society, then the exodus occurred. Those who departed were convinced that "Christendom" is a myth, seeing that the Church of Christ consists of the believing element of society and of it only. Their going only made the Reformers burn the midnight oil in an effort to provide an apology for the inclusive Church. And the Reformers grew progressively more hostile toward those who left. Here we are standing right in the middle of the battle at the Second Front.*

*With the exodus of the Stepchildren the vision of the Reformers became less ambiguous than it had been. Since the Stepchildren insisted that only

We have spoken of an *exodus*. That word is warranted. The people of the Second Front had indeed been at one time a part of the flock that had rallied to the cause of the Reform; in this sense the Stepchildren were the children of 1517. But they abandoned the Reformers because of an earlier conditioning; in this respect they were *not* the children of 1517. The Second Front resulted from an exodus of people who had come to the Reformation already conditioned, and this conditioning made it predictable that they would not feel at home there permanently and would, for that reason, depart again.

That this is what happened we have from the mouth of Luther himself. He wrote: "In our times the doctrine of the Gospel, reestablished and cleansed, has drawn to it and gained many who in earlier times had been suppressed by the tyranny of Antichrist, the Pope; however there have forthwith gone out from us *Wiedertäufer, Sacramentschwärmer und andere Rottengeister* . . . . for they were not of us even though for a while they walked with us."[1]

In this word from the hand of Luther we read the following three things: (1) that people who in earlier times had been suppressed by papal tyranny had joined his movement (they were therefore already estranged from the medieval order); (2) that these did not stay with him, seeing that they were really not homogeneous with him and his ideas; (3) that they thereupon came to be known as *Wiedertäufer*, etc. The present volume is in a large way an exegesis of this terse

---

a Church based on personal faith was acceptable to them and since they began to try for that kind of Church, the Reformers were left with the other alternative, a Church embracing all in a given locality. Of all the earlier Reformers it must be said therefore that they had an early phase and a later phase. This has been realized by many investigators. It has caused Alfred Farner, for instance, to say of Zwingli, in his *Die Lehre von Kirche und Staat bei Zwingli*, that "Seit dem Jahre 1526 beginnen bei Zwingli weltliches und geistliches Gebiet ineinanderzugehen." This was the logical outcome of Zwingli's drift toward the inclusive Church. At the end of his career he had come full circle, declaring "urbem Christianam nihil quam Ecclesiam Christianam esse." Another investigator, Hundeshagen, had discovered a century ago already that "Zwingli kenne das Prinzip der Gewissenfreiheit nur in den ersten Jahren seines reformatorischen Wirkens." A similar drift toward the right may be observed in the rest of the Reformers of the first decade.

statement made by Luther. The uncomplimentary names he used are nothing but synonyms for "Stepchildren of the Reformation."

Now that we have stated the nature of the Reformers' dilemma, we may well ask how they came to be in such an uncomfortable position. How did they happen to be torn between these two alternatives, these two irreducible views concerning the delineation of the Church? Why was it so painfully difficult to choose between these two possibilities? Whence came this problem that drained away a sizable part of the Reformers' following?

The dilemma resulted from the fact that the Reformers were torn between two loyalties. On the one hand was a loyalty to the New Testament Scriptures, which know no Church other than the believers' Church, a Church based on personal faith. On the other hand was a loyalty to what the Dutch call "het historisch gewordene" (that which has come about with the passing of time), in which the Church was construed so as to include all in a given locality. Only by repudiating history, twelve whole centuries of it, could one escape from the dilemma — unless he were prepared to repudiate the New Testament. This latter escape neither the Reformers nor the Stepchildren were willing to use. So there was the other escape, the repudiation of *het historisch gewordene*. To reject it was a radical step, too radical except for radicals, who took this way out and so came to stand alone, as Stepchildren.

As we have already said, in the dealings with the Stepchildren a great many terms of reproach were bandied about. Although these names were used in spite, they do, each in its turn, put in focus a phase of the master struggle, the struggle regarding the delineation of the Church. Each of these smear-words points up an aspect of the battle that raged at the Second Front. We shall in this study pick up some of the most commonly-used terms of reproach, examine them somewhat carefully, one in each chapter. Together these studies will sketch, so it is hoped, the essential outlines of the battle of the Second Front.

Before we delve into our subject we wish to point out that this neither was nor is a mere academic matter. The Stepchildren were not speculative theologians, eager to win an argument; they were deeply religious men, and the matter had a definitely existential dimension for them. We shall discover that for us also the matter is far from a mere monk's quarrel.

1   *Donatisten*

My kingdom is not of this
world . . . . John 18:36

ONE OF THE TERMS OF REPROACH USED BY THE REFORMERS
as an incriminating label of the Second Front was "Donatists";
the form "neo-Donatists" also occurs in the sources. This re-
proachful name was used very freely and frequently.

This name leads straight to the heart of the matter; that is
one reason for taking it up first.

To understand why the Stepchildren were called "Donatists"
or "neo-Donatists" one must go back to the fourth century, the
age in which the original Donatists lived. The original Donatism is
usually referred to as the Donatist Rebellion. To understand a
rebellion one has to know the thing against which the rebellion
was directed. Donatism was a reaction. To understand this
reaction one will have to know the thing against which the
reaction was aimed.

To get all this before us will take a little time and effort;
but it will be time well-spent, for the stage on which the
sixteenth century conflict was enacted was set in the fourth,
as informed observers in Reformation times saw very clearly.
We shall have to ʒ very rapidly, over the history of the first
four centuries of the Christian era, to understand what the
original Donatism was and why the Stepchildren were called
neo-Donatists.

We must begin by pointing out that with the launching of
the New Testament vision a new idea was being broached; the
world was being treated to a new and very revolutionary concept
of society, namely, that men can get along peacefully in the
market place even though they do not worship at the same
shrine. The New Testament conceives of human society as a

21

composite thing — that is, composed of factions. It expects that some men will glory in the very same Cross over which other men stumble. It anticipates that some men will make their boast of the very same thing of which other men are ashamed. And it assumes that such diversity on the plane of religion does not imply cacophony on the square. It thinks that even though men differ basically and radically at the shrine they need not clash in the market place.

This is one of the New Testament's boldest innovations, the sweep of which will not escape the thoughtful. In this novel view it is plainly implied that there are resources in the as yet not regenerated human heart, due to the remnants of the original righteousness left after the Fall, resources that are adequate for the affairs of state, loyalties that are adequate for the political level, over and above the loyalities that result of the New Testament's "Render unto Caesar the things that are Caesar's and unto God the things that are God's."

In the New Testament vision, that which we today call the State and that which we now call the Church are agencies that cater to differentiable loyalties. The State demands a loyalty that all men can give, irrespective of their religious orientation; the Church demands a loyalty which only he can give who believes in the Christ. The State has a sword with which it constrains men, coerces them if need be; the Church has a sword also, but it is the sword of the Word of God, a sword that goes no farther than moral suasion.

The New Testament envisions no trouble in the outworking of this division of labor — as long as both sides play in the register intended for them; it envisions trouble only if and when either of the two goes outside its province, as for instance when, as in Acts 4:18, men in the uniform of the State tell people whether they are to preach and what. The New Testament vision implies that as long as Church and State weed each in its own garden there will be a tolerable *modus vivendi.*

It must not escape the reader that this was a novel insight, so novel as to be revolutionary. The world had never seen the like of it before. For all pre-Christian society is *sacral.* By the word "sacral," which we shall be using frequently and which we request the reader to impress on his mind, we mean

"bound together by a common religious loyalty." By sacral
society we mean society held together by a religion to which
all the members of that society are committed.

The society of ancient Babylon, for example, was a sacral
society; all Babylonians were expected to bow to one and the
same Object (cf. Daniel 3); their society was pre-Christian.
The society of Ephesus was sacral; all Ephesians were expected
to join in the chant "Great is Diana of the Ephesians!"; Ephesian
society was pre-Christian. In our own day the society of the
Navajo in our Southwest is sacral; all members of that society
are expected to take part in the ritual; theirs too is pre-Christian
society.

According to this construction of things, the Old Testament
too was pre-Christian — as indeed it was in the chronological
sense. Every member of Old Testament society was considered
to be in the same religious category as was every other member of it. This makes Old Testament society sacral and pre-
Christian. It was a monolithic society rather than a composite
one. It had no room for diversity, for *for* and *against*.

If we are permitted to look ahead a bit here, there would
in all probability never have been a Second Front if the Reformers had been aware of the pre-Christian quality of the Old
Testament in this matter. It was the Reformers' refusal to admit
that there is this perspective in the relationship that obtains
between the two Testaments, it was their refusal to grant that
the one had outmoded the other at this point, that caused
the exodus of the Stepchildren. But we shall return to this
point later.

It was because the Jews of Jesus' day were pre-Christian,
and therefore sacralists in their conception of things, that the
problem "whether it is lawful to pay tribute to Caesar" seemed
to them to be an insoluble problem. How could a man, they
asked, be loyal to the political community by paying his taxes,
without thereby being disloyal to the religious community, the
Church. They, sacralists that they were, knew no answer to
this question. It vexed them every time they tangled with it.
And for that reason they confronted the Master with it, so that
He too might be embarrassed by it and be hopelessly pinned
in a corner. How great must have been their surprise at the
ease with which Jesus, acting on the new insight He had come

to convey, sailed through the dilemma with "Render to Caesar the things that are Caesar's and to God the things that are God's." In His way of thinking there wasn't even any problem.

As the thoughtful reader will have perceived, much is implied in this New Testament innovation. In it is implied that the State is a *secular* institution, secular in the etymological sense, namely, "pertaining to this age or era." The State is intended, by God himself, to regulate as best it can, with the insights available to it and with the resources at its command, the things of this age. It is implied in the New Testament vision that the State, being itself a creature of God's common grace, works with the resources which that non-redemptive grace makes available.[†]

It is implied in the New Testament vision that Christianity is not a culture-creating thing but rather a culture-influencing one. Wherever the Gospel is preached human society becomes composite; hence, since culture is the name given to the total spiritual heritage of an entire people, there can never be such a thing as a Christian culture; there can only be cultures in which the influence of Christianity is more or less apparent. The New Testament vision does not pit a "Christian culture" against a non-Christian culture; rather does it introduce a leaven into any existing culture into which it insinuates itself, a leaven whereby that already existing culture is then affected. New Testament ideology does not seek to make the not-yet-believer culturally sterile, nor even the outright unbeliever, the disbeliever; it is satisfied to add the Christians' voice to the cultural ensemble.

Again, if we are permitted to run ahead of ourselves a bit, we may at this point call attention to the fact that the house

---

[†]The State, which St. Paul does not hesitate to call "God's servant" (Romans 13) and for which he enjoins his followers not only to pray but to pray "first of all" (I Timothy 2), derives not from the redemptive enterprise of God but from God's desire to *conserve*. Emil Brunner, who has discussed this matter very helpfully in his *Die Christusbotschaft und der Staat* puts it this way: "Wir haben es hier zweifellos nicht mit einer Ordnung der Erlösung, sondern der Erhaltung, nicht der erlösenden, sondern der erhaltenden, der allgemeinen Gnade zu tun — die darum allgemein heisst, weil sie gerade wie Regen und Sonnenschein allen Menschen, auch denen, die nichts von Jesus Christus oder der besonderen Gnade wissen, zukommt."

of freedom and of democracy has been reared in those areas —
and we dare say in them alone — where men have made serious
work of the New Testament vision as to societal compositism.
It, more than any other single factor, has given us human
society with option built into it. For pre-Christian society is
optionless society — just as post-Christian society will again
be optionless society. The New Testament's idea of societal
compositism is the only real alternative to the stultifying ideologies that have given rise to the modern optionless and option-
forbidding totalitarian States.[g]

It was the outworking of the sacralist thought habits of
Roman society that occasioned the persecutions to which the
early Christians were exposed. The Roman State had its
officially designated Object of worship, and to it every Roman
was expected to give homage. It is significant that the early
Christians did not launch a crusade to have this Object ousted
and a new and better Object, the God of the Scriptures, put
in its place. The primitive Church did not propose to remove
the Object that had hitherto stood in the square and put its
own Object in its place. It was content to worship the Christian God in an off-the-street place and to ignore the Object
that stood in a place where none belongs, being careful that
no one would have reason to complain that by so worshipping
at an esoteric shrine the Christians were drawing themselves
away from the affairs of Roman life.

It must be said here, and with considerable emphasis, that

----

[g]One of John Dewey's smallest books, but one of his most important
ones, has the very un-American title: "A Common Faith." In its argument
Dewey asserts (very rightly) that historic Christianity is committed to
the distinction of sheep and goats; he also asserts (very wrongly) that
this differentiation must somehow be overcome if the American democratic
ideal is to be realized. The exact opposite, however, is true; the democratic
ideal of which Dewey speaks requires diversity, not sameness. It may be
argued, and quite correctly, that the very American ideal of democracy
of which the man speaks is the direct fruitage of the insight of historic
Christianity to which he refers, the insight which he wishes to see discarded. It is this insight that has given the world the idea of a society-
with-option. What Dewey is proposing is that we kill the goose that
lays the golden eggs. If ever the time comes that Americans have "a
common faith" America as we know it will be no more. In its place
will have come an optionless monolithic society — of the kind known in
our day as totalitarianism.

the New Testament vision of societal compositism did not lead
to any attitude of aloofness from the workaday things. We
point this out here because the notion is abroad that they who
take the New Testament seriously at this point must of necessity
become nonchalant concerning the affairs of public life. The
aloofness which was characteristic of the medieval and modern
"sects," an aloofness about which men have often complained,
and not without cause, was not a feature of the early Christians. Aloof Christianity comes later and then by way of
reaction. No, early Christianity was not aloof; it was deeply
involved in the affairs of society. The testimony of *The Epistle
to Diognetus* is enough, it seems, to bear this out. This literary
product, which according to modern scholarship dates from
near the end of the second century, draws a parallel between
the soul and the body on the one hand and the Christians and
society on the other hand, "The soul dwells in the body but
is not of the body and the Christians dwell in the world without
being of the world"; it then goes on to say:

> Christians are not distinct from the rest of men in country or
> language or customs. For neither do they dwell anywhere in
> special cities of their own nor do they use a different language,
> nor practice a conspicuous manner of life . . . . But dwelling
> as they do in Hellenic and in barbaric cities, as each man's lot is,
> and following the customs of the country in dress and food
> and the rest of life, the manner of conduct which they display
> is wonderful and confessedly beyond belief. They inhabit their
> own fatherland, but as sojourners; they participate in every-
> thing as citizens, and endure everything as foreigners. Every
> foreign country is to them a fatherland and every fatherland a
> foreign country . . . . They live on the earth but their citizenship
> is in heaven."[1]

Early Christianity, it may be said, took seriously Jesus' idea
about "in the world but not of the world." It knew that it
was the Master's will that they be "the salt of the earth," a
formula that speaks of deep difference going hand in hand with
close integration. The early Christians knew that they were
partakers of an *anointing*, a transaction whereby they were on
the one hand set in contrast with the world about them and
on the other hand set in context with it. They knew that one
must "follow peace" (of which the basic meaning is *together-*

ness) "and holiness" (of which the essential meaning is *separation*) if one is to "see God."

All told, early Christianity acted on the insight that Jesus had come to create "a people within a people"; it realized that it is by the act of faith that men become the Sons of God, with a sonship that is not simply continuous with the sonship that is by nature. Primitive Christianity knew that although God is the Savior of "all men" He is the Savior "in a special way" of them that believe. Early Christianity's world was peopled with folk who witness and folk who were witnessed to. It therefore conceived of a composite society, not a monolithic one.

One of the sayings of Jesus that has caused later generations trouble, if not embarrassment, gave the early Christians no trouble at all — namely His dictum: "Think not that I came to send peace upon the earth . . . . I am come to set a man at variance against his father, and the daughter against the mother . . . , a man's foes shall be those of his own household." To the early Church this was but a statement, somewhat hyperbolic perhaps, to the effect that Jesus came to usher in a new concept of society; in it He was setting forth His concept of the composite society, by carrying it even into the family circle. If societal compositism can and does occur even on this level what will it be in the great out-of-doors?

This concept was startlingly new. Roman society was sacral and non-composite. And its sacralism came to expression everywhere. In the instituiton known as the *idolothyta*, for instance, the placing of the meat supply before the Object. This ancient custom had grown to such dimensions that virtually all meat available at the butcher's was *placed* meat, and bore the stamp of the Object which Romans worshipped. It is a curious fact, one certainly not without its significance, that as far as we know, the early Christians did not so much as contemplate the possibility of having the public meat supply stamped with another stamp, the stamp of the Christians' Object; they seem not to have stirred a finger to have some Christian symbol, say the outline of a fish, put in place of the customary stamp. They seem to have proceeded upon the assumption that a religious mark upon a common meat supply is an anomaly anyway, one which a Christian does well simply to ignore. They walked

nonchalantly over the matter, with an "Eat anything and everything that they sell in the shambles, and never mind the questions." The only moral problem posed by the *idolothyta* was
the question whether it was in keeping with the Christian
attitude to walk roughshod over the sensitivities of a weaker
brother, the man who still heard religious overtones in the
butcher shop.

The Roman society, prompted by its sacralist view of things,
oppressed the Christians, especially when Rome was beset with
political worries. They ascribed their political troubles to the
fact that the religious pattern of uniformity was being shaken.
The religion of Rome was a religion of *do ut des* (I give in
order that you may give), and every adversity was interpreted
to be a frown of the Object for his loss of patronage, caused
by the Christians. If the Tiber went out of its banks or the
Nile failed to do so, the Christians were blamed for this
manifest gesture of divine displeasure. And then the cry rang
out, "To the lions with them!" So also if the earth moved or
the sky stood still.

Meanwhile the Christian cause went forward by leaps and
bounds. In an incredibly short time Christianity had insinuated
itself into every level of Roman society, all through the empire,
and beyond it. It had marched triumphantly to the ends of
the earth. So much has this remarkable growth been attributed
to the effect of the martyrdoms, so often has it been said that
"the blood of martyrs was the seed of the Church" that the
fact has been eclipsed that this phenomenal growth was
basically due to the techniques employed, the techniques prescribed by the New Testament concept of cultural compositism.
In a way that students of social dynamics will understand at
once, the Church grew and grew. After all, men change their
opinion primarily in contacts known as "bull-sessions"; and
Christians were forever engaged in bull-sessions with their
not-yet-believing associates. By the middle of the second century it was being said, by Justinus in his running encounter with
Tryphon Judaeus, that "There is not a race of men on the earth
among whom converts to the Christian faith cannot be found."
By the end of that century Tertullian could say, without fear
of contradiction, that "We came on the scene only yesterday
and already we fill all your institutions, your towns, walled

cities, your fortresses . . . , your senate and your forum."
The New Testament vision was paying off richly.

Meanwhile the empire had ceased to thrive. This, as we have
already said, was interpreted to be due to divine displeasure
at the sight of an eroding sacralism. The Christians posed a
new and strange problem. Rome had learned to live, somehow
and somewhat, with the Jews — even though they were a
standing exception to the sacralist pattern. True, once in a
while Rome persecuted these dissenters from the sacralist pattern, as when Claudias ordered all Jews to quit Rome (Acts
18:2); but this action was probably economic rather than
religious in origin. But the Jews never had been a part of the
Roman sacral society. In this respect the Christians were different. They were apostates; and that was a different matter.
We may say in passing, and return to this point later, that
sacral systems have a reason for dealing with apostates in an
especially severe way.

In one of the frantic moments, in a desperate attempt to
recover the erstwhile religious consensus (which, it was held,
had given Rome the golden days that were now past) the
emperor Decius invented the following scheme. Every householder was instructed to procure an affidavit attesting to loyalty
to, and recent participation in, the ancient religious behavior
vis-à-vis the Object; it read: "I, N.N., have always sacrificed
to the gods and now in your presence I have, in keeping with
the directive, sacrificed and have caused a libation to be poured
out, have tasted of the sacrificial victim; and I request that you,
a public notary, certify the same."[2] Then when a house-to-
house check-up was conducted the offenders were spotted. If
a man was unable to clear himself the failure to produce the
required billet was prima facie evidence of infidelity to the
Object, infidelity that was punishable with death. In this way
Decius not only hoped to inject a little life into the dying
religiosity of the empire by bringing the rank and file into the
temples once again, but he also welcomed the spotting of the
Christians. His concern was not so much a religious concern
as one which we would today call a political concern. It is
well to keep this remark in mind, for we shall come face to
face with this situation often in this study.

Since there is always the danger that the Christian innova-

tions are again lost, since there is always the danger of a
kind of atavism of the spirit, a reversal whereby things are
allowed to slip back into a supposedly superseded plane, it
was but natural that men should begin to toy with the possibility
of moving out the ancestral Object and moving in the Object
of the Christians, to make the religion of Jesus a substitute for
the binder that was eroding away. In a word, to carve out a
"Christian sacralism" (we print this expression in quotation
marks, to indicate that for us the combination of this noun with
this adjective is an anomaly) to take the place of the older
sacralism that was petering out. It seems that one of the first,
if not the very first, to toy with the possibility of having some
day a "Christian sacralism" was Meliton, bishop of Sardis, who
in the year 175 declared in the ear of the emperor that a *do ut
des* arrangement with the God of the Christians might be a
good thing, seeing that "Only when Christianity is protected . . .
does the Empire continue to preserve its size and splendor."
As early as the year 250 Origen was already hinting, broadly
enough, that "If now the entire Roman empire should unite in
the adoration of the true God, then the Lord would fight for
her, she being still [the reference is to Exodus 14:14]; then
she would slay more enemies than Moses did in his day."[3]
This is a broad hint in the direction of "Christian sacralism,"
the suggestion that it would be desirable to re-define the
Church of Christ, to make it a society embracing all in a given
locality, rather than, as it had been hitherto, a fellowship
of believers.

On the other hand, there were men, like Tertullian for
example, who early braced themselves against this eventuality.
The remark sometimes ascribed to him "Quid est imperatori
cum ecclesia?" (What does the emperor have to do with the
Church?) is the cry of a man who, mindful that in the authentic
Christian vision Church and State lie on different planes, is
ill at ease at the prospect of letting the one become confused
with the other.

What Tertullian feared came to pass in the "Age of Constantine," which was ushered in by the "conversion" of the
emperor. Much has been written about this event and much
remains to be written. One thing seems very evident; it is
that, as in the case of Decius before him, the problem to which

Constantine sought a solution was political rather than religious. The facts are that Constantine was a worried statesman, as well he might have been. The empire he had inherited was coming apart at the seams. He had his sleepless nights about this fact. How could he conquer this problem? How bind the sprawling domains together again? How regain the ancient stability and inner cohesion? Then came the much celebrated "vision," a cross in the clouds, and the words "in hoc signo vinces" (in this sign conquer). There he had it! Make the religion of Jesus the religion of the empire and then look to it to achieve the consensus that he, sacralist that he was, and remained, felt he had to have.

We wish to say in passing (for we shall return to this matter later in this study) that this was to read a new and totally strange meaning into the "Cross." Is the Cross of Christ then a thing whereby emperors' ambitions are realized? A device that sees the political aspirations of a power-hungry ruler through to victory? Surely Constantine had grasped little or nothing of the ideas set forth in the Cross of Christ! One need not go to the length of the writer who speaks of Constantine as "the murderous egoist who possessed the great merit of having conceived of Christianity as a world power and of having acted on this novel insight. We can easily imagine the joy of the Christians in having finally obtained a firm guarantee against the persecutions, but we are not obliged to share that elation"; but one cannot stomach any longer the hundreds of pages of extravagant praise heaped on Constantinus Magnus by his biographer, Eusebius of Caesarea! For it is and remains a fact that "Christianity grows alien to its essence when it is made into law for those who have been merely born instead of reborn." Yet that is what the Constantinian change effected.

It speaks volumes, it would seem, that the monogram which Constantine is said to have invented, and which has found its way into almost every Christian Church, the monogram that looks like the letter p with an X worked into its stem (the X representing the first letter of the Greek word *Christos* and the p being the second letter of it) was introduced on the *shields* of Constantine's *soldiers;* the "converted" emperor seems not to have had any interest in making it available as a badge for men not in uniform.

In the Constantinian change a tendency that had been developing for some time, was unleashed. A radical change of rôles occurred. The Christian religion would now enjoy the benefits, if benefits they be, which the ethnic faith had enjoyed hitherto. And the hardships which had in earlier times fallen upon the Christians would now become the lot of those who lingered at the ancient shrines; and for the same reason — that they posed a threat to the sacral order. By the end of the fourth century the simplest votive offerings set before the erstwhile Object, even in household shrines, made the bringers thereof subject to grievous penalty. Gatherings in the signature of the now outlawed faith were strictly proscribed. Indoctrination in the tenets of the ancient faith was strictly forbidden. Not yet baptized persons were required to attend catechism classes in preparation for baptism; all who after attending such classes refused to present themselves for baptism, or having received it then relapsed into the old ways, were subject to the ultimate sentence.[4]

It was at this point that Donatism appeared. Donatism was essentially a protest against the new sacralism. It was basically a rebellion against the Constantinian change. The tensions that had developed between the Donatists in North Africa and the Catholics were, as Professor Frend has put it, "not those of doctrine and philosophy; it was the question of the nature of the church as a society and its relationship to the world, rather than any distinctive beliefs, that formed the heart of the controversy between the Catholics and the Donatists."

The Donatist pastors were wont to tell their flocks that nothing had changed, essentially, now that the empire had embraced Christianity; the only difference, they said, was that whereas in previous times the devil had used force, he was now working in and with allies on the inside. For the true believer the result was the same, namely, persecution for the true follower of Christ. The Donatist bishop Petilian refused to entertain any difference between the persecutions once staged by a pagan government and the persecutions which his flock was now experiencing at the hands of the now supposedly Christian regime. The number of believers had not changed; only the tares had become more numerous. The Donatist pastors said that "the acre of the Lord continues in Africa alone." They looked upon the clerics who were promoting the change as "evil priests working hand in glove with the kings of the earth, men who by their conduct show that they have no king but Caesar." The Donatists continued to think of the Church of Christ as a "small body of the saved surrounded by the unregenerate mass." They insisted that the independence of the Church in regard to the emperor and his officials had to be "upheld at all costs."[5] When troops were sent to quell the Donatist rebellion the followers of Donatus were not the least bit surprised; the new regime was only acting in character.

This then was the original Donatism — a rebellion against the encroachments of "Christian sacralism," or — as we shall henceforth style it at times — against Constantinianism.[g] This then was Donatism — an attempt to conserve the concept of the Church "based on personal faith" and to obstruct the drift toward a Church "including all in a given locality."[h] These were the very same options before which the Reformers stood; small wonder that the name "neo-Donatists" came to the lips of men!

Donatism as a movement in the fourth century was successfully suppressed; but the ideas of Donatism lived on. They recurred in wave upon wave of dissent against the medieval sacralist order. There is probably a sound historical core of truth in the sentence written by Dostoevsky regarding the Constantinian change: "A compromise arose; the Empire accepted Christianity and the Church accepted Roman law and

[g]Some modern writers prefer the name Theodosianism, the reason being that much of the *legislation* in support of the new order originated with this emperor. (A good example of this preference for the name Theodosianism may be found in Emil Brunner's *Die Christusbotschaft und der Staat.*) Since the ideas of the new regime came to expression quite extensively in the days of Constantine already, we prefer to follow the school of thought that speaks of the *Constantinian* change.

[h]No one knew better than did Augustine just what was at issue in the conflict that had flared up between the Catholics and the Donatists. Said he, "The issue between us and the Donatists is about the question where this body is to be located, that is, what and where is the Church?" (Inter nos autem et Donatistas quaestio est, ubi sit hoc corpus, id est, ubi sit Ecclesia? See *Ad Catholicos Epistula* II, 2).

the Roman State. A small part of the Church retired into
the desert and there began to continue its former work." It
is with this continuing rebellion against the Constantinian
change that we are engaged in this study.

With Donatism begins a new variety of heresy, a heresy that
is theologically correct; we shall therefore refer to it as "heresy"
in the rest of this book.[1] To the theological correctness of
this "heresy" the sources bear eloquent testimony. Even the
inquisitors witnessed to it. These "heretics," they said, "have
the appearance of piety and this because before men they live
justly, believing correctly all things concerning God as well as
all the articles contained in the creed." It may be pointed out
however that there was one word in the Apostles' Creed at
which the "heretics" balked, the word "catholic" in the article
dealing with the Church. This word they could not and did
not utter. This is not surprising. The word "catholic" is
derived from the Greek *kata* (meaning "according to") and
holos (meaning "the entirety"); the combination means then
"according to the entirety" and fits into the language of "Christian sacralism." It is therefore not surprising that the "heretics"
avoided it. For them the Church was not "according to the
entirety" but consisted of the believing element only. Moreover, this word had a history. The proponents of "Christian
sacralism" had long ago seen the propaganda value which this
word could have in their scheme. Theodosius had given orders
that "all peoples over whom our rule extends shall live in that
religion which was revealed to St. Peter . . . . We give orders
that all these are to adopt the name 'Catholic Christians'; the
rest we shall let pass for fools and they will have to bear the
reproach of being called heretics. They must come first under
the wrath of God and then also under ours."[6]

It is therefore not at all strange that the "heretics" avoided
the word. The rejection of it must have been quite persistent;
for it became one of the tell-tale marks of the "heretic." It
is highly instructive that the Stepchildren of the Reformation,

---

[1]We do not wish to leave the impression that there were no dissenting
groups that entertained unorthodox theological ideas. There were, just
as there were such in the days of the Stepchildren. The fact is that
there were "heretics" and heretics, with the former disowning the latter
in very clear terms.

who continued in the tradition of the "heretic," also "recited the Apostles' Creed correctly, save for 'the word.'" The Clerk of Courts who has recorded this fact for us has added, in parenthesis, "i.e., the word *allgemein*"; he volunteered further that this was "*ut solent schismatici*" (as is the custom with the schismatic — which is a synonym for the "heretic").[7]

The one thing the prevailing Church had against the "heretics" was their refusal to go along with "Christian sacralism." This was their sin, their one and only sin. And it was this sin, and this sin only, that set the wheels of the Church's discipline going. (We shall return to this matter later.)

This "Donatism" was never absent from the medieval scene. In the words of Adolf von Harnack: "In the twelve centuries that went before the Reformation it has never lacked for attempts to get away from the State-Church Priests' Church and to reinstitute the apostolic congregational structurization."[8] What is this but to say that throughout medieval times there never was a moment in which Constantinianism stood unchallenged. In the company of the "heretics" the New Testament was honored (we shall return to this matter also); and wherever the New Testament is held in honor there its concept of the Church of Christ will continue to challenge. There a Church based on personal faith will challenge the concept of a Church embracing all.

The battle between these two concepts of the Church had been raging for twelve centuries when Luther put the trumpet of reform to his lips. The noise of this battle had by no means decreased. Contemporaries who were in position to know have gone on record to the effect that there were then more men committed to the views of the "heretic" than there had ever been before. In many areas the populace was so much on the side of the "heretic" that executions had to be carried out at night or early in the morning for fear of tumult. Sometimes the age-old provision that death sentences had to be announced with the tolling of the bell was conveniently ignored. At times jails in which "heretics" had been incarcerated were stormed and their prisoners set free. The frantic efforts used by the Church to keep in power are in themselves proof enough that "revisionism" was an ever-present threat. As a recent investigator has put it: "The Protestant Left was the heir of the

medieval underworld. It had categories of thought and a
vocabulary emerging from late medieval heresies . . . , a
vocabulary which pre-existed the Reformation and had its
own power and momentum quite apart from Luther."[9]

There is every reason to believe that the Reformers were
quite aware of the ancient battle. How could it be otherwise?
It may safely be said that a person could not spend the span
of a human life anywhere in Europe without coming in contact personally with the "heretic." There were inquisitors everywhere. Some of these had a record of consigning men to the
flames at the rate of almost one a day. How could an informed
person remain unaffected by the tradition of the "heretic"?

Moreover, there is every reason to believe that the Reformers
were at the first sympathetic toward much of the old heritage
of the "heretic." They said things that cheered the hearts of
people who had been conditioned by it. Sometimes they said
things that were definitely in the idiom of the old protest.
For a while it seemed, at least to onlookers who wanted to see
it that way, that the Reformers were going to be the answer
to the prayers of the "heretics."

When the Reformers presently gave evidence — as give it
they did — that they were not intent on sweeping the Constantinian heritage away, there was an arching of the eyebrows
among some who were walking with them. When the Reformers
accepted the proffered arm of the civil rulers — as accept it
they did — then there were frowns, frowns which soon changed
into audible groans of disillusionment. And then there was the
exodus. And with that the Stepchildren were on the scene.
And, the Second Front.

What caused the exodus was the Reformers' drift toward
neo-Constantinianism. As the Stepchildren saw things, history
was repeating itself. A new "Christian sacralism" was taking
shape, on a smaller scale to be sure and with some version of
a reformed faith in the saddle. It was this new "Christian
sacralism" that precipitated the neo-Donatists. Small wonder
they were called by that name.

The parallel between the things that had happened in and
with the coming of the Constantinian change and that which
was happening now was indeed close, so close as to be uncanny.
Just as his rounds with the original Donatists had made of

Augustine the unrestrained sacralist that he became, so did the Reformers, in their rounds with the neo-Donatists, become the uninhibited supporters of neo-Constantinianism that the record shows them to have been. The parallel can be drawn closer still; just as the original Donatism had its lunatic fringe, in the so-called *Circumcelliones*, so did the later Donatism have its lunatic fringe, in the men of Münster. Just as Augustine's experience with the Donatists led him to make certain *Retractiones*, in which he controverted his own earlier affirmations, so did their dealings with the neo-Donatists cause the Reformers to repudiate some of the things they had stood for earlier, so writing their own Retractions, as it were. (In its proper place we shall return to this about-face of the Reformers, a matter to which the Stepchildren were not slow to call attention.)

Just as the erstwhile Donatists had insisted that "the independence of the Church with respect to the emperor must be upheld" so did the later Donatists insist that "a true Church cannot exist where the secular rule and the Christian Church are blended together." It runs like a refrain through the testimony of the Stepchildren that, as they saw it, the Reformation had gone sour when the Reformers had made a league with the civil powers. It has therefore been very well said that the crystallization of the Reformation in territorial churches or in parishes led by city political authorities gave the impulse for the development of the Second Front. A good start had been made, so said the Stepchildren, but the enlistment of the magistrates had spoiled it all. One of the manifestoes that issued from the Second Front says, after relating a great deal of older history of the "heretic":

> In 1519 Martin Luther began to write against the frightful abominations of the Babylonian Harlot and to disclose all her wickedness . . . , yes, as with thunderclaps to bring it all down . . . . But as soon as he joined himself to the secular rule, seeking protection there against the cross . . . then it went with him as with a man who in mending an old kettle only makes the hole bigger, and he raised up a people altogether callous in sin.[10]

The charge, lodged with many variations, was that the Reformers had begun well but had spoiled their beginning when they reverted back to the medieval pattern of things. The

Reformers, said the Stepchildren, had "fallen back to the beast, that is, the Romish school, which now they defend; the kingdom of God which had previously come to them they have again cast away."[11] Now there were two papal systems, an old one and a new, both of them opposed to the Stepchildren and for the same reason, namely, the latter's rejection of "Christian sacralism."[J]

It was the coalition of the Reformers with "the arm of flesh" that grieved those who came to be treated as Stepchildren. One by one modern investigators have come to see this. "They would have nothing to do with a State Church and this was the main point in their separation from the Lutherans, Zwinglians, and Calvinists; this was the one conception on which all parties among them were in absolute accord"; "The real issue . . . was on the question of the type of Church which should take the place of the old Church"; "The real issue was . . . a bitter and irreconcilable battle between two mutually exclusive concepts of the Church"; "Luther stopped short of a full reformation, content to walk hand in hand with the State . . . , bogged down halfway between Catholicism and the New Testament Church organization." So runs the consensus.

While the radicals were defecting from Luther the Swiss Reformer Zwingli was having very similar troubles. At the outset Zwingli had been intimate with the people who later opened the Second Front. He had, in fact, to quite an extent shared their views, a fact to which the Stepchildren were not slow to point. He had, for example, said that infant baptism "nit sin solle," ought not to be. Then came the moment in which the City Council let it be known that all contemplated reforms in the religious area had to be officially approved by them first. To this Zwingli submitted; and it was at this moment, very precisely, that the Radicals began to peel off. One of the first mutterings of the storm that was brewing was the remark made by one who would soon function as a leader among the Stepchildren: "You have no business giving these decisions into the hands of the civil power." This marked not

---

[J]An incarcerated soldier of the Second Front spoke of his opponents, whether from the papal camp or the Protestant camp, as "bepstler, si seien vom alten oder neuen bapst."[12]

only the beginning of the tension; it also pinpointed the conceptual area in which it occurred, namely, that of the nature of the Church and the relationship in which it stands to society as such. Again, it was the question that had been in the minds of the Donatists, the same insistence that "the independence of the Church in regard to the magistrate must be preserved at all costs." Just as in the eyes of the Donatists the Church had disgraced itself when it accepted the flirtations of the emperor, so did the neo-Donatists frown upon the Reformers for letting themselves be seduced by the same siren voice, the same flirtations.

The flirtations to which we refer ended in a marriage.ᵏ It was this marriage that put in the status of stepchildren those who had hitherto walked with the Reformers but who had resisted stubbornly the coalescence of Church and State. Whether the marriage was one of convenience we shall not attempt to say; that it was diplomatically wise is of course evident. It made it possible for the Reform, which would otherwise in all likelihood have been choked in its own blood and dispatched as the Hussite reform had been dispatched, to have a future. By it the ancient sacralist system, armed to the teeth with military might available to it on a moment's notice, was challenged by a rival sacralist system, likewise backed up by a sword of steel. But from a principial point of view the marriage was a catastrophe; for it made inevitable the perpetuation of all the evils that had been spawned by the Constantinian change. As one of the first to attempt an objective study of the Second Front, C. A. Cornelius, has put it:

> As correct as this step taken by Zwingli was from the point of view of the State, and however much it was calculated to give his ecclesiastical endeavors greater dignity and status, it was a bad step from an evangelical point of view, one that was certain to lead to contention and schism in the party.[13]

ᵏAlfred Farner, in his *Die Lehre von Kirche und Staat bei Zwingli* traces Zwingli's gradual change from an ambiguous position to an outright espousal of "Christian sacralism." He sees Zwingli going past dead center, in his letter to Blarer in which, Farner says, it becomes clear "dasz für Zwingli Kirchgemeinde und bürgerliche Gemeinde eine Einheit geworden sind."

Of the momentous development, the marriage of which we have spoken, a present-day student of Reformation history has said, so very correctly:

> The product of the development from October 1523 to January 1525 was . . . the rejection of *Corpus Christianum*. Following the revolutionary change in the relations of the Church and the world which we associate with the names of Constantine, Theodosius, Augustine, medieval Christendom had no room for the Biblical concept of the "world." The consequences for ethics, for a doctrine of the Church, for evangelism, and for eschatology, were revolutionary and yet hardly noticed. So conscious and so all-pervading was the acceptance of the identity of Church and society that the Reformers, each working closely with the local magistracy and seeking to reform medieval Catholicism with as little commotion as possible, were not even aware of a problem and were able to pass off as political revolutionaries those who raised the question.[14]

In the eyes of the Donatists, whether early Donatists or late, the Church had "fallen" in the days of Constantine, with a "fall" as calamitous and as fraught with evil consequences as the "fall" in Eden. This "fall" had made a fallen creature of the Church, one "dead in trespasses and sins." And just as the catastrophe in Eden had made a re-birth necessary, so did the "fall" of the fourth century require a new creation. So said the "heretics." They felt called therefore to reconstitute the Church, to start all over. The medieval "heretics" may therefore be called Restitutionists, and their views, Restitutionism. Because the Stepchildren fell heir to this assessment of the Constantinian change they may likewise be called Restitutionists. We shall do so (and so fulfill a promise made in the Introduction of this volume). They were doubly entitled to this term; for, as they saw things, they were confronted with a twice-fallen Church, once in the days of Constantine and now again in the days of the Reform.

Restitutionists sought to recover the Church of the New Testament; their ambition, early and late, was to return the Church of Christ to its New Testament format. This ambition comes to expression constantly in the literature which the Stepchildren have left behind. We read, for instance, in an account drawn up by a man who fought at the Second Front:

> At the outset it must be confessed and granted that the first
> Church of Christ and the Apostles has in foregoing times been
> destroyed and laid waste by Antichrist, so that we do not
> need to waste many words or call in many witnesses, seeing
> that we to a man do know, as do all who call themselves
> Evangelicals, that the entire papacy has become a Sodom. . . .[15]

He then goes on to describe the steps which the Restitutionists
took in an effort to recover the erstwhile Church. Since the
Reformers, as the Restitutionists saw things, were now just as
"fallen" as the papists, their reformatory program held forth
no promise.

Let us not pass lightly over the implications of the Constantinian change. A "fall" is a serious thing. The change that
took place in the days of Constantine shook the ship from stem
to stern; nothing in the Church's theology, its organization, its
place in the world, escaped the effects of the virus that had
entered its bloodstream. Medication would have to be strong
and in large doses.

Moreover, let it be remembered that the Church which the
men of the sixteenth century had inherited had borne the
image of the Constantinian synthesis for well over a millenium
when the Reformation began to happen. Hence let no one
underestimate the headlong daring of the Radicals of Reformation times; they were out to turn the world upside down,
the world as it had stood for so long a time that men could
hardly imagine it had ever stood otherwise. Had it not been
for the fact that the blue-prints of the authentic Church were
still accessible, in the New Testament, there would never have
been any clamor for the restitution of it.

We shall spend the rest of our space in this chapter, and all
our space in the chapters that follow, setting forth somewhat
the effects of the "fall" of the Church. This will simultaneously
get us acquainted with the Stepchildren and their ambitions.
We shall travel from one sector of the Second Front to the
other, to see what goes on. As we do so we will probably have
the same experience which a modern historian, Walter Hobhouse, had when he travelled this same path:

> Long ago I came to believe that the great change in the re-
> lations between the Church and the world which began with
> the conversion of Constantine is not only a decisive turning

point in Church history but is also the key to many of the
practical difficulties of the present day and that the Church
of the future is destined more and more to return to the
condition of things somewhat like that which prevailed in the
Ante-nicene Church; that is to say, that instead of pretending
to be coextensive with the world it will confess itself the
Church of a minority, will accept a position involving a more
conscious antagonism with the World, and will, in return, gain
in some measure its former coherence.[16]

When Constantine came into the Church he did not check his
imperial equipment at the door. No indeed, he came in with all
the accoutrements that pertain to the secular regime. He was
not just a Roman who had learned to bow to the Christ; he had
been *pontifex maximus* hitherto, the High Priest of the Roman
State religion, and he entered the Church with the understanding that he would be *pontifex maximus* there too. And just
as his sword had flashed in defence of the old religion so would
it now flash in defence of the new. This put a new and novel
weapon in the hand of the Bride of Christ, the sword of steel.
Now her battles would be fought in the fashion to which the
Roman legions were accustomed. The implication was that He
who had come "meek and lowly and riding upon a colt, the
foal of an ass" would now come on a prancing war horse.
Almost incredible though it is, men do not seem to have noticed
how grotesque this was. Had it not been for the Roman
precedent the change would have been unthinkable.

It is true, the grotesqueness of the new situation did, it seems,
register to a degree with those who promoted the change, and
it registered enough to make them try to file down the rough
edges somewhat. They invented the ridiculous fiction that the
Church did not really sacrifice her dignity when the emperor's
sword flashed in her behalf, for it was the magistrate's man that
actually drew the blood — even though it was at her behest!·

Out of the words of Peter recorded in Luke 22:23, "Lord,
here are two swords," the Church distilled the ridiculous doctrine that Jesus intended His Church to have two swords, the
"sword of the Spirit" which the clergy wields, and "the sword
of steel" which the soldier swings. By the year 1150 this
formula of the two swords was already old, so old as to be un-
questioned: "Two swords belong to Peter; one is in his hand,

the other is at his command whenever it is needful to draw it . . . . Both the spiritual and the material sword belong to the Church; the latter sword is drawn for the Church, the former by the Church. One belongs to the priest and the other to the soldiery; but this one is drawn at the orders of the priest." By this colossal piece of sophistry the Church made herself believe that she could order the life-blood of men to be let, all the while getting none of it on her skirt!

This monstrous doctrine was put forth in dead earnest all through medieval times. It is set forth in the Bull *Unam Sanctam* issued by Boniface in 1302. It remains the unrepudiated doctrine of the Catholic Church to this day. As Thomas Aquinas has it: "The State, through which earthly objectives are reached, must be subordinated to the Church; Church and State are two swords which God has given to Christendom for protection; both these swords however are by Him given to the pope and the temporal sword is then by the pope entrusted to the rulers of State."

The Constantinian change made short work of Jesus' words: "My kingdom is not of this world . . . else would my servants fight, that I should not be delivered." It put Peter in the right for drawing the sword to promote the Cause and it put Jesus in the wrong for rebuking Peter for it. The "fallen" Church conveniently forgot that Jesus had been deeply displeased at the first suggestion of a second sword; it forgot that He had been so disturbed by Peter's rash act that He had stooped down to repair the damage Peter's sword had inflicted; it overlooked the fact that He had performed a miracle of healing, His last, to erase from the record the act so out of keeping with the work He came to do. The medieval Church boasted of being in the signature of this Peter — well, it was more like him than it knew!

Nor was this doctrine of the two swords merely a piece of scholastic subtlety. It was said and meant in dead earnest, and practiced, too. All through medieval times the heads of "heretics" rolled in all directions and the earth was dampened with the blood of men, the air abused with the smell of the roasting flesh of men — all in the signature of the Constantinian change. And at all times the priest stood by, to see to it that the secular power performed the gruesome assignment. In

order to be able to live with herself, the Church regularly
begged the executioner to "stop short of life and limb" — a
request that neither she nor he ever took seriously. The Church
would have been wholly embarrassed if anyone had taken this
bit of window-dressing seriously.[1]

To the credit of the "heretics" it may be said that they never
fell for this pious double talk, never let the Church proclaim
with impunity the idea that because she did not actually draw
the blood she was not guilty of murder. The Waldensians said
caustically: "The priests actuate the secular arm and then think
to be free from murder and they wish to be known as bene-
factors. Yes, just as did Annas and Caiaphas and the rest of
the Pharisees in the time of Christ so does Innocent do in our
times; they refrained from going into the house of Pilate lest
they be defiled and in the meantime delivered Jesus up to
the secular arm."

The horrible idea that the Church of Christ may move
the wrist of the hand that holds the sword was, of course,
carefully stated in the jurisprudence of the Middle Ages. None
put it more succinctly that did a jurist of the early sixteenth
century, Philips Wieland, who taught that "Heresy is punished
by fire;[m] the spiritual judge tries the case and the secular
judge performs the execution." Centuries earlier the famous
expert at Law, Philippe de Beaumanoir, had put it this way,
a bit more lengthily:

[1]The brutality and cruelty that accompanied the executions performed
under the supervision of the "fallen" Church were too frightful for
words. We shall give, but leave untranslated, the public announcement
that went with the execution of a certain Stepchild named Michel: "Das
Michel uf den mark gefürt werdenn, im die zange abgehewenn unnd
demnach 6 grif mit glüginen zangen zu im grifenn und mit lebendigem
lib in ein für geworfen und zu pulfor prent werdenn." It was considered
one of the lesser punishments to have the tongue pierced, a stick of
wood thrust through it, and so to stand in the public square for an
hour or so. It is understandable that men who knew the Christ of the
New Testament should begin to speak of the Church as "fallen."

[m]The custom of executing heretics *by fire* rather than by some other
means seems to have come up in connection with John 15:6: "If a man
abide not in me [which was identified with *not staying in the Church*],
he is cast forth as a branch, and is withered; and men gather them, and
cast them into the fire, and they are burned."

> If a lay person believes incorrectly he is to be returned to the true faith by instruction. If he refuses to believe but adheres instead to his wicked error then he shall be condemned as a heretic and burned. But in that event lay justice must come to the aid of the Holy Church; for when anyone is condemned as a heretic by the examinations conducted by the Holy Church then the Holy Church must leave him to lay justice and the lay justice must then burn him, seeing that the spiritual justice ought not to put anyone to death.[n]

Such then was "Christendom." The "fall" of the Church had so changed the visage of the Bride of Christ as to make her unrecognizable. She who had been sent on a mission of healing and helping had taken on the features of the modern police State. We make this comparison deliberately and seriously. The modern totalitarian State has added nothing new, not even that which we now call "brainwashing." The medieval world was a world in which minorities were unwanted. It was a world in which the rights of speech and of assembly were, as we shall have occasion to see in a later chapter, rigidly curtailed. Medieval society was optionless society, as optionless as any totalitarianism of our times. A small number of "party members" ran the entire show; the common man was completely and effectively defranchised. The parallel is frightening, as is the thought that in areas where the medieval monolithic society has not been successfully challenged the one totalitarianism readily makes way for the other.

The one encouraging fact is that there was at all times, all through the Middle Ages, a sustained protest against the distortions that had come with the Constantinian change — and that this sustained protest finally and ultimately was able to blow apart the Constantinian colossus. In and with this protest the New Testament and its delineation of the Christian Church remained a part of the heritage of man.

---

[n]In the original this passage (to which we shall return) runs as follows: "S' il a aucun lai qui mescroie en la foy, il soit radrecies à le vraie foi par ensegnement; et s' il ne las veut croire, ançois se veut tenir en se malvese erreur, il soit justiciés comme bougre et ars. Mais en tel cas doit aider le laie iustice à sainte Eglise, car quant aucun est condamnés comme bougre par l'examination de sainte Eglise, sainte Eglise le doit abandonner à le laie iustice et le laie iustice le doit ardoir, parce que le iustice espirituel ne doit nului metre à mort."[17]

To this the Stepchildren fell heir. Among them we find the ambition of the medieval "heretic" re-stated, to recover the Church of pre-Constantinian times. Among the Stepchildren we find therefore, from the very beginning, a studied attempt to expel the sword of steel from the affairs of the Church, an attempt to return the sword of the magistrate to its proper place. Among them we hear such cries as these: "All they have eternal punishment awaiting them who seek to sustain the Kingdom of God with recourse to the secular arm." Also: "In my opinion the rulers and their clergymen assign more to the magistrate than they should, for it is not the prerogative of any magistrate to sustain the Word of God by force, seeing that it is free."

Such then was the ideology to which the Stepchildren rallied. We shall have occasion to see that the attempt to recover Paradise Lost lay at the heart of the program that made the Second Front necessary, and that every feature of the vision of the Stepchildren was but a working out of this central thrust. It was the Stepchildren's evaluation of the Constantinian change that stood between them and the Reformers, this in essence, this particularly.

For the Reformers were not minded to repudiate the Constantinian change. Their ambition was not to get rid of "Christian sacralism"; rather was it their ambition to overlay the "Christian sacralism" that was partial to Catholicism with a "Christian sacralism" that was partial to Protestantism. The record is entirely plain in this matter, as we shall discover in some detail in the course of these pages. Suffice it to say at this juncture that a Reformed minister was deposed in sixteenth-century Strasbourg for adhering to "a new and Anabaptist error" which consisted in this: "that the magistrate must leave every man to his own devices in regard to religion, no matter what he believes or teaches, so long as he does not disturb the outward civil quiet."°

°In a *Ratspredigt* preached by the Reformer Hedio for the benefit of the civil powers "über die Pflichten der Obrigkeit" he stated the "error" of the Stepchildren to be that "die weltlich oberheit solle mit jrem ampt sich christlichs thuns unnd der religion nit annemen. . . , es stand jnen nit zu; wan sie eusserlichen friden halten und gute policey, das man bey einander leben möge, so haben sie inen gnug gethon . . . ."

The record shows very plainly that a frightful failure to understand the Stepchildren developed. We must by all means point this out; for unless we see through this misunderstanding, this failure to understand each other, we cannot hope to understand the Reformers' treatment of their Stepchildren. Unless we see through this misunderstanding we will be looking in the wrong place for the cause of the dissension; and this in turn will lead us to offer another, an erroneous, explanation. We must therefore look closely at the record touching this matter.

In the interrogations to which the Stepchildren were exposed, usually in prison, we constantly encounter the question: "Should there be a magistrate and should he sustain the Word of God?" It is plain that for the questioner this is *one* question; but for the one questioned this was *two* questions. For the questioner a simple yes and a plain no were the alternatives; for the answerer it was a matter of yes *and* no, yes to the question whether there should be such a thing as a civil ruler and no to the question whether it is his assignment to sustain the Word of God. For the questioner a negative answer to the question whether the magistrate has the duty to sustain the Word of God with his sword was tantamount to a statement that there should be no magistrate.

We who have lived for so long in a climate in which Church and State are separate institutions will have difficulty understanding how this misunderstanding could come about and persist so. But it did come about, and this is one of the darkest features of a dismal story. Let us explore the matter further.

For the man who stands in the Constantinian tradition, the things we call "Church" and "State" are essentially a single entity, the warp and the woof of a single fabric. The "parish" is in the tradition of Constantinianism at one and the same time a *religious* and a *political* unit. (Something of this usage survives in some of the southern States, where what we call *counties* are still referred to as *parishes*, the word having sloughed off its ecclesiastical connotation). The *gemeente* is, in the Dutch tradition of Constantinianism, at one and the same time a religious or ecclesiastical entity and a socio-political one. (This usage survives in the Netherlands to this day, where one never knows whether *gemeente* stands for the one or for the other.)

This fact will go far to explain the otherwise astounding fact that when the Stepchildren said that the sword had to quit the Church their opponents thought they heard them say that the sword has no proper place in human society. When the Stepchildren said that the idea of a sword in the affairs of the Church is an anomaly the Reformers thought they had heard them say that the sword has no rightful place in the community. As far as we have been able to make out no one in the Second Front ever advocated the elimination of the civil power from the society of men (they did in some cases tend to say that capital punishment was wrong — a matter in which many would in our day concur — but that is not the same as to deny the sword function). However, as far as we have been able to discern every last man among the Stepchildren stood for the expulsion of the sword function from the affairs of religion. It was because their foes were unable in their thinking to combine these two positions that the legend was born that the Stepchildren advocated the overthrow of the civil rule, a legend that finds its classic expression in Article 36 of the Belgic Confession, to the unending embarrassment of those Churches that adhere to this Confession.

One can understand this failure to communicate if he will for the moment divest himself of the terminology of "Church" and "State," and then attempt to discuss the matter. Without these terms, or others of like value, it is indeed difficult to distinguish between a clamor for the cessation of the sword function in things of the faith and a clamor for its cessation *überhaupt*.

Luther fell into the misunderstanding of which we are speaking. Mindful of the fact that the ancient Donatists had resisted the invasion of the civil power into the affairs of the Church, he ascribed to them the same nihilism that men thought to detect in the Stepchildren. He wrote, "The Donatists condemned the secular rule which we must allow to remain." In this Luther was, of course, in error historically, for there is no evidence that the original Donatists condemned the secular rule; there is no hint of anti-imperial ambition among them, no nihilism. How then came Luther to blunder so in the matter of history? The answer is that for twelve centuries the story had been around that he who challenges "Christian sacralism" challenges government as such; the Donatists had challenged emerging "Christian sacralism," hence the Donatists had been political nihilists! This was spurious logic on Luther's part, as spurious as was the logic that laid the same charge at the doorstep of the Stepchildren. The charge was, and is, false. When the Reformers asserted that the people of the Second Front "seek to overthrow government" they did them a gross injustice.

Perhaps the following is enough, for the space of this chapter, to prove that the Stepchildren were not nihilists. A Protestant minister, named Tilemann Noll, stole away one night to visit a conventicle of the Stepchildren, primarily, so he said, to have first-hand knowledge as to what went on there. (He was subsequently taken in hand by a Church court and made to confess in public his grave sin. At that, it almost cost him his cloth. What displeased his superiors especially was that on the Sunday after his visit to the nocturnal gathering of the "heretics" he had told his own parishioners that he had discovered that he had thus far preached nothing but the cold letter of the Scripture, *den toten buchstaben*. Part of his sentence was — and this throws an interesting light upon a matter that will engage us in a subsequent chapter, the latitudinarianism concerning conduct that marked the camp of the Reform — that he "shall keep himself apart from all gay parties and drinking sprees, for a whole year, upon pain of losing his ministerial status.") Upon pastor Noll's return from the conventicle he testified that of all that had transpired at the conventicle "the prayer pleased me the most, for they prayed for the needs of all Christendom, also for the emperor, the king, the nobles and prir.ces, that God might give them wisdom . . . ." It would appear that people who pray in that vein are not addicted to anything resembling an ambition "to overthrow the government." To charge them with this nevertheless was a gross injustice. It was an accusation born not out of observation but out of the thought-habits of an ancient sacralism.

The Reformers, we have said, were not ready to dismiss the sword of the magistrate from the affairs of religion. They justified, to the hilt, the idea that the sword of the civil ruler must throw the "heretic" in line and keep him there. We need only to quote from the writings of Urbanus Rhegius, Luther's trusted associate, in support of this. He said, "When heresy breaks forth . . . then the magistrate must punish not with less but with greater vigor than is employed against other evil-doers, robbers, murderers, thieves, and the like."[18]

The stance of the Reformers is plain enough from the following quotation, also from the pen of Rhegius:

> God raises up the magistracy against heretics, faction-makers, and schismatics in the Christian Church in order that Hagar may be flogged by Sarah [this allegory Rhegius had borrowed from the writings of Augustine — to which we shall return in a later chapter]. The Donatists murder men's souls, make them go to eternal death; and then they complain when men punish them with temporal death. Therefore a Christian magistrate must make it his first concern to keep the Christian religion pure . . . . All who know history will know what has been done in this matter by such men as Constantine, Marianus, Theodosius, Charlemagne and others.[19]

We dare say that no Protestant, at least no Protestant in the New World, will be able to be at peace with the position set forth in these quotations. And yet are they typical of the Reformers, who one and all refused to endorse the Stepchildren's contention that the sword is out of bounds when it invades the area of religious faith.

Since this study is published under the auspices of a Foundation that calls itself by the name of one of the major Reformers, John Calvin, it will be in place to take a close look at his thinking in regard to the matter in hand. We shall test him at two points, the Servetus episode and his reaction to the Stepchildren's first doctrinal manifesto, promulgated at Schlatten am Rande (also known as Schleitheim) in the year 1527.

Although Servetus was not typical of the Stepchildren as such, his case does throw a great deal of light upon the mind of John Calvin in regard to the matter we are discussing. For that reason this material deserves a place in this study,

the more so since the thinking that led to the burning of
Servetus was of a piece with the thinking that made the life
of the Stepchildren so hard.

The burning of Servetus — let it be said with utmost clarity —
was a deed for which Calvin must be held largely responsible.
It was not done in spite of Calvin, as some over-ardent admirers
of his are wont to say. He planned it beforehand and maneu-
vered it from start to finish. It occurred because of him and
not in spite of him. After it had taken place Calvin defended
it, with every possible and impossible argument. There is
every reason to believe that if it had not been for the fact
that public opinion was beginning to run against this kind
of thing there would have been many more such burnings.
The event was the direct result of the sacralism to which
Calvin remained committed, a sacralism which he never discarded.

In Calvin's defence it might be said, and not without some
justification, that since he arrived on the scene somewhat late,
after the first decade, after the neo-Constantinianism into which
the Reformation drifted had developed, he really didn't have
much choice in the matter. The die was already cast when
he appeared on the scene; the Second Front had already been
opened. Calvin never was in the position in which Luther
and Zwingli had been, in those early days when the heirs of
medieval Restitutionism were still looking on hopefully. When
Calvin entered upon his life's task the Reformation had already
lost those who had been conditioned by the medieval rebellion
against "Christian sacralism." If it was too radical for Luther
to go the way of Restitutionism it was much too radical for
Calvin, who came a bit later. If it was too much to expect
Luther to pry himself loose from twelve centuries of history,
it was much too much for Calvin to come clear of twelve
centuries plus a very important decade.

Be that as it may, the Servetus execution took place in a
sacralist setting and was the result of sacralist thinking. It
was medieval to the core. It reveals a Constantinian determi-
nation. Here was a man who posed no threat to civil serenity
in Geneva — unless of course it be granted that anyone who
deviates from the orthodoxy exposed by the State is *ipso facto*

a threat to that civil serenity.ᴾ Servetus started no parades, made no speeches, carried no placards, had no political ambitions. He did have some erratic ideas touching the doctrine of the Trinity; and he entertained some deviating notions concerning baptism, especially infant baptism. No doubt there was something of the spiritual iconoclast in him, as there is in all men of genius (Servetus was something of a scientific genius in that he anticipated the idea of the circulatory course of the blood). But he was not a revolutionary in the political sense. He was indeed "off the beam" in matters of religious doctrine, but he did not deserve to be arrested or executed — a judgment in which the man of sacralist convictions cannot of course concur. Only in a sacralist climate would men deal in such a way with such a man.

If the very burning of the unhappy Spaniard proves that Calvin's Geneva was a sacral State and Geneva's Calvin a sacralist thinker, the literature that sprang up in defence of the awful deed makes it doubly clear.

When the news was out that Servetus had died in the fire, a cry of outrage resounded over most of Europe. It is true that many of the leaders of the Reform applauded the burning (Melanchthon, for example, wrote that "the Church owes and always will owe a debt of gratitude to you for having put the heretic to death"); although it is also true that some, even in Geneva itself, refused to put their names to a document supporting the execution. But there was a chorus of protest that issued at once from those circles that had been deeply influenced by the humanizing tendencies of the times. Con-

---

ᴾIn the sacral pattern heresy is automatically sedition. The Codes of Justinian decreed that "Heresy shall be construed to be an offence against the civil order" (XVI, 5:40). It was this dogmatism that led to the burning of Servetus. It has been said that Calvin sought, late in the trial, to have sentence commuted to the effect that some mode of execution other than by fire would be Servetus' lot. The reason for this suggestion was that Calvin wanted Servetus eliminated as an offender against the *civil* order. Death by fire was for offenders in the area of religion. Hence Calvin's concern in the matter. It was this same sensitivity that made Margaret of Parma, in 1567, specify death by *hanging* for Guido de Brès. It would look better to have de Brès destroyed as a seditionist than as a heretic; hence death by the noose rather than by the flame. So also in the case of Servetus.

trary to the legend that is kept alive by over-ardent admirers of Calvin, the spirit of the age was already relegating such inhumanity to the limbo of the past. The Renaissance had not been without its fruitage of toleration.

There is reason to believe that Calvin and those about him who had engineered the Servetus killing had a vague foreboding that the news of the awful incident would cost them plenty. They seem to have been on the defensive from the moment the ashes of the fire had cooled.ᵠ They began to work furiously on a book which was supposed to calm the spirits and prevent a too great exodus. Early in 1554, a matter of months after Servetus had expired (he had died on October 27, 1553), a *Defence* (the full title was *Defensio orthodoxae fidei de sacra Trinitate*) rolled from the presses of Oliva Roberti Stephani. If Calvin and his colleagues had expected this publication to serve as oil on the troubled waters they were in for an unpleasant surprise, for its impact was more like oil on a fire. Almost at once (it was in early March) a scathing denunciation of the burning, as well as of the whole line of reasoning that had produced it, came from an unnamed press (it was published anonymously, moreover — such were the times that it was not safe to put one's name to a publication of that import) with the title *De Haereticis an sint persequendi* (whether heretics are to be liquidated). The Genevans were of course unwilling to let this be the last word; and so in early August they came out with a second publication, bearing the title *De Haereticis a civili Magistratu puniendis adversus Martini Bellii* (whether heretics should be punished by the civil ruler,

---

ᵠFrom Calvin's correspondence of the time we sense a feeling of insecurity, arising over the reception given to the news of the Servetus liquidation. In a letter dated October 5, 1554 he cried on the shoulder of a friend: "If you knew but the tenth part of how I have been hurt by these shameful calumnies you would, kind as you are, groan beneath the burden of grief by which I am being tried. Dogs bark at me from every side; whatever of slander they can invent is being hurled at me. Actually the unfriendly ones and the critical in our own camp attack me even more fiercely than the acknowledged foes in the papal company. Surely I have not deserved this at the hands of the Church!" It seems that the dissatisfaction even in Geneva itself was great enough to occasion the postponement of the celebration of the Lord's Supper. It was postponed at least once, and perhaps as much as three times, in that season.

against Martin Bellius, who, they suspected, was the author of the anonymous publication against which they were reacting).

Although Calvin and Beza complained bitterly about the tone of the anonymous criticism of what had happened,[r] anyone who reads it will have to agree that although it does not mince matters it is written with a poise that was quite unusual in those times and keeps itself from railing and invective in a surprising way. One must agree with a recent Dutch scholar as he says that "It is likely that future generations as they judge of the matter, will ascribe the violent tone of Calvin and Beza's reply to it to a conscious or unconscious sense of weakness rather than a well-grounded conviction that their position was right."

In the reply to the anonymous critic the burning of Servetus was defended, to the hilt, as well as the whole sacralist line of thought that had spawned the awful deed. Naturally there were proof-texts; and, again naturally, they were derived primarily from the Old Testament.

As the Genevan sacralists (Beza seems to have been the principal author) searched the New Testament for support, they (and again very naturally) were unable to come up with much. One is certainly not impressed with Beza's "proof-text" drawn from the Book of Acts: "With what power, pray, did Peter put to death Ananias and Sapphira? And with what power did Paul smite Elymas blind? Was it with the power that is vested in the Church? Of course not. Well then, it must have been with the power that is vested in the magistrate, there being no third kind of power." One gets the impression that this is a matter of a drowning man clutching at straws. This is atrocious hermeneutics and is far from responsible interpretation of Scripture. We shall not dignify this specious argument with more than the reminder that the part which Peter played in the matter of Ananias and Sapphira finds no parallel at all in the part which the Genevans had played in

---

[r]Calvin tried hard to keep up his spirits in the matter, writing to his friend Sulzer at Basel that "This book filled with slander against me has been patched together in order that a sudden opposition to me might occur. The Senate has decided to put it in my hands for study. It was not hard for me to cut short its slander; I was even able to turn it to my own profit . . . ."

the death of Servetus. Moreover, it is news indeed that "Paul blinded Elymas," and that this episode had been paralleled in the Servetus burning!

The plain fact is that Beza *cum suis* reeled before the onslaughts of "Bellius." What is there to say to a passage like the following?

> Who would not mistake the Christ for a moloch or some such god if indeed he delights in human sacrifice . . . ? Imagine him to be present, in the capacity of constable, to announce the sentence and light the fire . . . ! "Oh Christ, thou creator and king of all the earth, dost thou not see these things? Art thou so changed completely, become thus cruel and contrary to thine own proper self . . . ? Dost thou command that those who do not understand thy commandments and institutions as yet, are to be choked in water, struck until the bowels gush forth, these then strewn with salt, to be struck with the sword or made to roast over small fire, with every torment martyred in as drawn out a manner as possible?* Ah Christ, dost thou indeed command such things and dost thou approve of them when they are done? Are they indeed thy lieutenants who officiate at such burned sacrifice? Dost thou allow thyself to be seen at the scene of such butchery? Dost thou then verily eat human flesh, Oh Christ? If thou doest such things forsooth, or orderest them done, then what, pray what, hast thou left for the devil to do?"

What did Beza have to say to this sharp but not uninspired voice? Nothing more than this: "Of all the blasphemous and impudent gabs!" (The text from which we quote, a Dutch translation, of which we shall speak presently, made by a man whose knowledge of the Latin was superb, whose translation can therefore be trusted, has: "O des lasterigen ende onbeschaemden becx!") This rejoinder, needless to say, is not in the idiom of good theological discussion; it is a classic of *ad hominem,* and bespeaks only weakness and frustration.

The tract which we are discussing gains in significance for our present purpose when it is known that early in the seventeenth century a spiritual son and heir of Genevan sacralism,

---

*In the sentences whereby heretics were sent to the stake it was usually specified that the execution was to be by "small fire." It seems that in the case of Servetus green wood was used, so that it took three hours before he was pronounced dead.

one Johannes Bogerman (assisted by a ministerial colleague), the man who was destined two decades later to chair the Great Synod of Dordt, republished it, in the Dutch translation to which we have already referred, at Franeker and on the presses of Gillis Van den Rade, printer for the *Staten Generaal*.ᵗ Evidently Bogerman thought that Beza's book was still good reading, good enough to be reprinted and recirculated. That already speaks volumes; for it indicates that the sacralism that had precipitated the burning of Servetus, as well as the literature that came forth in support thereof, was still regnant in Dutch Reformed circles.

The plot thickens when it is known what it was that made Bogerman put Beza in a new suit. From the lengthy introduction prefixed to the translation we learn that this was the occasion. Bogerman and his ministerial associates at Groningen were just then starting a crusade against a group of Anabaptists who were holding worship services in the quiet of their own houses. The translation was made to get the magistrates to "Do your duty to the God who has put the sword into your hands . . . . Strike down valiantly these monsters in the guise of men!" From the lengthy introduction we learn that some years earlier, while Bogerman was stationed at Sneek, he had been instrumental in getting the magistrates to do their "duty" by driving apart a similar nest of "heretics." On that occasion he had come, uninvited and arm in arm with the constable, into the meeting, had, likewise uninvited, offered a lengthy prayer for the benefit of these "heretics" and had, once more without being asked, given them the benefit of a long "sermon," in which all their "errors" were neatly dissected. The most pathetic thing in the whole sorry account is that Bogerman wrote all this in the full confidence that his readers would applaud him for these feats of faithfulness. So sacralist was the thinking!

Beza had written, and Bogerman revived it, that the freedom of conscience for which the critics of the Servetus affair were clamoring was "worse than the tyranny of the pope, as much worse as anarchy is worse than tyranny."

ᵗThe public University of Amsterdam has a copy of this Dutch translation, which we were permitted to have and to use in the United States, through the facilities of the University of Michigan's Inter-library Loan service. It is from this volume that we quote.

The medieval doctrine of the "two swords" was roundly endorsed by Beza and Bogerman. We read that "just as the members of the body have, in spite of their several functions, one single assignment in one body, so also in regard to the Church, to the support of which both the civil power and the ecclesiastical have been divinely commissioned . . . . Let this then be the conclusion of this argument: those who would bar the Christian magistracy from the care of religion and especially from the punishment of heretics, contemn the plain Word of God, reject the authority of the ages [a not very Protestant argument, be it noted, coming too close for comfort to the Catholic idea of "tradition"], and as a consequence seek the total destruction and extermination of the Church."

There is a great temptation (but no need) to dwell longer on the Servetus matter and the literature produced in support of it. Enough has been said to make it quite apparent that the final strains of the Reformation were played in the register of "Christian sacralism." If more is needed we have only to point to the fact that the Belgic Confession lays upon the magistrate the "duties" which had led to the burning. It was not until the acids of time had bitten deep into the sacralist pattern that Article 36 began to embarrass Reformed people, and that did not take place until comparatively recent times. It did not take place in the Netherlands until the establishment-status of the *Hervormde Kerk* had been made fictitious by the Secessions.

Calvin's essentially sacral conception becomes apparent further in his reaction to the Anabaptists' manifesto promulgated at Schlatten am Rande in the year 1527. We pause for a brief examination of it and of Calvin's response to it.[20]

One of the points made in the Schlatten am Rande statement has to do with the sword function, in connection with the Church. It reads as follows:

> The sword is an ordinance of God outside the perfection of Christ; the Princes and Rulers of the world are ordained for the punishment of evil-doers and for putting them to death. But within the perfection of Christ excommunication is the ultimate in the way of punishment, physical death being not included.

We would submit that for any man who no longer thinks in terms of "Christian sacralism" this formulation is right and proper. The sword is said to be a divine institution, with power to coerce, if need be to inflict the death penalty. But this sword, so it is said, has no coercive assignment inside the Church; emphatically not, for in this area the highest sentence is excommunication. One would expect all right-thinking men to go along with this. It is true, the expression "the perfection of Christ" is a bit strange; but it must be kept in mind that those who were gathered at Schlatten am Rande were pioneering and had to create a vocabulary. The terminology that comes at once to our minds was not yet current; the terms "Church" and "State" were as yet undifferentiated. If for "the perfection of Christ" we substitute "the Church of Christ" (as we may) then this delineation of the functions of the two entities is altogether acceptable.

But not in the ears of a man of sacralist thought-habits. Calvin not only thrust Schlatten am Rande to one side but volunteered to refute it in print, saying: "The principal task of the magistrates is not the business of keeping their subjects in peace as to the body; rather is it to bring about that God is served and honored in their domains." For: "As the magistrates have the duty of purging the Church of offences by bodily punishments and coercions so do the ministers have the duty of assisting the magistrates by reducing the number of those who offend." Calvin rebuked Schlatten am Rande, saying, "The hand cannot say to the foot, I have no need of thee."[u] Knowing

[u]In so applying the words of 1 Corinthians 12:21, Calvin reveals his sacralist attitude; for him Church and State are but two aspects of one and the same thing. He will not hear of any separation. And in this Calvin was like all the rest of the Reformers. One must agree with Karl Rieker as he says, in his *Die Rechtliche Stellung der Evangelischen Kirche Deutschlands* . . . : "Es handelt sich also für die Reformatoren nicht um das Verhältnis zweier Gemeinwesen zu einander; sie kennen überhaupt nur *eine* Gemeinwesen, *eine* umfassende Verbandseinheit und das ist die *Christenheit* . . . . In diesem Stück sind also die Reformatoren nicht modern, sondern gut mittelalterlich" (pp. 53f., italics are Rieker's). One must agree also with Georges de Lagarde, who in his *Recherches sur l'esprit politique de la Reforme* declares that "L' Eglise calviniste n'est pas une société indépendent; . . . l'Eglise et l'Etat ne devaient former qu'un seul et même être."

full well that the authors of the manifesto had a way of going back to pre-Constantinian times, Calvin seeks to make them realize that they have no right to do so. For him the Constantinian change was a big improvement upon those earlier times, "those earlier days when the dignity of the Church still lay hidden," an idea which Calvin, as we shall see, owed to Augustine, that prime apologete for "Christian sacralism."

In fine, Calvin's reply to Schlatten am Rande was: "We ought not to shut out from among us the institution of civil justice nor drive it out of the Church" ("ny le chasser hors de l'Eglise"). In passing the reader will note that at this point Calvin falls into the fallacy of which we spoke earlier, namely of thinking that, when the Stepchildren clamored for the expulsion of the civil power from the Church, they were at the same time asking that it be terminated in the civil area. Calvin's sacralist thinking made it impossible for him to distinguish between terminating the civil rule and expelling it from the affairs of the faith.

From the monism that is reflected here Calvin never escaped. In his way of thinking, what we now call the Church and what we now call the State are woven into a single fabric; together they constitute a single entity. It was this monism that made it impossible for Calvin to understand what the Stepchildren were driving at. It was this monism that found expression in the creeds that grew up under his influence.

One can always learn where a man stands in regard to the tensions that came to expression between the Reformers and their Stepchildren if we ask him what he thinks of the Constantinian change as such. Exponents of "Christian sacralism" look upon the events of Constantine's day as the beginning of the golden age; Restitutionists look upon them as the end of the golden age.˙

That Augustine was of the former category we have intimated, and we shall have occasion to feel his pulse again. That Calvin was of the same school has been shown, and will be shown in greater detail in later chapters of this volume. That Bogerman was of a similar mind we already know; the following passage from his hand will make the matter clearer still:

> The service of the magistrate in the matter of the care of
> religion began in the New Testament times with Constantine
> the Great . . . , seeing that the preceeding rulers were heathen
> and hostile to the Church and that Constantine put forth
> proper zeal to procure for the Church outward peace and
> the true doctrine together with opposition for the teachings
> which he considered heretical.

(In passing it may be of interest to know that such lavish
praise for the man to whom the Stepchildren referred as "that
dragon" was too much for them. They shot back that Constantine had been an adulterer — to which Bogerman replied
"So was David, and a murderer moreover.")

This assessment of the Constantinian change was ingrained
in the Reformed tradition. How they felt about it at the Synod
of Dordt may be gathered from the lavish praise bestowed
upon the civil power, which had convened the Great Synod,
for "walking in the footsteps of your illustrious forbears, Constantine, Theodosius, etc."

Not only were the leaders of the Reform committed to Constantinianism, they also welcomed every invasion of the sword
into the affairs of the faith (provided of course that the magistrate supported the *right* religion). They constantly urged the
magistrate to draw the blood of the opposition. When Edward
the Sixth came to the throne in England, Henry Bullinger,
successor to Zwingli in the Swiss Reformation, jubilated (we
are able to quote him in an ancient English translation):

> Blessed be that bontuous lorde, which hath not suffered the
> prynces, whome by his divine providence he hath made and
> ordoned to be the supreme gouvernors of hys church, im-
> mediately under hym . . . to erre and bee deceved any longer,
> but dyd most mercyfull open their eyes to loke upon that
> comfortable sonne of rightuousness and lyght of the truth . . .
> who shall with all prudence shed the blode of them that dyd
> shed the innocent bloode . . . .[21]

(In passing be it noted that if this spirit had been allowed to
continue unabated, if this theology had not eroded away,
there would have been no end to the religious wars of
extermination.)

We spoke of erosion. Erosion is a slow process, and remnants of the Constantinian heritage were carried to the shores of the New World. Some of the colonies on the Atlantic seaboard excluded by law "all Ranters and Quakers and other notorious heretics." But there was also the leaven of the Stepchildren brought to these shores. The citizens of Providence refused to go along with the illiberal policy, saying that freedom of conscience was their "most prized possession." Thereupon the Massachusetts Commissioners retorted that these sectaries "tend to the very absolute cutting down and overturn of all civil government among you."

But erosion is also persistent. The colossus of Constantinianism fell, and as far as the New World is concerned, "great was the fall thereof." The First Amendment of the Federal Constitution, which provided that "Congress shall make no law establishing religion nor prohibit the free exercise thereof" was the death sentence of "Christian sacralism." This Amendment is a Monroe Doctrine in which the soil of the New World is closed to sacralist plantings from the Old World.

No doubt the very experience of carving out a new civilization in the wilderness hastened the day of the demise of Constantinianism in the New World. At any rate it lingered on much longer in Europe, where it has been said only lately that "The end of the Constantinian Age has come." Within very recent times, however, an exponent of the Reformation tradition in the Netherlands gave clear evidence that in his mind Constantinianism was still very right and proper. We find this evidenced in his assessment of the Constantinian change. Wrote Dr. Abraham Kuyper:

> When the first contest eventuated in this that the emperor bowed to Jesus, then . . . the kingship of Christ began to be triumphant in society . . . . The kingship of Christ from this time on stood as a direction-giving power above the imperial power, which, in order to strengthen its influence, tried for an ever-increasingly close integration with the kingship of Jesus . . . . When in the fourth century persecution ceased and the imperial power showed a readiness to accommodate itself to Jesus, then the basic victory became apparent . . . . This

principial victory continued on during the entire course of
the long long period known as the Middle Ages.ᵛ

Wherever there are remnants of Constantinianism there one
detects a sort of nostalgia for what for these people were "the
good old times," the days of "Christian sacralism"; wherever
the Constantinian formula has been effectively repudiated there
this nostalgia does not occur; in its place one finds a nostalgia
for the world depicted in the New Testament. Among the so-
called Younger Churches, where there is no Constantinian
tradition, separation of Church and State is taken for granted.
It seems safe to conclude that if the cause of Christ still has
a future (and we have His word for it that it has) it will be
in the climate of the composite society. This is but to say
that it will be in the kind of world for which the Stepchildren
agonized, an activity that earned them the hateful name of
"Neo-Donatists."

ᵛA curious monism comes to expression here. The confluence of Church
and State in the days of Constantine (which Kuyper celebrates as a
great triumph) required the rule-right that comes to expression in the
State to coalesce with the rule-right that comes to expression in the Church.
This monism, if allowed to go its way, will cause men to slide imperceptibly
from the common grace of God (which has given us the State) to the
special grace of God (which gives us the Church). It will cause men
to slide imperceptibly from the sonship that results from the Creator-
creature relationship to the sonship that results from the Redeemer-
redeemed relationship. This monism bites as a caustic into the distinction
of General Revelation and Special Revelation. It tends to erase the distinction between *Volk* and *Volk Gottes*. It is not surprising that the
Stepchildren, who opposed this insidious monism consistently, were spitefully called dualists by those who continued to adhere to it!²²

2 *Stäbler*

W E HAVE SEEN, IN THE PREVIOUS CHAPTER, THAT "THE SWORD was welded to the cross" at the time of the Constantinian change. From this point on the cause of Christ had the benefit, if benefit it was, of a second sword, one made of steel. And we have begun to point out that the Reformers were not minded in their day to sweep this alien weapon out of the Church. The men of the Second Front, however, were convinced that the Constantinian change had perverted the Gospel, had by bringing the sword into the Church and its affairs admitted a foreign body into the tissues of Christ's Church, a foreign body that had to be removed if suppuration were to cease.

The sword of steel is basically a weapon with which to coerce. The Constantinian change, therefore, caused the technique of coercion to be imported into the affairs of the Church. Because of it the cause of Christ lost the dimension of voluntaryism, which is native to true Christianity, and with it the cause of Christ picked up the dimension of coercionism, which is foreign to the true faith. It is with this matter of coercionism versus voluntaryism that we shall be engaged at the present time.

Quite understandably the "heretics" made an issue of this change. They assailed coercionism and advocated voluntaryism. As they sought to reconstitute the Church, they — like the rebuilders of the temple in the day of Nehemiah — worked with the sword in one hand and the trowel in the other; the sword, to banish coercionism; and the trowel, to rebuild voluntaryism.

63

In this program the "heretics," in some instances at least, adopted a distinguishing badge. In protest against the sword-wielding ones they themselves carried a harmless staff such as shepherds use.

For this they were, in Reformation times, sometimes referred to as *Stäbler*,[a] staff-carriers. So widely was the carrying of such a harmless cane thought of as a mark of "heresy" that we find this feature mentioned in the sixteenth century as *prima facie* evidence of addiction to the "heresy" that characterized the Second Front.[b]

Such cane-carrying was not invented in the 16th century, however; it seems to have been a distinguishing feature of the "heretic" from very early times. We read that the Waldensians taught men not to confess their sins save to a cane-carrying cleric. This was apparently taken over by an element among the Bohemian Brethren, as a mark testifying to the conviction that the sword of steel is not a proper weapon in the hands of a follower of the Christ.[c] The innovation caused one of the leaders of the Bohemian evangelicals, Lucas of Prague, to say angrily, "I highly disapprove of these vain Pharisees wandering around with staffs, who display their righteousness."[1]

The Scotch-Irish, who long resisted the "Constantinian change" in northwest Europe, carried a staff, known as a *gambutta,* to differentiate between themselves and the Rome-sent clerics. Here the issue seems also to have been the matter of voluntaryism versus coercionism.

The Donatists may have been the first staff-carriers. They carried a harmless cane, which they called their *"Israel,"* a

---

[a]At the root of the German word *Stäbler* lies the word *Stab,* meaning *staff*; with the suffix *el* it becomes *little staff*. *Stäbler,* then, are people who carry a little staff.

[b]At a hearing, held in 1590 to ascertain whether there had been any Anabaptists in the area, a witness based his testimony, that there had indeed been some, on the fact that he "had met them often enough when with their little staff . . . they were on their way to their preachings or whatever it is they do."

[c]Sometimes the anti-coercionism of the Restitutionist vision came to expression in the practice of carrying a wooden (and therefore harmless) sword. So, for example, among some of the Bohemian Brethren. This symbol of anti-coercionism also occurred among Restitutionist groups in Poland and Lithuania, especially among the followers of Peter Gonesius.

term that in all probability is of Semitic origin (it will be re-called that there was considerable Semitic influence in North-west Africa), possibly a corruption of "*Azael*," meaning "strength of God." If this is accepted then the man who carried such an "*Israel*" was contrasting himself with those who were making the arm of flesh (the emperor) their strength. It would then again be a matter of the propriety or impropriety of coercion.

However common or uncommon the carrying of a staff may have been, we shall in this study let the term *Stäbler* stand for the "heretic" as he resisted the encroachment of coercionism in matters of the Faith.

It was Augustine, he perhaps more than any other, who sup-plied the Constantinians with arguments from the Scriptures (or rather with arguments fastened upon the Scriptures) where-by coercion was rendered theologically respectable. The ex-pression found in Luke 14:23, "Constrain them to come in," rendered in Latin *Compelle intrare*, was exactly what he needed in his running battle with the Donatists.

The followers of Donatus were offering to secede from the "fallen" Church and to go their own way, a step which the advocates of "Christian sacralism" could not permit, for it would strike at the very heart of their dream of a faith common to all in the empire. Hence they let it be known, early in the conflict, that schism would not be permitted but would be opposed, if need be with arms. Thereupon the Donatists pointed out that this would be to deviate from the policies of the Master, who had not raised a finger, much less a sword, to restrain people from going away. More than that, when a sizable group walked out He had confronted His disciples with the wistful question, "Do you not also want to go?"

To this line of thought — the cogency of which had not escaped him — Augustine replied:

> I hear that you are quoting that which is recorded in the Gospel, that when the seventy followers went back from the Lord they were left to their own choice in this wicked and impious desertion and that He said to the twelve remaining 'Do you not also want to go?' But what you fail to say is that at that time the Church was only just beginning to burst forth from the newly planted seed and that the saying had

not as yet been fulfilled in her "All kings shall fall down
before Him, all nations shall serve him." It is in proportion
to the more enlarged fulfillment of this prophecy that the
Church now wields greater power — so that she may now
not only invite but also compel men to embrace that which
is good.[2]

Here we have an early representation of the notion that
the Church of Christ was intended by its Founder to enter
into a situation radically different from the one depicted in
the New Testament. Here we have the beginnings of the
notion, which reigned supreme in the minds of men all through
medieval times, that part way into the Christian era a change
was intended by the King of the Church himself — a change
whereby the world of apostolic times would become obsolete.
This change was identified with the Constantinian innovation.
This idea set forth by Augustine controlled the thought and the
theology of European man all through medieval times. It
led to all sorts of theological absurdities — as, for example, that
the Great Commission was intended for the pre-Constantinian
era and had with the Constantinian change been fulfilled. Here
is the beginning of the un-Protestant deference to *het historisch
gewordene,* to which we have called attention earlier. Augustine's notion of a new regime that coincided with the Constantinian change and that constituted a "larger fulfillment"
continues to be in vogue wherever men have not sloughed
off their Constantinianism.[d]

[d]In the year 1953 the present author wrote an article for *The Reformed
Journal* (October issue, article entitled "Biblical Christianity and Cultural
Compositism") in which the idea was set forth that the New Testament
anticipates a composite society. The contents of this article did not seem
right to those of the Reformed Church of the Netherlands who feel
that separate and antithetical social organizations are implied in the
Christian vision. Several meetings were held to refute the idea of societal
compositism and a series of articles appeared in the periodical *Patrimonium,*
which regularly speaks for that faction. In these articles we read (I
translate): "We must point out with emphasis that any proof from
Scripture becomes extremely dangerous if historical development is lost
sight of. We all are acquainted with the shadow-boxing of the sects,
who seize upon random texts to 'prove' their theses, forgetting that there
is such a thing as history and the unfolding of human existence. What
is really the value of recourse to texts in the New Testament? Does
Verduin not know that in the as yet diversified culture of those times

For this notion of the "larger fulfillment" Augustine had managed to find "Scriptural warrant" — with the help of exegetical form that is not much short of acrobatic stunting. For he goes on to say:

> This He shows [namely the "enlarged fulfillment" idea which now puts the Church in position to coerce] plainly enough in the parable of the wedding feast; after He had summoned the invited ones . . . and the servants have said "It has been done as you ordered and yet there is room" the Master said "Go out in the highways and hedges and compel them to come in in order that my house may be full." Now observe how that with reference to those who came in during the former period it was "bring them in" and not "compel them," by which the incipient condition of the Church is signified, during which she was but growing toward the position of being able to compel. Since it was right by reason of greater strength and power to coerce men to the feast of eternal salvation therefore it was said later . . . "Go out into the highways and hedges and compel them to come. in."

Here then is the vision, regnant from Augustine to Reformation times and beyond them, that the "fall" of the Church was a fall upward. And here, at the very outset we find it worked out that one of the features of this fall upward was the acquisition of the power to coerce.

Fully confident of himself, Augustine concluded tauntingly:

> And so if you [Donatists] were strolling quietly outside the feast of eternal salvation and the unity of the holy Church then we would overtake you on your "highways"; but now that you verily by many injuries and cruelties which you perpetrate upon our people, are full of thorns and spines, now

---

the situation was altogether different from our own, that moreover a *different* [The italics are by us; but they are called for by the accent mark in the original] task was laid away for those early Christians — the Church had still to explode, as it were, in the world . . . . I should think we should first of all get together to discuss the use of Scripture as such." Here, as the reader will see, we have Augustine in modern dress, the "greater fulfillment" having rendered the New Testament obsolete as it stands, so that its texts become "extremely dangerous" if quoted without being filtered through "het historisch gewordene." Needless to say, this is a "Protestant" equivalent of the Catholic notion of "tradition" and wholly unacceptable.

we come upon you in your "hedges" to compel you. The
sheep which is compelled is coerced while it is unwilling, but
after it has been brought in it may graze as its own volition
wills.

Augustine managed to overpower° still another Scripture
passage that he could turn to suit his purpose, great allegorizer
that he was. He found it in the family situation of Abraham,
where there were two wives, one a free-woman and the other a
bond-servant. The former lived her life in the climate of
voluntaryism and the latter lived hers in that of coercionism.
In this way Augustine justified the presence of two kinds of
Christians in the Church, one there by choice and the other
by coercion. Moreover, the allegory also justified it that the
former afflicted the latter — had not Sarah pommelled Hagar?

This bit of sophism also became a part of the panoply of the
medieval exponent of "Christian sacralism." It was repeated
in Reformation times, as we shall see.

All through medieval times the "fallen" church, acting on
the teachings of Augustine and others, resorted to the use of

°The length to which Augustine went in his effort to find New Testament warrant for coercionism is almost unbelievable. In his letter to
Vincentius he wrote: "have you not read how Paul . . . was compelled
by great violence . . . to embrace the truth? For, the light of men's
eyes, more precious than money or gold, was suddenly taken away from
him . . . . He did not get it back until he became a member of the
Holy Church. You think no coercion should be used to deliver a man
from his error; and yet you see . . . that God does this very thing." In
a sermon on Luke 14:16 Augustine puts these words into the mouth of
Christ: "Whom thou shalt find, wait not until they choose to come,
compel them to come in. I have prepared a great supper . . . , I cannot
suffer any place to remain vacant in it. The Gentiles come from the
streets and lanes; let the heretics come from the hedges . . . . For those
who make hedges have as their object to make divisions. Let these be
drawn away from the hedges, plucked up from among the thorns. They
have stuck fast in the hedges, unwilling to be compelled. 'Let us,' say
they, 'come in of our own volition'; but this is not the Lord's directive.
He says, 'Compel them to come in.'" In his De Correctione Donatistorum
Augustine comes back once more to this passage in Luke: "Wherefore if
the power, which the Church has received by divine appointment in its
due season through the religious character and faith of kings, be instrumental in compelling those who are found in the highways and hedges —
that is, in heresies and schisms — then let these not find fault for being
thus compelled."

force wherever it went. When, for example, Amandus came to what is now Flanders, early in the seventh century, he began his "missionary"[t] efforts with a visit to the local king, Dagobert II. His request for aid granted, to the extent of coercion by the king's sword, he went to his task, carrying papers on which it was stated for all to know that the king's orders were: "If anyone does not of his own accord have himself regenerated by baptism he shall be coerced to it by the king." This Amandus a little later complained to his superiors in Rome that he had once and again been obliged to pick himself out of the Schelde River — the explanation for this not very kind reception seems to be that this was the way the natives sought to pay him back in his own coin, replying to his forced baptisms by a forced baptism of their own.[r]

Amandus' colleague Winfrid, (who was beatified as St. Boniface for his many services rendered in the interest of Constantinianism), was similarly committed to the idea that coercion by the secular arm was right and proper. He went so far as to say that "Without the patronage of the Frankish princes we are unable either to rule the Church or defend the priests and clerics, the monks and the nuns; nor can we without their orders and authority prevent the pagan rites and the idolatrous sacrilege of the Germans."

Quite in keeping with this doctrine, taught him by the "fallen" Church, Emperor Charles, who for his many services in the Constantinian scheme came to be known as Charlemagne (i.e., Charles *the Great*) helped the "missionaries" by decreeing that "all who stubbornly refuse Christian baptism shall be put to death."

Among the "heretics" this philosophy whereby coercion was justified was from early times under attack. This attack became an integral part of the total vision of men of Restitutionist

---

[t]We place this word in quotation marks because it is anomalous to refer to these activities as "missionary." As we shall point out at a later juncture, missions in the New Testament sense of the word did not and do not occur in the Constantinian climate.

[r]*Zwangtaufe*, baptism by force, was common enough in medieval Europe. We shall see that the Stepchildren were in their times exposed to this indignity.

convictions. The following description of medieval "heresy" makes this quite apparent:

> The heretics preach much from the Gospels and the Epistles and say among other things that a man should do no evil, should not lie nor swear. When they preach from the Gospels and the Epistles they corrupt them with their explanations — as masters of error who know not to sit at the feet of truth, teaching and expounding the Scriptures being altogether forbidden to lay-folk. They say that their Church is the true Church and that the Roman Church is no Church but a Church of malignants. They reprobate Church wealth and ecclesiastical regalia, the high privilege of bishop and abbot, they seek to abolish all ecclesiastical privilege. They maintain that no one is to be coerced to the faith. They condemn the Church's sacraments and say that a priest living in mortal sin cannot make the body of the Lord. They hold that transubstantiation takes place not in the hands of the priest but in the heart of him who receives worthily.[3]

Similarly a man of "heretical" bent in faraway Poland, Peter Chelcicky, was saying a century before the Reformation:

> By the use of force no man is brought to faith in Christ, as little likely as that a man can learn Bohemian by studying German . . . . By means of the secular power Anti-Christ has pulled all power to himself under cover of the Christian faith. Since we believe that it was by meekness and humility unto the Cross that Christ delivered us from the power of Satan we cannot allow that the perfecting of our faith comes by worldly power; as if force is a greater benefit than is faith . . . . When Emperor Constantine in his heathen mode of existence was taken up into the Church by Pope Sylvester and the latter in turn was fitted out with external power — it was then that the destruction of the Church was inevitable.

These were voices that issued from men who had broken with the "fallen" Church; there were also some individuals who remained in it but repudiated its ideas as to voluntaryism and coercionism. Just as, according to the Belgic Confession, the Fall in Eden left some "little traces" of the glory that once was, so also did the "fall" of the Church leave some such small vestiges of the former state of rectitude.

Outstanding among these was Hilary of Poitiers, who wrote in 365, when the Constantinian change was taking place:

> The Church now terrifieth with threats of exile and dungeon and she who of old gained adherents in spite of dungeons and exile now brings men to faith by compulsion. She who was propagated by hunted priests now hunts priests in her turn . . . . This must be said in comparison with that Church which was handed down to us and which now we have lost; the fact is in men's eyes and cries aloud.

Similar evidence of the "little traces" occurred off and on throughout medieval times. Here is Wazo, bishop of Liège, who in the eleventh century replied to his colleague, who was prodding him to proceed against certain "heretics" that reportedly were sojourning about Liège:

> Although the ideas of these heretics have been condemned by the Church long ago yet should these men be dealt with gently and in the spirit of Him who cautioned against pulling up the tares. We ought not to resort to the judgment of power to put out of the way those whom the Creator lets live. Nor must we think that upon our ordination as bishops we come into possession of a sword, the sword of the civil ruler; we are anointed unto making alive not unto putting to death. The faithful must of course be warned against the heretics seeing that he who handles pitch gets his fingers soiled.

These were sentiments uttered by individual men, men in whom the darkness had not become complete. But officially the "fallen" Church thought and taught and wrought otherwise — all through medieval times. The Church of the Middle Ages was not a company of believing folk joined in voluntary association; it was a mass of human beings brought together and held together by the symbol of coercion, the sword of the secular power. The official doctrine was, as Pope Pelagius was putting it as early as the year 553, "unto the coercing of heretics and schismatics the Church possesses the secular arm, to coerce in case men cannot be brought to sanity by reasonable argument."

When the medieval Church called these Restitutionists "heretics" it used that word in its etymological sense. In this sense the word does not connote theological deviation, as it does in modern usage. The "heretics," as we have said, were not off the beam theologically; and yet they were "heretics." The word "heretic" is derived from the Greek verb *hairein* which means "to exercise option in the presence of alternatives." Those who saw the Christian life to be a matter of choice between alternatives were for that reason called "heretics," by those who thought in terms of a "choiceless Christianity." For this reason the word "heretics" was used interchangeably with "schismatics" — as the quotation just recited from Pelagius illustrates.

We see then that the Reformers had to choose between two alternatives, to continue in the tradition of "Christian sacralism" or to go in the tradition of the long rebellion against that concept. The latter alternative was fraught with very great difficulty. It would mean to go it alone, without the help of the princes. This would expose the reformatory movement to almost insuperable danger — for, over against it stood the Catholic order, armed to the teeth with weapons which, as history had shown for a thousand years, it was not loath to use. How oppose such a power? With empty hands? That would be similar to fighting against army tanks with bare fists — as the Hungarian rebels did in Budapest in 1956. The alternative was to make a deal with the local rulers. This would give the reformatory movement its own sword and the promise of success. After all, what had become of John Hus? And what was there to save Luther from a similar fate? The wits of the day were already referring to him as "the German goose" (i.e. the German Hus, for the slavic word for goose is *hus*). Luther had a decision to make, a hard decision. Let no one belittle the extremely cruel nature of the dilemma which he and his fellow Reformers faced. Humanly speaking, the only thing that offered any hope was to construct a rival Constantinianism, a new territorial Church, which could then offer the older Constantinianism some formidable competition. There seemed to be no workable alternative.

But Luther also had his other moments, when he was more in accord with the New Testament. Then he spoke from the point of view of the old Restitutionists. "Heretics must be converted with Scripture and not with fire!" In these early days, in 1523, Luther gave voice to the following: "The soul's thoughts and reflections are revealed to no one but to God; therefore it is impossible to compel one with physical force to believe this or that. It takes another kind of compulsion to accomplish this; physical force is incapable of it." In these moments Luther stood close to Tertullian, who had said in his day that "It is a fundamental right, a privilege of nature, that every man should worship according to his own convictions. One man's religion neither helps nor harms another man. It is not in the nature of religion to coerce to religion, which must be adopted freely and not by force." But just as this Tertullian had his other side, so that he also said, later in life, that "Heretics may properly be compelled, not enticed to duty; obstinacy must be corrected, not coaxed," so did Luther also shift his weight to the other leg. His stance was determined by what was at the moment uppermost in his mind, the New Testament delineation of the Church or *het historisch gewordene*. There were moments in which Luther cherished the ancient Restitutionist hope of having some day a Church of believers. He spoke sometimes, to his most intimate friends, about this pipe-dream. But each time he was jerked back into the world of reality and its harsh requirement. Then the other alternative beckoned.

Those in his following who had been conditioned by medieval "heresy" soon grew weary of this halting between two opinions. For them there was no problem. For them there was only one solution, that of making a clean break with the past and starting from scratch. There were hot-heads among them, men who wanted to go "full steam ahead, come what may!" Their recklessness made Luther look the more kindly toward the other alternative. This only made the radicals the more impatient. Disappointed with the Reformers' halting between two opinions they skulked off by themselves.

Soon we find Luther launching a full-scale attack upon his erstwhile friends and associates. Now that they had abandoned him there was nothing further to lose. The Reformation had crystallized in the pattern of neo-Constantinianism; there was nothing left but to turn the guns on those who had deserted the Reform because of it.

Luther assigned to his associate Urbanus Rhegius the task

of leading the attack, telling him to write a book against
the *Schwärmer*, as he now began to call them. Rhegius complied, with a volume in which lavish praise is heaped upon
Constantine and his successors for the direction they had given.
Rhegius endorsed to the hilt the policy of coercing those who
stand in the way of sacralism, liquidating them if need be:

> The truth leaves you no choice; you must agree that the
> magistracy has the authority to coerce his subjects to the
> Gospel. And if you say, "Yes, but with admonition and well-
> chosen words but not by force" then I answer that to get
> people to the services with fine words and admonitions is
> the preacher's duty, but to keep them there with recourse to
> force if need be and to frighten them away from error is
> the proper function of the rulers . . . . What do you suppose
> "Compelle intrare" means?[4]

Meanwhile the Radicals went about to organize a Church
as they thought it should exist — by voluntary association. As
one of their leaders, Felix Manz, put it, their ambition was
"to bring together those who were willing to accept Christ,
obey the Word, and follow in His footsteps, to unite with
these by baptism, and to leave the rest in their present conviction." It will not escape the observant that here we have
voluntaryism secured, (in the words "willing to accept") and
coercionism precluded (by the phrase "leaving the rest in their
present conviction").

This was certainly Restitutionism, without any ambiguity.
For this ambition Manz was placed in a boat with his hands
tied together at the wrists and passed over his knees, a heavy
stick then thrust between his knees and his bent elbows. Thus
bound, he was rowed to the far end of the Limmat and thrown
overboard, so that he perished in the murky waters. This
happened on January 5, 1527.

Another of the Radicals, Georg Blaurock, gave expression
to the Restitutionist vision in these words: "to gather by ourselves as Paul has it." Such a Church cannot be a Church of
the masses. To raise up such a Church is to put an end to
the sacralist program. No wonder Blaurock was a hunted man.

Still another, Pilgram Marpeck, a Restitutionist of the higher
classes, put the issue of voluntaryism and coercionism thus: "By

infant baptism men coerce people to enter the Kingdom of God; and yet there should be no coercion there. All they have eternal punishment awaiting them who seek to sustain the Kingdom of God with recourse to the civil power . . . the magistracy has no assignment touching the Kingdom of God."

To quote still another, Hans Denck: "Let everyone know that in matters of faith things ought to be on a voluntary basis, without coercion."

In these testimonies we hear the voices of the leaders of the Second Front; if we listen to the voices of the common soldiers we hear the same sentiments. About eighty young men, selected because of their physical fitness from among some two hundred who had been arrested, were held at Trieste until the galleys (on which they had been sentenced to serve as beasts of burden) came into port to take them on. While they waited they drew up a statement of their faith. In it the matter of the propriety of coercion was also taken up. We read in the quaint dialect of these simple folk: "Where has God commanded His child saying 'Child, go into the whole world . . . teach all nations, him however who refuses to accept or to believe your teaching you are to catch, torture, yes, strangle until he believes'?" When the representative of the "Christendom" which was responsible for the incarceration of these people, a cleric who had been dispatched to convert these "heretics," replied by saying, "Does not Christ say in the parable . . . 'go into the highways and hedges and compel them to come in so that my house may be full'?" they shot back, "It is by His Word and His judgment that Christ constrains men!"

All this is plain enough, no doubt. The rejection of coercive techniques from the area of Faith was an integral part of the platform of the Radicals — from the most intellectual leader to the simplest peasant. That this was the case may be known still more clearly from testimony given by the Reformers themselves. Henry Bullinger, for instance, Zwingli's successor, recited the following to show what "intolerable" people these Restitutionists were:

> They say that one cannot and may not use force to compel anyone to accept the faith seeing that faith is a free gift from God. It is wrong, say they, to compel anyone by force or coercion to embrace the faith, or, to put anyone to death

because of erring faith. It is an error, they assert, that in
the Church any other sword is used than that of the divine
Word. The secular kingdom, they hold, should be separate
from the Church and no civil ruler ought to exercise his
authority there. The Lord has commanded, they hold, simply
to preach the Gospel and not to compel any one by force to
accept it. The true Church of Christ, according to them, has
this characteristic that it suffers and endures persecution but
does not inflict it upon any.[5]

The passage just quoted should go far to refute the argument, heard only too often, that it would be an anachronism to
expect from the Reformers an open espousal of the principles
of religious freedom since those principles had not been for-
mulated as yet. Bullinger knew them and was able to recite
them — only to reject them. The same is true of Bucer, who
had been exposed to the following, addressed to him personally:

This work of the Lord will be done without the help of the
sword and without show of physical force, solely by the
spiritual power and grace, not without many afflictions and
tribulations . . . . The Sacred Scriptures do not teach that the
mighty ones and the glorious must build the Church . . . with
the help of force and coercion utilized knowingly and un-
knowingly . . . . Those who have the sovereignty and the faith
also . . . ought to be subject to the discipline of God together
with the other members of the Church . . . for the magistrates
have not been called by God to uproot and exterminate the
tares by persecuting them or by confiscating their goods and
industry or by depriving them of their life for the cause of
religion. It is not for this end that God has given them power;
quite to the contrary, Christ forbids that the powers be used
to these ends in the bosom of the Church. It is their duty
to administer in an equitable and impartial way temporal
affairs and material things . . . . It is not fitting that they who
love the Word of God in truth should constrain to the faith
by tyrannical violence those who are outside, or, to make
those who share in their own religion to continue in it contrary
to their own volition. It is impossible to believe that it is in
any way useful to necessitate a man to attend the Holy Supper,
in the vain hope that this will eventuate in a voluntary and
lasting acceptance of the faith . . . . The law of grace does
not desire to have men serve contrary to their own choice,
but, quite to the contrary, leaves to every man his own free

> choice . . . . The Lord has not given any other rule nor any
> other means of constraint for forcing men to faith and to
> religion, none other than the Word of Truth alone . . . . In
> this matter you take recourse to imperial law and to the views
> of Augustine . . . but we hold that such constraint brings the
> Church more of evil than of good.

Far from giving in to this, Bucer only retorted:

> It is the magistrates' duty not to tolerate that anyone assails
> openly or reviles the doctrine of the Gospel . . . . The notion
> that this is because such a person is seditious and constitutes
> a threat to the peaceful regiment is not of itself enough; for
> he also is not to be tolerated in a Christian republic who
> refuses to be taught[h] the things pertaining to the Kingship
> of Christ.[6]

It is apparent that the Reformers knew the principles that
lead to religious freedom; they knew what was meant by
separation of Church and State. It is also apparent that they
rejected this line of thought. And they did so because it
was an axiom with them that the State must have a religious
confession, must be a "republica Christiana." It was this conviction, a conviction that leads straight to "Christian sacralism,"
that made them what they were.

Bucer's associate, Adam Krafft, added his bit to the propaganda in favor of coercionism, saying that "It can happen that
he who is coerced today may come willingly tomorrow . . .
and then is saved, and thanks his magistrate for coercing him."
In an attempt to justify coercionism he added "Thus did also
the king of Nineveh when he commanded his subjects to
fast . . . . So did also Nebuchadnezzar when he threatened with
death all sacrilegious persons. This imperial edict of Nebuchadnezzar teaches all Christian magistrates that they certainly have
the prerogative to coerce men to the faith."[7] This Protestant
pastor was blissfully unaware that by saying this he was in
reality cutting his own throat; it was only too true that the
policies he recommended were of pagan origin and fit into
pre-Christian ways of thinking and into them only. He was

---

[h]With this we are back to the forced attendance at indoctrination
classes invented when "Christian sacralism" was first launched.

asking the Church of Christ to unlearn what its Master had taught it and to sit at the feet of pagans instead!

The apologetes for "Christian sacralism" were able, as we have seen, to find support for their views with the heathen. They also fared fairly well at the hands of the Old Testament — where there are indeed examples of religious uniformity enforced by the coercing sword of the civil rulers. But even the Old Testament — which the men of the Second Front insisted was obsolete in this matter — was not quite stern enough for the Reformers. The aforementioned Urbanus Rhegius asserted that "It follows that our magistrates should punish heretics and faction-makers and exterminate them, not with less but with greater zeal than did the kings in the Old Testament."[8]

The advocates of "Christian sacralism" fared extremely less well in the light of the New Testament, which failed to provide a decent argument. When a Restitutionist, Leendert van Maastricht, maintained that evil men persecute the good but that the good persecute no one, Bucer came back with "That evil men persecute the good we grant; but that the pious do also persecute evil men, this the Scripture teaches. What did Christ do in the temple-cleansing and what did Paul do to Ananias?"[9] This was the best they could find in the New Testament, a lamentably weak support.

To arguments drawn from the Old Testament the Restitutionists turned a deaf ear. One of them, who had been imprisoned for his anti-Constantinianism, said as follows:

> We are right in saying that the magistrate is not commanded with so much as a single word to rule in matters of the faith, no matter how many in our day scream that it is so and give the sword into the hand of the ruler to judge in matters of faith, supporting their contention with reference to the Judges and Kings of Israel. They do so without warrant; for although we were to grant that it was commanded to some rulers in Israel to punish idol worship and such like, this was because Israel was a servile people of the law (*ein knechtisch volck des gzetz*) among which everything was by constraint, also their religion. Now however ,in the free doctrine of the Gospel of Christ all coercion has ceased, so that it is not proper either by the use of force or the secular rule to saddle anyone with the faith against his will; nor is it proper for the magistrate to penalize anyone for lack of faith; for this is the prerogative

exclusively of the Son of God and of no creature on earth —
as indeed some have acknowledged who now fight against this
with all their might, this because they were then, the only
ones who opposed the bad situation, until others began to
resist their erroneous notions and their doctrines (just as they
had resisted those of the Pope), then it was that the trouble
began. They forgot their former teachings; they began to
speak a different language and persuaded the magistrates to
sustain their false teaching; they sustained then that against
which they had earlier written and clamored, as namely whether
the magistrates should keep their hands off matters of religion —
all of which we shall leave to God to punish, seeing that it
is something that was done to us.[10]

The reader will have noted the Restitutionist complaint,
heard at the Second Front constantly, that the Reformers had
gone back upon their earlier selves, that although they had
at the outset spoken against coercionism they were now defending it. This shift of position was inevitable once the Reformers had accepted the hand of the civil power. The Stepchildren however never accepted such a hand, and for principial
reasons. When the Reformers went back to the doctrine of
coercion in matters of faith, the Stepchildren remained convinced that freedom of conscience and voluntary affiliation
with His cause are of the very essence of the teachings of
Christ. This is something which the sacralists, whether early
or late, did not and do not fully realize.[1]

It was their failure to realize this that caused the Reformers
to write those things that now embarrass their followers. The
embarrassment which Article 36 of the Belgic Confession causes
virtually all who have to do with it is well known. Men have
tried by various devices, radical surgery included, to get rid

---

[1]Abraham Kuyper, for example, wrote: "If coercion by the State only
worked we would not for one moment hesitate to employ it" (Baatte
staatsdwang we zouden geen oogenblik voor staatsbemoeiing terugdeinzen)
(*Ons Program,* p. 325). Kuyper also wrote: "I do not draw back if
someone should say, 'Then you desire and propose that if need require
it idolatry and similar sins be punished capitally!' If need be, very
certainly . . ." (*Dictaten Dogmatiek, Locus de Magistratu,* pp. 420f.).
Evidently Kuyper was still sufficiently caught up in the toils of sacralism
to see no *principial* reason for opposing the use of force, only *practical*
ones.

of what it plainly says. But said Article 36 is symptomatic of
a deep-seated ideology; to "doctor up" the symptoms is not
enough; much more drastic treatment is needed if the embarrassment is to cease.

Article 36 is not alone in vexing us. Who is not similarly
vexed by Calvin's rejoinder to the Stepchildren's idea that the
magistrate has no assignment inside the Church: "Let us remember the rule laid down by Paul, to the effect that each
must remain in the calling in which he was called, and that
we are one body in our Lord, so that the arm cannot say to
the eye, nor the hand to the feet 'I have no need of you.' "[11]
Who among Calvin's spiritual children does not wish that the
great Genevan had not said that? What — the magistracy by
definition a member of the body of Christ? The magistrate's
office one of the organic functions of His Body? Related to
the other functions and agencies of it as the hand is related to
the foot and the arm to the eye?

We are likewise embarrassed by the things Calvin said when
the Stepchildren asserted that the rule-right of the magistracy
is "of the flesh" and the rule-right in the perfection of Christ
is "according to the spirit." Even if we should grant that this
terminology is subject to improvement (let it be remembered
that the Stepchildren were struggling to create a vocabulary:
the words, to which we are accustomed, "Church" and "State,"
were as yet unintelligible), they can be given a sense that is
at least traditional. Has it not always been the custom to
refer to the regime of the magistrate as the "temporal power"
or the "secular arm"? Why then did Calvin have to belabor
the Stepchildren with:

> Just as a drunkard after he has belched then vomits out the
> vile stuff that lies heavy on his stomach so do these miserable
> ones; after they have spoken evil of this holy office which
> our Lord honored altogether, they vomit up blasphemies much
> more out of order; the government of the civil ruler, say they,
> pertains to the flesh and that of the Christian company per-
> tains to the spirit . . . . But this is as nothing in comparison
> with that which follows, namely, that the seat of the magistracy
> is confined to the earth [the Latin text has *tantummodo in
> hoc mundo est*] but that of the Christians is in heaven. In
> God's name, I pray you, all faithful believers, and admonish

you, to consider well that which Saint Paul and Jude have
said about those who in their day already perverted the faith
of the simple.

One could wish that Calvin had not written that; at least not
in those words. In his haste, so it seems to us, to reprimand
the Stepchildren for distinguishing between the rule of God
that comes to expression in the magistrate and the rule of God
that comes to expression among those who are of the household of faith, he himself gets too dangerously close to identify-
ing the two. If, as we say today, the State results from common
grace and the Church from special grace, then what the Stepchildren were saying was not blasphemous, as Calvin would
have us believe. Then his own confusion of the two alarms us.
Calvin continued his attack upon the Restitutionists with:

> The principal purpose of the office of the magistrates is not
> this, to maintain their subjects in peace as to the body, but
> rather this, to bring about that God is served and honored in
> their lands and that everybody leads a good and honest life . . . .
> We see how that the devil speaks through their mouths, in
> order to turn the Princes from their course and keep them from
> their duty . . . . They show that they are enemies of God
> and of humankind.

One can only wish that Calvin had never written that; it
is of a piece with the Article 36 that has caused his followers
great embarrassment. Calvin's thinking at this point reflects
the medieval monism which saw in the magistrate and in the
priest two complementary arms of one and the same body; the
time was ripe for someone to call attention to the fact that a
new dimension is reached when we come to "the perfection
of Christ." They are not "enemies of God and of humankind"
who point this out. The civil magistracy is indeed *of God*
(as the Stepchildren said in words of one syllable) but it is
not good to say (as Calvin said) that "The civil magistracy is
a calling not only holy and legitimate but by far the most
sacred and honorable in human life."[12] Does the burgomaster
hold down a position more sacred and honorable "by far" than
that of a minister of the Gospel? Then one finds it easier to
accept Schlatten am Rande, with its: "The sword is an ordinance of God outside the perfection of Christ; thus the Rulers

of the world are ordained for the punishment of the wicked and for putting to death."

How did Calvin come to write all these things which we who in so many matters are his followers find it impossible to repeat after him? The answer must be sought in the fact that Calvin, beset by the same dilemma that tortured Luther, attempted the same impossible solution, that of combining two irreconcilable views of the Church of Christ. Like Luther he had learned to see that the New Testament delineates the Church as the company of believing folk; like him he had on the other hand inherited the medieval concept of the Church, in which the Church embraces all in a given locality.

As we have already intimated, the favorite device for keeping the one from cancelling out the other was the device of "Church visible" and "Church invisible." Calvin's visible Church is the Church of Constantinianism; his invisible Church is the Church of the New Testament. The latter is for Calvin infinitely smaller than the former, "a small and contemptible number hidden in a huge multitude, a few grains of wheat tucked away in a pile of chaff."[1] The picture is that of many "christians" among whom there is a sprinkling of "Christians."[k] This

---

[1] We submit that the New Testament nowhere envisions a Church in which a tiny *ecclesiola* lies hidden in the folds of a massive *ecclesia*. To sustain this idea of *ecclesiola in ecclesia* sacralists of all ages have been obliged to go back to the Old Testament situation, where one can indeed find a mere "seven thousand who have not bowed the knee to Baal," of true Israelites, hidden away in the masses of an outward Israel. In the New Covenant they "do not teach every man his brother, saying 'Know the Lord'" for all [in that company] shall [already] know me . . ." (Hebrews 8:11).

[k] The category of "Christian," i.e., a person who is neither a heathen man nor a Christian is foreign to the New Testament. One would expect that people who have had occasion to witness the rise of the reign of terror under Nazism would let go of the notion of a "Church" that embraces a total society; one would expect that men who can themselves recall how that when these Nazis began to say "Gemeinschaft des ganzen Volkes hat die Kirche zu sein, nicht Gemeinschaft für sich in separativer Bildung," the clergy had no objection (until it was too late — so accustomed were they to this sacralist representation); one would expect that they would review their theological heritage which made this possible. But instead we find men toying still with the sacralist formula. In the Netherlands, Noordmans pleads for an enlargement of the structurization of the Church so as to make room in it for believer and disbeliever alike,

whole concept of "Church visible" and "Church invisible" is foreign to the New Testament; it was fashioned in order to provide a formula whereby men could escape from the Stepchildren's clamor for a Church of believers; it was invented in order that men might be excused from repudiating the inclusive Church of *het historisch gewordene.*

If Calvin wrote things we cannot digest, Theodore Beza satisfies even less. In support of the killing of heretics he wrote:

> After God had launched Christianity by unarmed apostles He afterward raised up kings by whose wisdom He intended to protect His Church . . . . They do not like it that civil laws are enacted against their wickedness, saying that the apostles have asked no such thing of kings — but these men do not consider that those were different times and that all things agree with their own times. What emperor had at that time believed in Christ, in days in which Psalm 2 was still in effect: 'Why do the nations rage . . . .' When we invoke lawfully and divinely instituted protection against stubborn and incorrigible heretics we only do what the Word of God and the authority of the holy prophets assert.[13]

This is undiluted Constantinianism. It accepts without question Augustine's notion of the "larger fulfillment." It breaks a lance for coercive procedures in the cause of Christ's Church.

Actually Beza outdoes even Constantine. His only criticism of Constantine is that he was not severe enough in his repressive techniques. Hear Beza say:

> Will not Constantine be judged to be guilty in this matter? He would have been wiser if he had defended more sternly the majesty of Christ so wickedly and stubbornly attacked . . . . While the imperial protection was still a novel thing in the Church it is really no wonder that the more lenient use of it at the first pleased both emperor and bishop.

"een uitbouw van de gemeentelijke inrichting, waarin de schare meer betrokken is dan tot dusverre." He thinks that the time has come for us to ask whether "next to the presbyterial structurization of the Church in which they are served who are consciously of the Church there is not room for an organizational form over and above this, whereby the masses which are now but loosely connected may have their place." But Noordmans will be unable to eat his cake and have it, as unable as was Luther, who also toyed with this very notion.

Beza took it ill of Augustine that he had at the first been of the opinion that the Donatists should not be put to death.

It was this hyper-Constantinianism, fostered by Beza, that became regulative in the Low Countries. Small wonder that Dutch Protestantism, when it encountered the Stepchildren, drew the sword with a vengeance. And small wonder also that, when Reformed clergymen scanned the world of publications for material that would serve their purpose, their attention went at once to Beza and his book written in support of the killing of heretics. As has already been said, Bogerman reprinted it, in Dutch translation, in 1601.

He also added to it a lengthy introduction or preface, which was even more Constantinian than was Beza — if that is possible. The occasion was this. During his pastorate at Sneek it had come to Bogerman's attention that there were Anabaptists in his city, people who were holding meetings by themselves.[1] Although these religious gatherings were being held off the street and in the quiet of private homes, without the faintest hint of seditious intent, Beza, accompanied by the local police, came, uninvited, into these meetings. Unasked, he began to recite a lengthy prayer and to offer an exposition of Scripture. Subsequently the local authorities were prevailed upon to publish stern prohibitions against any further "non-reformed" services.

All this we have from Bogerman's own pen. He recited his exploits with manifest confidence that his Reformed contemporaries would applaud his actions. He complained that the Restitutionists had had the "temerity" to quote (before the city hall some years earlier) from Matthew 22, the passage about "rendering to Caesar the things that are Caesar's and to God the things that are God's," and from Acts 4, the passage about "obeying God rather than men," in order that the magistrates might know that they were not to make men's religion their business. Bogerman cried out at this point, "Imagine a conscience so seared! . . . for what does more to break down the kingdom of Satan . . . than when the Church with its spiritual

---

[1] We shall, in Chapter 5, discuss the Reformers' attitude toward the unauthorized religious gatherings of the Stepchildren, their *Winckelpredigten,* as these gatherings were spitefully called.

weapon and the civil rulers with their physical ones join hands"
— as they had done, literally, when Bogerman and the constable,
walking arm in arm, had invaded the meeting of the "heretics."

When Bogerman had moved to Groningen (it was here that
he translated Beza's work) he came upon the same kind of
situation — more Anabaptists and more illicit gatherings.
Naturally he acted on the same insights. He and his Reformed
colleagues prevailed upon the local magistrates to publish the
notorious *Groninger Edict*. It begins: "Burgomaster and Council
hereby decree that henceforth no religion other than the Reformed shall be permitted in their city; he who attends any
meeting of the papists or the Anabaptists shall be fined . . . ."
Then follows a list of civil penalties adequate to liquidate any
opposition to the sacralism that had entrenched itself in the
city.

To the Restitutionist argument, that the magistrate "must
not assume responsibility in matters of religion but must leave
it to the ministers of the Word working by themselves . . .
to achieve whatever is achievable by spiritual means," Bogerman put forth the remarkable wisdom that "nothing is more
useful toward health on the political scene and the prevention
of commotion than the practice of a single religion, seeing that
no bond of unity and of fidelity occurs among human beings
who are committed to diverse religions." (In passing the reader
will observe that here again, as when "Christian sacralism" was
first launched, it is concern for things political that determines
the policy.)

To the Restitutionist distinction between infractions punishable by the magistrate and infractions punishable by Church
discipline, Bogerman turned a deaf ear, adding, "If we follow
this . . . then what remains but to spare all culprits — just so
they add the offence of heresy to their other misdeeds" —
not being exactly fair to his opponents. One could wish that
Bogerman had taken to heart what the "heretics" were saying,
for the distinction they were making was valid enough.

To the Restitutionists' argument that "It does not appear that
there was a magistrate's office in the apostolic Church, for it
is written in Ephesians 4 that he 'set some to be shepherds
and teachers etc.' . . . . if He had also instituted a magistrate's
office in the Church then the apostles would not have omitted

a reference to it," Bogerman replied, "If from this silence it follows that the office of the magistracy has no place in the Church then these heretics must reject all the offices not mentioned in Ephesians 4." This was not a very telling rejoinder, if we may say so.

Although there were individual voices that spoke a different piece — so that here again we are reminded of the Belgic Confession's "little traces" — the position taken by Bogerman was the position taken by the Reformed Church of the Low Countries. Of this there should be no argument. If the enactment of Article 36 of this Confession is not enough to settle the matter, we could point to an almost endless array of evidence.

The *Groninger Edict* was duplicated in other cities. At Deventer, for example, the following was decreed in 1620, as the result of Reformed pressures:

> The magistrates of the city of Deventer instruct all citizens and residents of their city that no Mennonites, etc., shall hold any secret or public assembly . . . where any preaching . . . marriage, or any other exercise of religion, is practiced, under whatever pretext . . . on pain . . . of perpetual banishment . . . . Any person found at such a place or in such an assembly shall forfeit his upper garment plus 25 *florins;* the second offence, the upper garment plus 50 *florins;* the third offence to be followed with arbitrary punishment. He who lets his house be used for such a gathering shall forfeit 100 *florins;* the second time, 200; the third time perpetual banishment.

It may be said that the Reformed Churches of the Netherlands were officially committed to the Constantinian formula. At the Disputation held with the Stepchildren at Emden in 1578, Menso Alting, official spokesman for the Reformed Churches declared:

> The civil authority is an ordinance and vocation of Almighty God, one which he has instituted within the Christian Church . . . . The Church of the New Testament has certain special promises in the Old Testament touching the office of the magistrate; such as Isaiah 49:23 ("Kings shall be your nursing fathers"). Therefore the office of the magistrate cannot and may not be excluded from the New Testament Church — otherwise the promises of God touching this office are

made null and void. And so this office belongs in the Christian Church; and they who serve in it must themselves be Christians . . . . And so we have proved from Scripture . . . that the magistracy is an ordinance of God that of right belongs in the Church.[14]

This illustrious exponent of the Reformed State Church reinforced his idea of the sword as a legitimate weapon *in* the Church with these words:

Even the heathen, although unacquainted with the true God, when they wished to make political ordinances felt that their first duty was to institute their religion, erroneous though that religion was. By this it becomes apparent that the law of nature taught them that they were responsible for religion in connection with their vocation.

Little did he realize, it seems, that this only proves that the sacralist formula is pre-Christian and therefore pagan.

From all of this it is apparent that the theology of the Reformers remained entangled in the medieval synthesis of "that which is Caesar's" and "that which is God's." They continued in the signature of such a man as Peter Damian — who drew a parallel between the "mystery" whereby the human and the divine flow together in Christ and the "mystery" whereby the civil rule and the ecclesiastical flow together. This entanglement continued until the forces of erosion had whittled down the medieval world and its sacralist *Weltanschauung*.[m]

---

[m]There were two forces in history which contributed heavily toward the eroding away of the neo-Constantinianism of the Reformers; they are the French Revolution and Anabaptism. It is significant that both of these are "black beasts" in the estimation of those Calvinists in the Netherlands who still have not sloughed off their Constantinianism. It is significant that the political party that seeks to continue much of the old sacralism calls itself *anti-Revolutionair,* that is, anti-French Revolution; for it was the French Revolution that put an end to the world which this party would recover. Needless to say, Calvinists in the New World do not take such a dim view of the French Revolution, feel that there was much good in the cry "Liberty, Equality, Fraternity." It is likewise in the circles of the *anti-Revolutionairen* that the Anabaptists continue to be looked upon as nihilists. This too is not surprising, seeing that the Anabaptists contributed significantly to the eroding away of the world-view which the *anti-Revolutionairen* would like to recover. Nor is it at all surprising that in the New World the Anabaptists are being given a new and sympathetic hearing.

It will hardly be necessary to marshal more evidence that
the Reformed Church of the Low Countries was Constantinian.
Was not the Synod of Dordt a civil gathering first of all? As-
sembled by the States General (upon the insistence of the
consistories of course), presided over by a person from City
Hall? And were not the sentences pronounced upon the de-
feated party civil in nature — banishment from the land?

It is part of the record that hardly a meeting of classis or
Synod in the southern Low Countries was held without passing
a resolution to pressure the local government officials to put
an end to the practice of any religion save the Reformed.
Measures were taken against the Anabaptists and others.[n]
Especially, however, did the new Reformed sacralism put forth
efforts to squelch the remnants of the Catholic cult. At the
Classis meeting held at Breskens on October 2, 1582, it was
decided "to send a request to the city authorities to bring about
the extermination of the papists" ("om te vercrijghene uuy-
troeynghe der papen"). Similar action was taken at the classis
meeting held at Sluys in 1582; at Ramscapelle, action was taken
to have the "duyvelsche afgodische dienst" of the papists
obviated as well as to procure the extermination of the catholic
priests ("vuytroudynghe vande eerloose ende goddeloose
papen"); so also at the meeting held at Sluys on April 12, 1583;
likewise at the meeting of November 3, 1578, scheduled to be
held at Deinze but held at Ghent because the plague was
raging at Deinze.

It appears that the civil magistrates were not very coopera-
tive in this matter of suppressing all religious exercises but the
Reformed. We read that at a meeting of Classis, held at
Brugge on February 13, 1582, it was decided: "in view of the
fact that we get no support from the magistracy, to send a

---

[n]For example, in the Acts of the Provincial Synod of the Flemish
churches, held at Ghent on March 8, 1581, one of the Churches asked
the question: "Hoe ende op wat maniere die doopers ende dierghelijcke
ketters moghen geweert worden?" To this the Synod replied: "dat men
dien angaende niet beter doen can, dan achtervolgens die articulen des
Dordrechsen Synodi; ende indien zulcke ende dierghelijcke middelen niet
souden helpen, dat alsdan de Christelicke overheyt haeres officii stichtelijck
zal vermaent worden . . . ." See H. Q. Janssen, *De Kerkhervorming in
Vlaanderen*, Part II, p. 75.

request to every Classical gathering to supplicate the civil rulers, along with us, to get the services of the papists stopped, following the precedent of Holland and Zeeland."[15]

This was the situation commonly, the leaders of the Reformed Churches putting forth every effort to get the civil power to suppress all other religious factions and the magistrates refusing to cooperate in this illiberal program. We find, for example, the States General administering a severe rebuke for the city of Aerdenberg, which was walking in the treadmill of the Reformed pastors:[o]

> We have learned with surprise that contrary to our resolution announced to your honorable body by our clerk, Jan Bogaerd, you still hinder the members of the fellowship of the Anabaptists . . . in the freedom of assembly and exercise of their religion. Whereas we desire that the aforesaid shall be allowed to enjoy just as much freedom . . . in their mind and conscience and assembly, in Aerdenberg as elsewhere . . . therefore we instruct you to govern yourselves accordingly.

The Prince of Orange had to come to the rescue of these Anabaptists in a similar way in 1578; a second time in 1579. His successor, Maurice of Nassau, had to repeat the orders in 1593.

We see that whatever tendency there was toward religious toleration in the areas where Protestantism was "established," this tendency characterized the secular power rather than the consistories. This situation has led a modern investigator to declare that "It is certainly wrong to attribute to any of the Reformers an attitude of religious voluntaryism which modern countries take for granted.[p] The Reformers can hardly be

[o]In these years the Reformed Church leaders addressed an admonition to King Stephen of Poland, urging him to suppress the Catholic religion, an admonition to which that liberal monarch replied with a firm refusal, saying that one of the things he refused to reign over was men's consciences. His reply, a classic of liberal thought, has been printed and discussed by H. Q. Janssen in *Bijdragen tot oudheidkunde en geschiedenis, inzonderheid van Zeeuwsch-Vlaanderen*, Deel III.

[p]There is sound truth in the words of William Warren Sweet as he asserts: "There is a widespread notion among Protestant groups that the separation of Church and State, and thus religious liberty, was one of the immediate products of the Reformation, that the early Protestants were advocates of a large tolerance, and that religious liberty was but

quoted in support of religious liberty . . . . They were horrified
by the implications of the free Church."[16]

This is a strange situation indeed — the magistrate preparing
to give the societal compositism of the New Testament a try
and the clergymen resisting it! Yet that is the situation. Hear
the Reformed pastor at Middelburg, Johannes Seu, declare as
he urges the local ruler to "do his duty" by enforcing religious
uniformity:

> How can there be a quiet and a peaceful life and how can
> a country flourish if its citizenry is divided by diverse con-
> ceptions of religion? There is nothing so baneful for the com-
> munity as disunity, diversity, and contention in matters religious.
> Therefore a magistrate must stand guard diligently that false
> doctrine and heresy are precluded and eliminated, for these
> are the well-springs of all disunity among the citizens . . . .
> It is as clear as the noon-day sun that unity achieved by the
> sword of the magistrate is the one and only beginning, the
> middle, and the end, of peace and prosperity in the land.[17]

There were also some, happily, who continued in the spirit
of the days before the coming of neo-Constantinianism. One
such was Huibert Duifhuis, a native son of and minister in the
Reformed Churches of the Netherlands. He had declared in a
sermon, "Let the civil rulers permit no one to mislead them
so as to employ force in matters of faith and of conscience,
nor to persecute any for such matters, seeing that these things
belong to God." For this the prevailingly sacralist Church took
action against him. At the meeting of Classis in 1578, they
read for his benefit from Beza. Duifhuis listened just long
enough to identify the work. Then he interrupted with, "If
those are your sentiments then my soul may not linger in your

---

the logical development of the principles held by all the reformers. Just
where this notion arose is difficult to say, and no reputable historian
of our times would endorse it. The fact is that the rise of Protestantism
was accompanied by an unprecedented outburst of intolerance . . . "
(*Religion in Colonial America*, p. 320). One can and should tone down
the idea of an "unprecedented" intolerance, for there had been outbursts
of intolerance far more ruthless; but one can hardly quarrel with the
assertion that the Reformers were not protagonists of religious liberty.
For that we must go to the camp of the Second Front.

council; with such I do not care to be identified." Thereupon
he walked out of the meeting unceremoniously. One of the
leading ministers, Hendrik Alting, asserted that the forty-seven-
year-old Duifhuis was "a wolf in sheep's clothing, whom men
should first resist in private and who, that failing, should be
brought to the attention of the magistrates." In due course
of time Duifhuis was deposed.

His views are taken for granted among Protestants everywhere today; they are part of the heritage of freedom, so
that it has been said:

> These views are on the North American continent among
> those truths which we hold to be self-evident: the voluntary
> Church, the separation of Church and State, and religious
> liberty. From the days of Constantine . . . these principles, to
> us so cardinal, had been in abeyance.[18]

How came these "self-evident truths" to be held on the North
American continent? That is a study by itself. No doubt the
erosion of sacralism in the New World was — like all erosions —
the result of a variety of causes; but among these the pioneering
by the Stepchildren deserves a prominent place. No one has
seen this more clearly than that great student of social history,
Ernst Troeltsch, who wrote of the New World: "Here those
Stepchildren of the Reformation have at long last had their
history-making moment . . . . Here the end of the medieval idea
of culture was effected and in the place of the coercive culture
of the State-Church came the beginning of modern culture
separate from the Church."[19]

As another German scholar has put it in this century: "To
a modification of the Protestant conception of the State the
Anabaptists drove the Protestant State-Church proponents; and
in so doing they have rendered the Reformation a stupendous
service, a service for which they have not as yet been given
the praise which in the forum of history is rightly theirs."[20]
Certain it is that the arguments employed by the men of
the Second Front had much to do with the development on
these shores of the "self-evident" truths of the voluntary Church,
separation of Church and State, religious liberty. When one
reads, for example, William Penn's "The Great Case of Liberty
of Conscience once more briefly debated" (1687) it is as if

one hears voices from the past, the voices that emanated from
the Second Front.

History seems to have established beyond reasonable doubt
that, as a recent Calvinist authority has pointed out: "Every
religious cultus that gets tied up with coercion must of necessity
become corrupt." The Reformers' collaboration with the secular
power, the consequent resurgence of "Christian sacralism," was
a thing fraught with much evil. And certain it is that we
today will be increasingly embarrassed by it. Equally certain
is it that in our embarrassment we will find ourselves judging
very differently concerning the "Stepchildren of the Reformation" than did our forebears. As we speak of Anabaptists we
find ourselves unable to digest what our Reformed fathers
wrote about them. We find ourselves adjusting our evaluation
of them as did one of the authors of the Heidelberg Catechism,
Olivianus, who had also been taught that the Anabaptists
should be exterminated, but who, when he had listened to
them, changed his mind quite radically concerning them.[q]

The American Protestant is certain that the magistrate is
out of bounds when he with his coercing sword invades the
area of religion — just as certain as were the Reformers that
he belongs there. We are certain that such physical coercion is
principially wrong. Even more passionately confirmed in this
belief were the Stepchildren, who because of this conviction
went by the spiteful name of *Stäbler*.

We have discovered anew that voluntaryism is of the essence
of the Gospel. This discovery has brought us close to the
position held by the Stepchildren in their day. We live in a
world where by legal enactment the only structurization of
Christ's Church that is permissible is the structurization for
which the Stepchildren agonized. And as we become acquainted
with the Stepchildren as they really were we find ourselves
saying what Castellio reportedly said to Beza:

> With regard to the Anabaptists I should like to know how
> you know that they condemn legitimate marriages and the

---

[q]In the year 1598 the Oberrat of the city of Heidelberg testified that
he "Weisz sich sonst wohl zu erinnern das D. Olivianus der meinung
gewesen, inen die köpf herunder schlagen zu lassen; ist aber uf dem
creuzenachischen hofgericht einer andern und miltern meinung worden."[21]
He was referring specifically to the Stepchildren.

magistracy and condone murder. Certainly this is not to be
found in their books and even less in their words. You have
heard these things from their enemies, Beza; but if enemies
are to be believed then know . . . that it is being said of your
Farel that he has as many devils in his beard as hairs, and
that whenever he eats he feeds the crumbs to these devils.
Beza, I do not believe what you say about these Anabaptists.

America calls itself the "land of the free" and has shown
itself to be willing to give all it has to preserve its "freedoms."
One of these is the freedom to believe and to disbelieve. This
is the fruitage of the vision for which the Stepchildren agonized;
it is, as even foreign observers have noted, "not the progeny of
the Enlightenment but rather the ripe fruit of the Freechurchism
of the Left-wing reformers." If this seems far-fetched let it
be recalled that the first voice to be raised against another
variety of coercionism, human slavery, was a voice from the
sector of the Stepchildren. As early as 1688 the son of a
German-speaking Restitutionist, an immigrant who had come to
these shores to find freedom of conscience, wrote back to his
people in Europe: "Here there is freedom of conscience, as
is right and proper; what there should be moreover is freedom
from slavery." This was but an inference drawn from the
voluntaryism for which the Stepchildren pioneered. Nor is it
in any sense a mere coincidence that the State that took such
a leading part in the abolition of slavery was that State that
had been influenced greatly by the ideas of the Stepchildren —
Rhode Island.ʳ When it is recalled that bond-service was officially approved (in the case of Saracens and other non-members
of "Christendom," of course) in the heyday of "Christian
sacralism," we begin to see a pattern, namely that the voluntaryism of the New Testament begets human freedom, even as the

---

ʳIt is refreshing to see a European scholar, Emil Brunner, recognize
that the end of Constantinianism with its *Zwanggleichschaltung* was not
in the New World simply occasioned by the *Aufklärung* but that back
of this development was "zum Teil auch die christliche Kirche selbst."
(See Brunner's pamphlet on *Die Christusbotschaft und der Staat*, p. 45f.)
Brunner says in this connection that "der erste Toleranzstaat ist bekanntlich
eine christliche Gründung, der kleine Neu-England-Staat Rhode Island."
It is significant that it was precisely this "kleine Neu-England-Staat Rhode
Island" that had been most deeply influenced by the heritage of the
Stepchildren.

coercionism of "Christian sacralism" spawns servitude. The people who were spitefully called *Stäbler* had a point to make. And they made it, even though it took a long time.

3   *Catharer*

A people zealous of good
works . . . . Titus 2:14

W E HAVE OBSERVED IN THE PRECEDING CHAPTERS THAT IN
the Constantinian change the Church of Christ came to be
viewed as coextensive with the empire. The side effects of
that change were many. We shall be dealing in this chapter
with the side effects which the Constantinian change had in
the area of *conduct,* or more correctly, of conductual requirement.

In the unfallen Church, those who belong to it contrast with
their environment in the matter of deportment. It is written
large in the New Testament that they who have accepted
Christ no longer live as do the rank and file. They have begun
to walk "worthy of the calling wherewith they have been called."
They have begun to "bring forth fruits worthy of repentance."
They have been "raised with Christ" and as a consequence they
have begun to "seek the things that are above."▪

But if the Church becomes inclusive, so that "all in a given
locality" are in it, then all this has to change; then a leveling-
off takes place. Then the "world" is no longer something that
lies around the Church but has become identical with the
Church. Conductual-averagism is the inevitable consequence
of the inclusive Church; when the premise of the Church as
a body of the elect has been dropped, then most of the puri-

▪It seems that the moral rectitude of the early Christians was almost
proverbial in their day. We find it said, without fear of contradiction,
in the *Octavius* of Minuscius Felix, that "The prisons are crowded with
your followers whereas they contain not a single Christian — unless it
be a renegade or one whose crime is his religion."

tanical beliefs with which this concept is associated become obsolete. Then Christian behavior and ordinary human behavior become indistinguishable.

Conductual-averagism was the immediate result of the Constantinian change. And resistance to the leveling-off was instantaneous. It was plainly present in the Donatist rebellion.

As everyone knows, the conflict between the Donatists and the Catholics turned immediately about the question whether a worldly *cleric* can convey salvation; but this is only a refinement on the theme of conductual-averagism. The "fallen" Church, already on its way toward substituting salvation by sacramental manipulation for salvation by response to the Word, was ordaining priests with little or no attention to the candidate's status as a believer. It was filling the countryside with clerics who gave no evidence of being regenerate and all sorts of evidence that they were not. It was against this alarming development that the Donatists protested — saying that a cleric who lives in sin cannot convey salvation. In other words, Donatism was a protest against conductual-averagism and it brought that matter to a head at the level of the ordained man. Donatism was basically concerned for the perpetuation of the righteousness that had been a mark of the follower of Christ; it was particularly concerned about the perpetuation of *priestly* righteousness. It saw that the "puritanical beliefs" of primitive Christianity were becoming obsolete and it took steps to recover them. In this program it concentrated on the priesthood because the loss of the "puritanical beliefs" was especially serious at the level of the leader.

This Donatist concern, refinement and all, continued to be heard long after the Donatist rebellion had been suppressed. It runs, refinement and all, through the literature dealing with the "heretic" of the Middle Ages. So much was the "heretic" a man who harps on conductual requirements that any person who talked of the changed life was automatically suspect.[b]

---

[b]The French writer Beuzart has observed, in his work on pre-Reformation heresy, that "le gravite et le serieux de la vie loin d'etre une sauvegarde devenaient plutôt un motif de suspicion . . . ." Ralph of Coggeshall, a notorious inquisitor, himself relates the story of a virtuous young woman suspected of heresy because she resisted the amorous advances of a priest and who was also burned as a heretic (cf. Coulton, *Inquisition*

So much was the issue of "a walk worthy of repentance" in the forefront of the clash between the sons of the "fallen" Church and the "heretics" that it gave to people of Germanic tongue their most common word for the "heretic" — as we shall see in a moment.

All of this came to renewed expression in the age of the Reformation. The men of the Second Front were to the neo-Constantinians what the Donatists had been to the Constantinians twelve centuries earlier. The argument touching conductual requirements was very prominent in the sixteenth-century scene. It is this spectacle that we shall be observing in this present chapter.

The "fallen" Church in her effort to discredit the "heretic," who was incessantly nagging her concerning her conductual averagism, dug up an old term of reproach, the name by which an ancient dualistic heretic had been known, the name *Cathar*, a word meaning *cleansed*. The Church changed this proper noun into a common noun, so that she could use it of any and every "heretic." It was this *Cathar*, now as a common noun, that gave the Germanic languages their most common word for *heretic;* for the High German *Ketzer* is nothing but the word *Cathar* pronounced with High German vocal equipment, just as the Low German *ketter* is nothing but the word *Cathar* pronounced with Low German vocal equipment.[e]

After the word had become a common noun, applicable to any and every person who dissented, it continued to be useful however in the smear campaigns to keep alive the insinuation

---

and Liberty, p. 35ff.). This inquisitor tells the story with the understanding that his readers will side with the priest rather than with the girl! That such situations were by no means unusual is apparent from the writings of Peter the Precentor, who speaks of "certain honest matrons, refusing to consent to the lasciviousness of the priests . . . who have by such priests been written into the book of death, and accused as heretics and even condemned . . ." (*op. et loc. cit.*).

[e]Medieval man seems to have lost track of the etymological derivation of the word *Ketzer*. Luther derived it, erroneously, from *Götzen* (idol) (cf. *Werke*, St. Louis ed., III, p. 1692). Bullinger, likewise in error, associated the word *Ketzer* with the idea of *dividing* (cf. John H. Yoder, in "Recovery," p. 207, quoting from Bullinger), so confusing it with *heretic*.

that the *Ketzer,* or the *ketter,* was a dualist. The original Cathars had indeed been dualists; they had indeed taught that ultimate reality is dual, that there is an Evil Principle and a Good Principle; but it was a grave injustice to carry over this charge upon all who were later covered by the word after it had become a common noun. This injustice is the more serious in that it is committed still.

It was an injustice committed all through medieval times to lay the charge of dualism upon any and all who opposed "Christian sacralism." For, as that expert in medieval dissent, Herbert Grundmann,[1] has shown, there is from the beginning of heresy in the western world, as far as research has been able to make out, no addiction to any dualistic traits. The reports in which the charge of dualism is made commonly begin with "It is said . . ."; this is in and of itself evidence enough that the writers are dealing with a cliché, an ancient tradition, a legend. This puts all they say under suspicion.

When, to give but this one example, that great heresy-hunter Eckebertus of Schonau, charges his victims with dualism he, as Grundmann has shown, "copies from Augustine." Augustine had been obliged to fight dualists, in his contest with the Manicheans, also known as Cathars; and Eckebertus derives his image of the heretic, not from observation, but, in true medieval style, from the authorities, in this case from Augustine. And so Eckebertus belabors his contemporaries with the very same verbal lashings which Augustine long before him had constructed in his rounds with the Manicheans. It follows that we cannot take Eckebertus at face value.

The charge laid at the door of the medieval "heretic," the charge that he was given to a basic dualism, was a false charge, by and large. This is the more serious because men have not to this day escaped from it.

The charge of dualism, was taken over by the Reformers and continues to be heard among their followers to this day. Especially is this true in the Netherlands. For reasons which we shall discuss in another connection, in this area Anabaptism has always been considered a major threat to what is conceived to be Biblical Christianity. To this day the polemic against this Anabaptism is almost certain to begin with the charge of dualism.[a] It is time to abandon this approach to the Step-children of the Reformation. They were *not* addicted to any intolerable dualism — unless it be dualism to insist that the rule-right that comes to expression in the State (which is a creature of common grace) and the rule-right that comes to expression in the Church (which is a creature of redemptive grace) are discrete, as discrete as are the universal sonship and the redemptive sonship, general revelation and redemptive revelation.

We are not saying that there were no groups in medieval times in whom traces of pre-Constantine dualism lingered on. There were such, perhaps more than what we have reproduced from Grundmann would seem to imply. There seem to have been dualistic tendencies among the Albigensians; but it also appears that these dualistic touches led to grave tensions between this variety of heretics and those whose system revolved about the repudiation of Constantinianism. We have the word of a medieval inquisitor for it that although all heretics saw eye to eye in regard to an aversion to the "fallen" Church they disagreed vehemently in regard to dualistic assumptions. Well has Professor Ebrard said, a century ago, that "The basic error in the prevailing representation is that when men hear the word *Cathar* they straightway think of a gnostic sect, whereas the more . . . honest of the medieval opponents of the Cathars themselves distinguish very clearly between two varieties of Cathars." It is certainly an error to think of dualism whenever one hears the word *Cathar*. The term was borrowed from one situation and applied to another — in an effort to discredit.

The same dubious transfer of terms occurred at many junctures. For example, the Bogomils were Manichean or Manichean-like heretics that had their headquarters in the Balkans and who were for that reason known as Bulgars. This word became *bougres* on the lips of French-speaking peoples. And this word, at first a proper noun connoting a specific dualistic

[a]Dr. Berkouwer, for example, derives just about all that was characteristic of the Anabaptist vision (he mentions by name: doop, eed, Overheid, Staat, oorlog, incarnatie) from a "pronouncedly dualistic premise" (een uitgesproken dualistisch standpunt). (Cf. his *Karl Barth en de Kinderdoop*, pp. 79ff.)

heretic, became a proper noun signifying a heretic of any descrip-
tion.ᵉ Here again is a word borrowed from one situation and applied to a quite different one — in order to discredit.ᶠ It became a
mere cliché, a feature of the stereotyped image of the heretic.

There were many such stereotypes and they were unbelievably persistent. For example, all through medieval times
it was said that heretics were *pale*. We read of a medieval
bishop who "when he looked at men he could tell by their
pallor whether they had been to the Waldensians' conventicles."
So much was pallor a mark of the heretic that when the city
of Münster fell, the soldiers "killed on the spot all who were
pale of face." The reason for this ascription of paleness is not
expressly indicated. It may have a very natural explanation;
who, knowing himself to be a "heretic," would not grow pale
when an inquisitor spoke to him or even looked in his direction?
Moreover, the "heretics" spent a great deal of their time in
hiding, coming out mostly at night (for which reason they
were often called *turlupins*, wolf-people. One reads the pathetic
phrase "sad of heart — like the child of a *turlupin*"); for this
reason their visages were not tanned by the sun. In all events
this cliché was extremely tenacious; one may hear to this day
in rural France the expression "*blanc comme un huguenot.*"
So also with the ascription of a basic dualism. These clichés
were features of the stereotype of the "heretic" and passed
from father to son.

Two considerations aided the "fallen" Church as it sought

ᵉThe word *bougre* as a common noun designating a heretic *überhaupt*
occurs twice in the quotation contained in note 17 of Chapter 1 of this
volume. We read of a Dominican inquisitor, called Robert le Bougre
because he was himself an ex-heretic, who brought about "a very great
and acceptable holocaust to the Lord, in the burning of Bougres; for
183 Bougres were burned in the presence of the King . . . and many
prelates" (Coulton, *Inquisition and Liberty*, p. 113).

ᶠThe expression *bougre* survives in the unsavory English word *bugger*.
Just as the sacralist world of pre-Constantinian times had accused the
Christians of unnatural vice so did the medieval sacralist world accuse
the "heretic" of similar things. In Reformation times these ancient slurs
were thrown after the Stepchildren. This old cliché seems to be hard
to kill; when the present writer was in the Netherlands in 1950 he was
informed, by a professional man, that when the Baptists celebrate the
Lord's Supper the whole affair ends in an orgy of sexual abandon!

to discredit the Cathar by flinging at him the charge of dualism.
One of these was the fact that he posed a threat to the monism
which the Church had embraced. Although primitive Christianity had recognized the State as "an order of creation but emphatically not as an order of redemption," this distinction was
blurred at the time of the "fall" of the Church, it being at once
undigestible in a sacralist system. In sacralist Rome the emperor had been sacrificed to as *soteer, dominus, et deus* (savior,
lord, and god) and men did not differentiate between the State
and the Church. This monism recurred, now in a "Christian"
version, when the Constantinian change took place. It comes
to expression constantly in Roman Catholic theology. Perhaps
the formulation in which Peter Damian (who died in 1076)
put it is as succinctly as any we could quote: "Just as, in a
mystery, the human nature and the divine flow together in
Christ so, likewise in a mystery, do the rule of the magistrate
and that of the priesthood flow together." The Restitutionists
were chargeable with dualism, if by dualism is meant the views
of him who rejects the monism on which the sacralist system
rests.

Then too the Restitutionists attacked the monism that identified *Volk Gottes* with *Volk*. They held that society is composite,
that it consists of believers and non-believers. This two-camp
vision can be called a dualistic vision — if by dualism is meant
anything that cuts across the monism implied in the sacralist
vision. The Restitutionists, early and late, have thought in
terms of "those inside" and "those outside"; they have always
thought of some as being in the category of "heathen and
publicans" and some as being in the category of "brethren
in Christ." No doubt this "dualism" aided the "fallen" Church
in its policy of fastening the ancient label of dualism upon
those who criticized its fallenness.

Still another matter that made the charge of dualism appear
at least outwardly plausible was the fact that the Restitutionists
had a tendency to down-grade the Old Testament (for reasons
which we have already pointed out, namely that the Old
Testament can be cited in favor of sacralism). It was well-
remembered that the original Cathars had ascribed the Old
Testament to the Evil Principle and the New Testament to

the Good Principle. It was therefore possible to slide adroitly
from the one down-grading of the Old Testament to the other
down-grading thereof — not precisely honest and fair, but
highly effective. The Restitutionists' attitude toward the Old
Testament and the Reformers' attitude toward it were an integral
part of the Reformation scene; while the former looked upon
the Old Testament as pre-Christian, and therefore outmoded
now, the Reformers looked upon it as the ideal, reflecting a
societal situation to which the apostolic Church had not at its
inception been able to come, a situation to which it was,
however, destined to come later, in the Constantinian change.

There is another thing that must be said here. It is that
when the Cathars said that the Church consists of changed
men and women, they were not saying that it consists of sinless
men and women. It was easy, very easy, to slide from the
"heretic's" censure of conductual-averagism to the charge that
he was given to Perfectionism. But this would be quite unfair.
The Reformers made themselves guilty of this unfairness, times
without number.ᵍ   No one knew better than did the Restitu-

ᵍCalvin also made himself guilty of this unfairness; in *Institutes* IV,
1:23, he writes: "Long ago there were two kinds of heretics, Cathars
and Donatists. These, the former as well as the latter, were in the
same phantasy in which the contemporary dreamers are when they seek
for a Church in which there is nothing to censure. They cut loose
from Christendom so as not to be soiled by the imperfections of others.
And what was the outcome? Our Lord confounded them and their
understanding so presumptuous. Let this be proof for us all that it is
of the devil, who under cover of zeal for perfection inflates us with
pride and seduces us by hypocrisy so as to get us to abandon the flock
of Christ . . . . For since there is no forgiveness of sins nor any salvation
anywhere else, Acts 4:12 [The reader will observe that Acts 4:12 says
nothing about the matter Calvin is treating here; it says that there is
no salvation apart from *Christ*, which is quite a different thing from
saying that there is no salvation apart from the everybody-embracing
Church]. Therefore even though we should have the appearance of a
sanctity more than angelic, if by such a presumption we come to separate
ourselves from a Christian society we have become devils." Calvin commits the same error, of ascribing Perfectionism to the Stepchildren, in
Institutes IV, 8:12. Like Augustine before him (who had sought to
escape from the unwelcome fact that the Donatists excelled in the matter
of conduct by calling it a "quasi laudabilis conversatio") and in chorus
with the Reformers in general, Calvin speaks of an "apparent" (i.e.,
not real) sanctity.

tionists that a Church of wholly sinless people is unattainable; and it is historically not defensible to imply, much less to assert, that they visualized a Church of unambiguous saints.[h] What they did say is that there are saints who *fall* into sin and sinners who *live* in sin — a distinction that is essential to authentic Christianity. It may be difficult or even impossible to say in any given instance whether a man is a sinner living in sin or a saint falling into sin; but one cannot reject the distinction and retain the New Testament delineation of the Church.

It was by the formula of living in sin and falling into sin that the Stepchildren avoided on the one hand the quite un-biblical notion that the Church of Christ cannot be known by the conductual distinctiveness of its members and on the other hand the equally unbiblical idea of unambiguous saints. This middle way the Stepchildren walked; they rejected conductual-averagism and they rejected Perfectionism. Their most influential thinker, Menno Simons himself, made this clear enough. His assault upon conductual-averagism is known to all; but his rejection of Perfectionism is just as evident. Said he[3]: "Think not that we boast of being perfect and without sin. Not at all. As for me I confess that often my prayers are mixed with sin and my righteousness with unrighteousness."[i] The charge of addiction to Perfectionism is therefore to be rejected. It was not derived from the Stepchildren's doctrine but was an inference, an unwarranted one at that. It arose in the heat of battle and was invented in the camp of the Reformers as an escape from the Stepchildren's assault on the idea that the Church consists of converted and unconverted alike.

Why, it may be asked, were the Reformers so quick to attack the Stepchildren for their puritanism? Surely an em-

---

[h]Balthasar Hübmaier, an influential leader among the Stepchildren, was well aware that the Reformers were twisting the "heretics'" clamor for the changed life so as to make it add up to Perfectionism. He rejected this in these words: "Sye giessen auch von uns ausz, wie wir uns berümen, wir mögen nach dem tauff nymmer sünden . . . . Wir wissendt, das wir vor und nach arm und ellend sünder seyent."[2]

[i]In another connection Menno declared that "meyne gherechtigheit gaarniet en is dan eenen vule bevleckte laken."

phasis upon "fruits worthy of repentance" is always in place;
in those violent days it was doubly necessary. Why then did
the Reformers raise their hackles when they heard about this
emphasis?

Resistance to it was not prompted by a concern for theological correctness. It came up because it was felt that the
idea of a Church to which only believers belong bites as a
caustic into the sacralist system. After twelve centuries men
still had, as it were, a sort of tribal memory whereby they recalled that once a troubled statesman had stood before the
problem as to how to hold the empire together. Men remembered vaguely that then the solution had been found in binding the Church of Christ and the empire of the Caesars together. And they recalled distantly that this had been possible
only by submitting to conductual-averagism. Men of Reformation times had the vague conviction that conductual-averagism
was necessary to political peace and stability and that for
that reason anyone who talked of terminating conductual-
averagism was rocking the boat. That this was the motivation
behind the angry cry that was raised when the Restitutionists
clamored for a Church of believers becomes apparent when we
hear Justus Menius, one of Luther's trusted associates say:

> Like the Donatists of long ago, they seek to rend the Church
> because we allow evil men in the Church. They seek to
> assemble a pure Church and wherever that is undertaken the
> public order is sure to be overthrown, for a pure Church is
> not possible, as Christ cautioned often enough — we must
> therefore put up with them.[4]

We are in position now to see through the oft-repeated
assertion that the Stepchildren were political nihilists, that they,
in the language of the Belgic Confession, "seek to overthrow
the magistracy." This charge was a gross injustice; it did not
rest upon observation but upon a syllogism. Only a sacralist
society could have invented it, resting as it does upon the
(mistaken) notion that society cannot hang together unless
it is bound together in a common religion.

The rift between the Reformers and the Restitutionists first
appeared in Luther's world in connection with the issue of
conductual-averagism. As early as 1524 there were already signs

that the Reformers and the Radicals were drifting apart in regard to conductual requirements. In that year a book appeared with the title *A Dialog between an Evangelical Christian and a Lutheran in Which the Offensive Life of Some Who Call Themselves Lutherans is Exposed and Fraternally Reproved.*

In the same year, 1524, Hans Hut, pioneer Radical, cautioned men against the Reformers because of their failure to attack conductual-averagism; said he: "whoever leans on them will be misled, for their doctrine is nothing but faith and goes no farther . . . . Oh, how lamentably do they in our times mislead the whole world . . . with their false and trumped-up faith, a faith from which no moral improvement follows."[1]

In a more positive vein, they said at the Second Front: "Christ has indeed died for us and has redeemed us; but no man is saved by this redemption unless he in his conduct follows in Christ's steps, does and has done to him what Christ did and had done to Him."

Another representative of the Second Front, Michael Sattler, one of the first to die for the Restitutionist cause, said that the Reformers "throw works without faith so far to one side that they erect a faith without works."

A famous leader of the sixteenth-century Restitutionists, the man who has given his name to their modern descendants, also rebuked Luther for his one-sided emphasis upon the forensic

---

[1] Balthasar Hübmaier complained that in the camp of the Reformers men had learned only the first two of three pivotal doctrines of the Christian faith, that "das volckh nit mer denn zway stuck geleernet hat." The first doctrine was "der gloub macht uns selig." (We are saved by faith.) The second was "of ourselves we cannot do any good" (wir mugen ausz uns selbs nichts guts thon). Both of these are true enough, says this teacher at the Second Front. But then he goes on to say that "Under cover of these two half-truths all evil, unfaithfulness and unrighteousness have gained the upperhand completely . . . so that the old saying is fulfilled "Ye alter ye böser!" . . . . "Everybody wishes to pass for a Christian and a good evangelical as far as taking a wife is concerned, eating flesh [in Lent], making no further sacrifice, fasting not, saying no prayers any more;" but otherwise one sees nothing but drinking, gourmandizing, blaspheming, practicing usury, lying, cheating, abusing, forcing, stealing, robbing, playing, dancing, flirting, loafing, committing adultery, tyrannizing, slaying, etc., etc. The third lesson, which men in the Protestant camp had not mastered, said this Hübmaier, is that faith without works is dead.[5]

aspect of salvation and said reproachfully that "one does not find among Turks and Tartars such godless conduct as one sees in those so taught." He added glumly, "And if one rebukes such behavior he is dubbed a heaven-stormer, a *Schwärmer*, a work-saint, or an Anabaptist."

In Zwingli's world some of the earliest signs of tension appeared in connection with the Stepchildren's demand concerning conductual requirement. Zwingli, who was at the first quite sympathetic toward them, turned against them when he heard of their agitation for a Church of people who contrast with their environment in the matter of conduct. It happened this way:

> First of all Simon of Höngg [i.e., Simon Stumpf, who became a leader among the Stepchildren] had come to him and to Master Leo [i.e., Leo Jud, one of Zwingli's colleagues] and had belabored them to the effect that they ought to raise up a separated people and Church and embrace in it a Christian people leading non-offense-giving lives and adhering to the Gospel, a people not up to their ears in usury. They turned a deaf ear to this, albeit in a kind and friendly spirit. Afterward Grebel came to them exactly as Simon had done. Him they likewise turned down. Nevertheless these men went ahead anyway, holding meetings at night for to raise up a separated Church.[6]

The constantly recurring reason given for the defection of the Restitutionists is this matter of conductual-averagism. We read the following account, penned in 1538 by one of the Stepchildren:

> While we were still in the national church we obtained much instruction from the writings of Luther, Zwingli, and others . . . . Yet we were aware of a great lack in regard to repentance, conversion, and the true Christian life. It was on these things that my heart was set. I waited and hoped for a year or two, since the minister had much to say about amendment of life . . . . But I could not close my eyes to the fact that the doctrine which was preached . . . was not carried out; no beginning was made toward true Christian conduct . . . true repentance and Christian love were not in evidence . . . . Then God sent His messengers, Conrad Grebel and others, who had surrendered themselves in the doctrine of Christ by conversion. With their assistance a congregation was

formed in which repentance was in evidence by newness of life in Christ.[7]

Conrad Grebel, mentioned in this quotation, said as early as 1524 that "nowadays everyone thinks to attain salvation by a make-believe faith, one devoid of fruits . . . without Christian deportment."[k]

Luther was quite aware that protest against conductual-averagism had led to the exodus of the *Schwärmer*. Wrote he:

> From the beginning of the Church heretics have maintained that the Church must be holy and without sin. Because they saw that some in the Church were the servants of sin they denied forthwith that the Church was the Church, and organized sects . . . . This is the origin of the Donatists and the Cathars . . . and of the Anabaptists of our times. All these cry out in angry chorus that the true Church is not the Church because they see that sinners and godless folk are mixed in her and they have separated from her . . . . It is the part of wisdom not to be offended at it when evil men go in and out of the Church . . . . The greatest comfort of all is the knowledge that they do no harm but that we must allow the tares to be mixed in . . . . The *Schwärmer*, who do not allow tares among them, really bring about that there is no wheat among themselves — by this zeal for only wheat and a pure Church they bring about, by this too great holiness, that they are not even a Church but just a sect of the devil.[9]

So one could continue. Example after example leaves no doubt that one of the facets of the quarrel that had erupted at the Second Front was the disagreement as to the need for distinctiveness in conduct. Two things stand forth with unmistakable clarity. They are: (1) that in the camp of the Reformers there was no full-scale attack upon the conductual-averagism that is the inevitable corollary of sacralism; and (2) that the Stepchildren made serious work of challenging

---

[k]In the argument that arose in connection with conductual-averagism, the Stepchildren's preference for the New Testament came to expression also. According to the Reformer Bucer, thy were wont to say "Es soll die christliche gemeynd reiner sein dann der alten. Darzue käme man basz, so nit iederman getauffet unnd in Christlich gemein, sonder allein die bekennenden eingenommen wurden."[8] We shall, in a later chapter, return to this idea of the Restitutionists, that baptism should not be done wholesale fashion but should be restricted to the believing element.

the old order with its laxity in the matter of conduct — and, that they in a large way set a better pattern. Since both of these theses will strike some readers as being quite novel, we must document both of them at some length.

To begin with, Philip of Hesse, one of the sanest men of his times, wrote, to his sister, Elizabeth of Saxony, with reference to the Stepchildren, "I verily see more of moral improvement among them than with those who are Lutheran."

Capito declared in a letter that the Radicals "guard themselves against the offensive vices which are very common among our people."

Luther himself acknowledged that his Reform had done little to correct conductual-averagism, but had left things in the main as they had been before. It is a sad fact that he sought to justify this, moreover. In an attempt to get away from the evidently indisputable fact that the Stepchildren were doing much better, he said: "Doctrine and life are to be distinguished, the one from the other. With us conduct is as bad as it is with the papists. We don't oppose them on account of conduct. Hus and Wyclif, who made an issue of conduct, were not aware of this . . . but to treat of doctrine, that is to really come to grips with things."[10]

To Schwenkfeld (who had come to feel out Luther and his associates as to their sentiments in regard to the lineaments of the Church that was to be, and who had advocated the creation of a believers' Church with disciplinary techniques for expelling the impenitent) Luther acknowledged that "among us there is no betterment of life."

On the other hand the record leaves it unmistakably clear that the Restitutionists with their insistence upon "conduct becoming saints" were doing rather well. This fact came out in the court hearings quite constantly. We shall select a few of the almost endless list of examples.

When certain people were being investigated for suspected Anabaptist leanings, this testimony was offered: "Because their children are being so carefully and devoutly reared and because they do not have the practice of cursing and swearing, therefore they are suspected of being Anabaptists."[11] Similarly at the hearing of Hans Jeger, under similar suspicion, it was said: "Now because he does not swear and because he leads

an unoffensive life, therefore men suspect him of Anabaptism . . . .
He has for a long time passed for such, because he did not
swear, nor quarrel, nor did other such-like things."

Conversely, we read of people cleared of Anabaptist leanings
by their *bad* deportment. Of Casper Zachers it was testified
in court: "He is not commonly by the rank and file thought
to be an Anabaptist, because he is a churlish fellow who can't
get along with others, starts fights and discord, swears and
curses, disturbs the peace and carries weapons on his person."

The simple fact is that in the camp of the Restitutionists
of the sixteenth century a "conversation such as becometh saints"
was in evidence — as everybody knew. The Reformed preachers at Berne admitted as much, in a letter which they sent to
the City Council: "The Anabaptists have the semblance of
outward piety to a far greater degree than we and all the
other churches which in union with us confess Christ; and they
avoid the offensive sins that are very common among us."[12]

Henry Bullinger declared, "There are those who in reality
are not Anabaptists but who do have a pronounced aversion
to the sensuality and frivolity of the world and for that reason
reprove sin and vice and are as a consequence called or mis-
named Anabaptists by petulant persons." Schwenkfeld complained that they were doing this very thing to him, saying,
"I am maligned, by preachers and otherwise, with the charge
that I am an Anabaptist, even as all who lead a true and
devout Christian life are almost everywhere given this name."
So much was an unusually good deportment a mark of Restitutionist "heresy" that as early as 1531 it was already said of
the Protestants in general: "So far has their idea of Christian
liberty carried them that any person who talks about God
and the Christian way of life or who is seriously exercised
concerning his own moral improvement passes with them for
an arch-anabaptist."[13]

Similarly a Roman Catholic contemporary:

> Among the existing heretical sects there is none that in ap-
> pearance leads a more modest or pious life than do the Ana-
> baptists. As to their outward life they are without reproach —
> no lying, deception, swearing, strife, harsh language, no in-
> temperate eating or drinking, no outward personal display;
> but humility, patience, uprightness, neatness, honesty, tem-

perance, straight-forwardness, in such a measure that one would suppose that they had the Holy Spirit of God.

It is apparent that the undeniably good way of life of the Stepchildren was an uncomfortable fact to the Reformers — so that they sought to escape it. In this mood Henry Bullinger wrote:

> Those who unite with them will by their ministers be received into their church by rebaptism and repentance and newness of life. They henceforth lead their lives under a semblance of quiet spiritual conduct. They denounce covetousness, pride, profanity, the lewd conversation and immorality of the world, the drinking and the gluttony. In fine, their hypocrisy is great and manifold.[14]

The Reformers, in an attempt to get away from the mortifying fact that the Stepchildren were actually succeeding in their onslaught against conductual-averagism, resorted to the argument — an old one — that the good works were nothing but bait with which the devil baited his hook so as to catch a lot of fish. Bullinger, for example, wrote that the exemplary lives of the Restitutionists "are hypocrisy, for . . . even Satan can transform himself into an angel of light . . . . he who wishes to catch fish does not throw out an unbaited hook." After granting that the Restitutionists, Pilgram Marpeck and his wife, were "people of devout and blameless lives" he added: "But this is an old trick of the devil, with which he has in all churches, from the days of the Apostle Paul, sought to catch his fish."[15]

Manifestly the changed life of the Restitutionists wore well. The saying was that the Restitutionist preachers carried a little bottle with them wherever they went; out of it each new convert was required to take a little swig, the result of which was to fix him forever in his "heresy." This story (which may have come up in connection with the fact that the Restitutionist preachers carried a wooden bottle of wine — for use in their celebration of the Lord's Supper) even entered the Court records. When Leonard Schiemer was on trial he was told "what evil comes from this Anabaptism, also community of wives and of goods, and that it leads to shameful affairs and lusts, and that they give to drink out of a bottle containing I know not what, a matter contrary to God, and more such matters." To this the prisoner said simply, 'I verily don't know anything about any bottle nor of any evil allegedly coming out of it." This bizarre idea of a "fixing" heresy potion is in itself an eloquent witness to the fact that after a man had become an Anabaptist he led a life of rectitude from which it was not easy to deflect him.

No one squirmed more painfully in view of the unwelcome fact that the Restitutionists were successfully attacking conductual-averagism than did Martin Bucer. He was constantly urging the magistrates to greater rigor in the use of the sword, saying with a glance at the Stepchildren:

> Their most pointed argument is always this that we keep house so badly; with this argument they lead astray many people. God help us, so that we may one day be able to take this argument away from them, yes from our own conscience and from the Lord our God. Of a truth it is getting to be high time that on the day of Saint Catherine we deal seriously with the matter of our housekeeping . . . for if this is not considered and remedied all our counsels against this rod of the Lord will be in vain.[16]

At another time this Reformer complained:

> The magistrates are rather coarse and carnal men and the preachers are very neglectful; many of them frequently get drunk. Since the lords and the council-men are that kind of people . . . they drive the poor people away with their wild way of life [mit irem überbolderen]. The plain man cannot bring himself to recognize the Church of Christ among such wild persons, and, to distinguish correctly between doctrine and life.[17]

In writing about this, Bucer was able to remain composed and dignified — more so than when he was talking to a Restitutionist face to face. Then he found it hard to keep his poise. To one of the Stepchildren, Leonhard van Maastricht, he cried out, in 1538: "How can the conclusion be good that 'it is an evil tree for I see no good fruit on it!' How about the fact that the tree may be standing in Calcutta, whereas I am way out here, and see no good fruit on it? Does that prove that it doesn't have any? He, this Leonhard, hasn't seen everybody. Therefore he judges flippantly."[1]

In his dialog with the Restitutionist Jörg Schnabel, Bucer said, likewise in the year 1538:

> They are forever accusing us that things are getting worse instead of better. Now is this our teaching: "Repent and improve your way of life." It is not the doctrine's fault that nothing happens. In the Old Testament as well as in the New God's Word has always had this quality that it makes worse those who do not embrace it . . . . They who do not accept the doctrine after they have been sufficiently taught, these fall daily deeper; and these give occasion for the saying that "Since the new doctrine has been preached, many people have gotten progressively worse."[18]

Ever since the launching of "Christian sacralism" the "heretics" had been characterized by much emphasis upon a conduct whereby the believer is set off from the non-believer — so

---

[1]At this point Bucer is dependent on Augustine, who had scolded the Donatists in very similar vein, saying: "They who say that they know for sure that specified men are wicked and unworthy of the communion in the Sacrament . . . , whatever it is that they know, they will be unable to persuade the universal Church, spread out as it is throughout the nations, to give credence to their tale . . . . The unity of the Church dispersed through the whole world must on no account be forsaken because of other men's sins." The idea of a "congregation," an ecclesiastical unit with autonomy sufficient to exercise discipline was not a part of Augustine's thinking, nor of the Church of the Middle Ages. The Christian world owes the recovery of the *congregation* to the Restitutionists, a fact that has led Ernest A. Payne to say (in his *The Anabaptists of the Sixteenth Century and Their Influence in the Modern World*, London, 1944, p. 13): "To the Anabaptists is due not only the machinery of a single congregation, which was presently taken over by Calvin in his Institutes, and put to practice in Geneva, but also the machinery for an alliance of congregations, adopted in France during 1559, and in Scotland the next year, and so well known as the Presbyterian scheme . . . . Early Anabaptist Church organization antedated and influenced that of the Calvinists . . . . But the 'Brethren' had one feature which was dropped by the French, Scotch, and the Dutch, an order of evangelists whose business it was to travel and propagate the faith." (We shall return to this item, which according to Payne the Reformers did *not* take over from the Anabaptists, in a later connection. For a discussion of the "daughter Church," i.e., the *congregation*, cf. Hübmaier's views, in "*Quellen IX*," p. 478.)

much so that Bucer said, "This has always been Satan's nature and practice, to introduce false religion with strictness as to conduct . . . . This was proved in the case of the Manicheans and the rest who have distorted the holy religion very grievously."[m]

When one of the Stepchildren, Bernhard Knipperdollinck, had written that the true Church is the believers' Church, Urbanus Rhegius was commissioned to reply to him. At this point he wrote:

> Aha, there Bernhard resorts to a genuinely Donatist trick. They condemned and abandoned Christendom on account of some evil and false Christians . . . . Nevertheless there have always been some true and devout Christians in the masses, and we hope they are present also with us. Moreover the fact that wicked rascals are present with us . . . does not concern us; we haven't told them to drink and gourmandize, to be immoral or covetous . . . . We don't want to rend the net because there are some bad fish in it, as the super-saintly Anabaptist Bernhard is doing. He gives himself away at this point and shows that he has the Anabaptist devil in him which blinded also the Donatists in Africa. They also opened their eyes wide and saw with a hypocritical face that many wicked people were wearing the name of Christ, folk who were in reality genuine heathen; and they proceeded to go off by themselves, apart from Christendom, and made off that they wanted to build up a truly reformed Church, one in which there were nothing but saints. And they were so pure in their own eyes that they declared the baptism performed in Christendom by evil priests to be no baptism, and baptized anew. By this method they thought to raise up genuine holiness. They scolded Augustine for abiding in the gathering of the wicked — to which Augustine replied that there were indeed evil people in his fellowship . . . and saying that external fellowship of good with evil does not harm the former's salvation, seeing

[m]Back of this strange argument, used throughout the centuries by men of sacralist principles, lies the notion that theological correctness is infinitely more important than behavioral correctness, so much so that the Evil One impels men to righteous living in order to get theological aberration across. This scale of values does not comport with New Testament teaching, where doctrine without life is as bad as life without doctrine.

that they don't approve of the latter's evil and godless way of existing. We are not to cause a separation; he who separates from the Church becomes a heretic and a schismatic. Let Bernhard consider himself told off — for he is a neo-Donatist who has taken offence at the evil lives and has . . . tried to raise up a holy and unspotted Church, one in which there are only saints, a pure net without a foul fish, he and his company, cut loose from Christendom . . . . I would forsooth prefer to be a coarse publican in the Christian Church, or a patent sinner, rather than be the most holy Pharisee of all. in Bishop Bernhard's *spelunk*![19]

This was an impassioned plea for a Church "including all in a given locality" without any such thing as entrance requirement. But our Stepchildren could be quite as impassioned. So for example, Hans Kuchenbacker, spokesman for their group at Marburg. Said he in connection with Ezekiel 22:26 ("Her priests put no difference between the holy and the profane . . . ."):

Here God complains that the priests make no difference between holy and profane . . . of which we poor people also complain. For this reason the Lord says in Malachi 3:18 'Return to me and make a distinction between the righteous and the wicked, between him that serveth God and him that serveth Him not.' This distinction the apostles as true servants of God observed; even though they spoke the Word to the masses, yet have they accepted only such as received the Word and turned to God and said farewell to sin, to be members of the congregation, to the breaking of bread, fellowship, and prayer. In this matter they remained constant and practiced brotherly love and no one else dared join himself unto them, as we see from Acts 2:38. From this it is clearly evident that even though good and bad are together in the gatherings where the Word of God is being taught, yet must a distinction among them be preserved . . . . We cannot believe that the present evil world, living as it does in darkness, in unbelief, and in accordance with the desires of the flesh, in deliberate blasphemy, in avarice, usury, pride, and intemperate eating and drinking, blasphemy of God's name — that this is the Christian Church and congregation of God. And we hope that no one who fears God and has the mind of a Christian . . . will forbid us this way of thinking or reckon it against us as an error.[20]

Or take this passage, penned by Jorg Leinhardt and Peter Los from the jail at Marburg, concerning the sacralist practice of putting all men in the category of "Christian":

> Very well then, then one man has as much to lose as the other . . . even though Saint Paul says (2 Cor. 5:10), "We must all appear before the judgment seat of God in order that each may receive according to his deeds whether it be good or bad"; even though Christ says (John 14:21), "He who keeps my commandments he it is that loves me"; and in chapter 15 vs. 9 and 10, "Abide in my love, even as I have kept my Father's commandments and abide in His love"; in 1 John 2:4 the Apostle says, "If any man says that he knows God and keepeth not his commandments, the same is a liar and the truth is not in him." Therefore Paul says, in Romans 2:5-16, "You however, O man, after your own obstinate and impenitent heart, treasure up for yourself wrath against the day of wrath and the revelation of the righteous judgment of God, who will render to every man according to his deeds." *Deeds* it says, not according to an imagined or trumped-up faith but to each according to his works, namely "glory and honor and eternal life to him who by patient continuance in well-doing seeks after eternal life; but to them that are contentious and obey not the truth but obey unrighteousness," what will God give him? The same as the scoundrel — as the false apostles say? Paul says, No, but "displeasure and wrath, tribulation and anguish to every soul of man that doeth evil." Oh God, that your Excellencies, yes all men, might ponder this testimony of Paul. Then the false apostles would not hold captive so many God-fearing souls in a lying comfort! Paul goes on to say that God will "give praise and honor and peace, in the day of His wrath, to those who have done the good . . . whether they be Jews or Gentiles." But the false apostles revile those who in our day try to follow this, calling them hypocrites and comparing them with the man who stood in the temple bragging of his piety . . . . O what has become of the words of Christ (Matt. 12:36) "I say unto you, that every man will have to give an account in the day of judgment of every idle word!" And then the false apostles say that if a man can only say that he believes that Christ has paid for him, has suffered for him, has atoned for him before God, no matter how he lives, then all his sins are forgiven him and left behind — which they deny in their deportment. If one takes account of their flock, their children whom they have

begotten by their Word, you will find it to be as we say. Therefore we pray your Excellencies in all humility to ponder the
Holy Scriptures and to judge our writings, our speech, and
our deportment in their light.[21]

As has been said earlier here are two irreconcilable delinea-
tions of the Church. The one camp wanted to raise up a
"confessional Church based on personal faith," and the other
camp was determined to keep a Church "including all in a
given locality." For the former, one's way of life sets him off
as a Christian; for the other, the happenstance of being an
inhabitant of a given locality qualifies him, and conductual
patterns are not definitive.

In the course of the conflict, the Restitutionists in Hesse
recited what they believed to be the proper description of
Christ's Church: "We believe and confess one holy Christian
Church, a fellowship of the saints, namely of all believing regenerate Christians and children of God, born again from
above by the Word of God and the Holy Spirit." To this the
Protestant pastors raised serious objection. Said they:

> When men talk about the marks of the Christian Church,
> the characteristics by which men may find it, so as to be
> joined to it, then we call the Church that mass among which
> the Word of God is purely preached and the Sacraments are
> administered according to the institution of Christ. Where
> these two marks are in evidence there we are not to question
> it but that God has most certainly, among this unwieldy mass
> [*diesem grosen haufen*] of called ones, His own little group
> [*sein heuflein*] of true believers, let them be few or many . . . .
> Christ has taught in parables how it stands with Christ's
> Church on earth: "The kingdom of God is like a man who
> sowed good seed on his field but . . . ."[n]

---

[n]The portion of Scripture to which these Protestant pastors go to sustain
their sacralism, the Parable of the Tares, has been cited so often in
support of the idea of a Church embracing all in a given locality that
it may well be called the *locus classicus* of the sacralists. These teachers
take this passage to support the idea of togetherness *within the Church,*
the togetherness of good and bad alike. The "heretics" have quoted it
quite as frequently, contending that this Parable supports their position,
namely that the togetherness of which the passage speaks is a togetherness
in the world. It must be pointed out that in this disagreement over the
essential meaning of the Parable the "heretics" plainly had the better

Since so much was hung on this recital of the marks whereby the true Church may be known and since it is still current in the Reformed Churches, it may not be amiss to notice that it was manifestly invented to serve as a rebuttal to the Step-children's delineation of the Church. It is not patently Biblical. It is not the outcome of exegesis of the New Testament. The idea that the Church is delineated according to these marks is a piece of polemics, devised in order to have something with which to escape from the Stepchildren and their patently correct delineation of the Church.

The New Testament delineation of the Church is not that of a tiny constituency, lost, as it were, in the massive crowds. Perhaps we would want to splice out the Restitutionists' definition of the Church; we might want to make room in it for the children of believing parents. (The Restitutionists would have been willing to make this adjustment once their criticism of the territorial Church had been granted.) The Restitutionists would have been quite willing to grant that as men see the Church, there may be an admixture of hypocrites (they said plainly enough that such was likely to be the case). But they were dead set against the Church as described in the Constantinian vision, as "including all in a given locality," without any reference to a conduct "such as becometh saints."

In the light of this Restitutionist emphasis on inner renewal the remark attributed to a Restitutionist pastor becomes highly significant; he is reported to have said to his audience, "Go home and die first; I never bury living people." The reference, of course, is to baptism. Just as it would be premature to offer to bury a man who had not as yet died, so was it pre-

---

of the argument, for Jesus' own commentary on the Parable indicates specifically that the scene of the togetherness is "the world," not the Church. The Parable does not teach that compositism is right and proper *in the Church;* it teaches that compositism is right and proper *in the world.* The Parable sustains the idea of societal compositism, not that of sacralism. The sacralist use of this Parable spawned two evils; on the one hand it gave the totally unspiritual man a comfortable place within the Church; on the other hand it deprived the dissenter of any place for the hollow of the foot in the society of which he was a part.[22]

mature to offer to baptize a man who had not as yet died unto sin.°

The Church as seen by the Restitutionists is an organization with entrance requirements. One has to qualify in order to be admitted, not in the sense of being in possession of earned credits but in the sense of having submitted willingly to the humbling concept of grace. And since no one can go through this experience without being inwardly renewed, the Church looks for signs of this inner renewal. In this sense a "walk worthy of the calling" is a prerequisite for membership.

Knowing full well that in her evaluation of men the Church is not omniscient and that therefore she must always be prepared to scrutinize her holdings, she must check to see whether her lists need to be revised. If it then becomes apparent that there are unfruitful branches, the Church is confronted with the pathetic task of removing the manifestly dead timber.

This implies discipline, Church discipline, the kind of thing Jesus was talking about when He said something about "Let him be unto you as a heathen man or a publican," the kind of thing Paul had in mind when he laid it upon the Church at Corinth to "put away that wicked man from among you." Although the New Testament leaves the impression that such drastic action is called for rather infrequently, it plainly teaches that such disciplinary action must in extreme cases be resorted to. Needless to say, if the Church exists by voluntary association the incidence will be much lower than it would be otherwise. If, as is the normal situation, a certain amount of opprobrium attaches to the Christian confession, then the incidence will be low indeed. But conditions are never such that the Church is allowed to drop the keys into the well, as it were.

Needless to say, sacralists will be embarrassed at this point.

°The story is told, of the Anabaptist leader Leendert Bouwens, by Guido de Brès in his book against the Anabaptists. Needless to say, de Brès tells the story rebukingly. The Reformers were not sympathetic toward the idea that one must have died unto sin if he is to be a fit candidate for baptism. The doctrine of "presumptive regeneration" which developed later is a left-handed acknowledgement that the Stepchildren had been right in their insistence that where baptism is rightly administered there regeneration is presumably present.

They have no receptacle into which to put a person who can no longer be carried on the church's rolls. If he is to be put out of the Church, he will also and simultaneously have to be put out of society, that is *exterminated* (from the Latin *ex* and *terminis*) — that is, put "outside the boundaries."[p] If the ecclesiastical community and the societal community are one and the same thing, merely seen from different vantage points, then he who is expelled from the former cannot be allowed to remain in the latter. Church discipline as set forth in the New Testament is impossible in "Christian sacralism."

It is a fact that Church discipline was in a hopeless mess ever since the Constantinian change was affected. In the first place, there was no discipline for aberrations in conduct. Men could live in sin and debauchery, dissipate to the full extent of their physical powers, and never come to know that the Church of Christ has keys with which it is supposed to lock out such rough-necks.

The Church stirred not a finger -- unless and until someone challenged the sacralist formula. This was the one "sin" which made the "fallen" Church reach for her keys. In her catalog this was the unpardonable sin; this was *the* sin of the "heretic," the "sectary," the "schismatic," the Carthar — all of them names that hark back to *this* quarrel. When the "fallen" Church saw or heard of anyone who was "rending Christ's robe" then, and only then, did the wheels of discipline begin to turn. With a fury that reminds one of that of the twentieth-century communistic world when it hears of revisionism — and no wonder, for it was similarly inspired — the Church bared its claws when men challenged the sacralist formula.

When the "fallen" Church did discipline, it went much too far; for it then expelled not only from the company of the redeemed but from the company of men as such.[q]

[p]It is doubtful indeed that the Church ever intended the word *extermination* in its etymological sense merely. Certain it is that very early indeed it was already being used and intended in its modern connotation, namely, that of liquidating. The word seems to have been one of the many euphemisms which the medieval Church used so freely and so cleverly to enhance its own "image."

[q]This monism-inspired confusion — this failure to see that punitive measures in the area of society lie on a different plane than do punitive

Church discipline was in dire need of a major overhaul at the end of the Middle Ages.

It was with the Stepchildren that the idea of the restoration of such discipline as the New Testament requires was first set forth.[r] Men who are accustomed to hearing that the Church has a third note ("where Church discipline is observed"[s]) will find it hard to believe that time was when this was not only absent from the Reformers' delineation of the Church but was looked upon as a piece of Anabaptist fanaticism. The record however, speaks plainly.[t]

Conrad Grebel is usually looked upon as the man about whom the Restitutionists first rallied, and his letter to Thomas Müntzer, who he thought could be won for the Restitutionist cause, may be looked upon as one of the earliest writings

---

measures in the area of faith — receives its classic expression in the teachings of Thomas Aquinas, with whom we read that heresy is a thing for the perpetration of which the guilty one deserves "not only to be separated from the Church by excommunication but also barred from the world by death" (non solum ab ecclesia per excommunicationem separari sed etiam per morte a mundo excludi; cf. Summa, II, 2, Q. 11, Art. 3).

[r]There had been hints in the earliest years of the Reformers' careers that they were not insensitive to the need for the recovery of Church discipline. But their views were at best ambiguous. When thereupon the Restitutionists waved all ambiguity aside, also in the matter of discipline, the Reformers drew back. This development has lead Farner to say of Zwingli that with him "tritt seit dem Jahre 1526 der Bann zurück" (op. cit., p. 18).

[s]The quotation is from the Belgic Confession's Article. When it was written, in 1559, the idea of the exercise of discipline as the "third note" of the Church had become a part of de Brès's thinking. In that same year, however, the French Confession, which had Calvin's approval, did not as yet include it.

[t]It was the medieval image of Donatism that stood across the Reformers' path as they contemplated the restoration of Church discipline as portrayed in the New Testament. It was looked upon as a piece of Donatist fanaticism. When the Stepchildren broached the idea of a return to Church discipline the Reformers said "Shades of Donatism!" Calvin, for instance, wrote "The Donatists who when they observed faults in the Church which the bishops reproved in words but did not punish with excommunication . . . inveighed fiercely against the bishops as betrayers of discipline, and in an impious schism separated themselves from the flock of Christ" (Institutes IV, 12:12). He added in the same breath that the Anabaptists of his day "act in the same way."

originating among the Stepchildren. In this letter, dated 1524, we read:

> Try with the Word to create a Christian congregation, with the help of Christ and his rule, as found in Matthew 18 and as we see it in practice in the Epistles . . . . He who refuses to reform . . . resisting the Word and the work of God, and who continues in that way, such a man, after Christ and His Word and rule have been preached and after he has been admonished by two or three witnesses and the congregation . . . such a man must not be put to death but classified as a heathen man and a publican and be let alone.[23]

With this Grebel was proposing a procedure whereby such discipline as was currently known in Christendom — a discipline which ended in death for the victim — would be discontinued; and a new discipline — one in which excommunication is the ultimate in punishment — would be introduced. Grebel's program was calculated to terminate the Church as it had been known for twelve centuries and to substitute for it the Church of the New Testament. This put the whole issue between the ideals of the Restitutionists and those of the neo-Constantinians in sharpest focus. During the course of his trial, Grebel stated his position on Church discipline thus: "no avaricious person, no usurer, no gambler, none other of the sinners set forth in Scripture, shall have a place among the Christians — rather are they to be excluded by the ban."

Grebel's companion, Felix Manz, spoke similarly of the Restitutionists' ideal: "As to the Church, my understanding has always been and is now that all those who live in revilings and sin, such as drunkards, fornicators, adulterers, gamesters, fighters, usurers, and such like, are to be excluded from it." (He added here, "If however a person should carry on in this way without people knowing it and without revealing himself, these we would allow to remain.")

As the leaders spoke, so spoke also the followers in the camp of the Stepchildren. Some who had been jailed in Hesse, in the year 1538, spoke as follows:

> If the Christian ban were exercised according to the institution of Christ and the Apostles then we would not in any sense distance ourselves . . . . Yes, as soon as we shall see that all that is feasible is done, in keeping with the wisdom

and power of Christ, the exercise of the ban as ordained by Christ and the Apostles, then we will be prepared with all our hearts to betake ourselves to that communion.

Bernard Wiek, a plain man from these circles, said during his trial, "In New Testament times there was a punishment among Christians for those who misconducted themselves, a thing that is not in evidence now." Testimony like this could be extended to great length.

Needless to say, the matter of Church discipline engaged the attention of the Restitutionists who had gathered at Schlatten am Rande. In the manifesto drawn up there (which we have already mentioned) it was declared: "The temporal sword is an ordinance of God outside the perfection of Christ; the princes and rulers of the world are ordained to punish the wicked and put them to death. But in the perfection of Christ excommunication is the utmost penalty, not physical death." It would seem that this would find acceptance with all right-minded people. As a formula it is actually very good. It puts the sword and its function where they belong, and it points to a second kind of disciplinary power, one that is within the Church, and according to which excommunication is the maximum penalty. This formula prepares a division of labor, a much needed one, whereby the State has its function (which in extreme cases leads to capital punishment) and the Church has its function (which in extreme cases leads to expulsion from the society of believers). As such, this formula puts an end to much that was evil. One would expect Bible-believing folk to agree with it.

The article goes on to say that "Excommunication ought to be practiced upon those who profess to be Christians, having been baptized, but who nevertheless fall into some sin by inadvertance and not deliberately. These ought to be exhorted and pleaded with in private, once and again. At the third time they are to be publicly banned before the entire congregation, to the end that we may be able in one mind and one zeal to break the bread and drink the cup." This also has much to recommend it. It proceeds upon the assumption that a believer may fall into offensive patterns of behavior, from which he is then to be reclaimed by pastoral visits. This failing, he is moved from the category of one who has fallen into sin and is placed in the category of those who live in sin. Since such are not to be considered part of Christ's Church, they are to be officially read out of the company. This article provides for leisurely procedure — by arranging for repeated visits. It provides for secrecy in the early stages. It gives, as the first objective to which the disciplinary action looks, the improvement of the offender, and, as a second objective, a concern for the dignity of the Sacrament. Surely this would not be opposed by Reformed men!

But to think that would be to minimize the strangle-hold which the sacralist tradition had upon the minds of men, the Reformers included. For this plan would create islands of "outsiders" right in the sea of Christendom. It would be to reach back of the Constantinian change. It would be as radical as the Constantinian change had been in its time — albeit in opposite direction. In the light of the revolutionary implications of the Restitutionists' proposal to raise up a believers' Church kept that way by Church discipline, Calvin's reaction to it becomes at least understandable.

He set himself to refute Schlatten am Rande. He wanted no part in the idea that "excommunication has come in the place of the physical sword in the Christian Church, in such a way that instead of punishing a crime by death we must now punish the delinquent by depriving him of the company of the faithful."

It is true that Calvin in his refutation says that excommunication is a good and necessary policy. In fact, he says that "it is from us that these poor ingrates have learned whatever it is that they know about the matter; they by their ignorance or presumption corrupt the doctrine which we teach in its purity."[u] He asserts that it is a "great fault and vice" if dis-

---

[u]It is hard indeed to figure out how Calvin could accuse the Step-children of being "ingrates" who had pilfered the idea of Church discipline from "us." If by the "us" he means his own person then we must find a way to explain how the believers of Schlatten am Rande could, in 1527, appropriate from Calvin, at that time a lad in his teens. Moreover, it must be recalled that as early as 1524, in the letter to Müntzer, Grebel already set forth a well-articulated doctrine of Church discipline. In 1524 Calvin was but fifteen years old! And if we take the "us" to refer to the Reformers then we are still in a quandary. For in 1527, to say

cipline is neglected. However, he disagrees with the people
of the Second Front when they say that a Church without
discipline is no church. "The first question," says he, "is whether
or not we are to consider a company which does not practice
discipline to be the Church." Calvin points to the congregation
at Corinth to find the answer to this question. Discipline was
lacking there, but Paul honored them with the name of Church.
Calvin says that if there is no excommunication, "the form
of the Church is thereby disfigured but it is not destroyed
altogether."

Against the Restitutionist position that the Church has room
in it for believers and for them only, Calvin urges that "we
must think so highly of the Word and the Sacraments that
wherever we see them we are to conclude without a doubt
that the Church is there, regardless of how much vice and
evil there may be in the corporate life of men."ᵛ Manifestly
Calvin held, along with Luther, that the Church of Christ
cannot be empirically known and that conductual distinctiveness is not definitive of her. How this can be harmonized with
Christ's maxim "By their fruits shall ye know them" is indeed
hard to see.

Calvin in his refutation is particularly offended by the
Restitutionist position that if there is no discipline, and knaves
and scoundrels are therefore in attendance at the Lord's Supper,
the true believer must withdraw lest he be polluted along
with the rest. To organize a rival Church for this reason is
intolerable — no matter how bad the situation is. Did the

---

nothing about 1524, the Reformers had not as yet published anything
looking to Church discipline; what was there for "ingrates" to pilfer?
Moreover, when the Reformers came across Church discipline, as practiced
among the Bohemian Brethren (it was in 1540), they gasped in surprise
and envy at what they heard. How they were in position to teach prior
to 1527 (or 1524) what they were themselves amazed to see in 1540
remains a mystery. It seems that what Calvin says here is just another
example of the misrepresentations to which the Stepchildren were constantly exposed.

ᵛ". . . nonobstant les vices et macules qui pourront estre en la vie
commune des hommes." The reader will observe that Calvin does not say
"en la vie des gens confessants" or "en la vie des gens d'eglise" or some
such expression; no, he says "des hommes," for in his system the two are
coextensive, "les hommes" are the Church.

prophets of the Old Testament have "an altar or a temple apart?"[24]

To support this idea Calvin says that when Paul speaks of not eating or drinking with men of scandalous lives (1 Cor. 5:11) "this has to do with private association and not at all with the public communion. If the Church puts up with an unworthy person then let him who knows it keep himself from that man in his private contacts . . . but he is not to make a schism nor separation in regard to the public communion." The plain implication is that it is normal to sit at the communion table with a man of such evil report that one would not want to be seen in his company on the street!

This idea, that one may have to avoid the company of people because of their wicked lives but have no qualms about sitting at the communion table with them, Calvin endorses with an example:

> There is a man still alive who, because he was infested with this error, so that he feared to receive communion with us because of some men's imperfections, deprived himself of the communion of the Church. And all this while he had two servants in his house of very wicked and slanderous lives. I being informed thereof declared to him that he ought certainly to endeavor to purge his own house, of which he had charge, if he thought of being defiled by the faults of people over whom he did not have governance. He thereupon realized how foolish he had been.

Calvin also defended the inclusive Church (as Constantinians had done for twelve centuries, beginning with Augustine) with the Parable of the Tares in the Wheatfield. It is a field, said Calvin, "in which the good grain is so mixed with the evil that frequently you can't see it at all."[w] Calvin, like

[w]Calvin asserts in *Institutes* IV, 1:2 that "often no distinction can be made between God's children and the ungodly, between His own flock and wild beasts." This was said, of course, of that entity which Calvin chose to call the visible Church, a term invented in order to make room for a civilization-wide Church. To the extent that the Reformers swerved to the right did the concept of the "visible" Church find acceptance with them. This fact has led Farner to say of Zwingli that the concept of the visible and the invisible Church "characteristisch ist für die zweite Periode von Zwingli's Kirchenbegriff" (*op. cit.*, p. 5, n. 7). The Restitutionists would of course have nothing to do with the distinction.

all who before him had argued in favor of the Church as a body "including all in a given locality," read right over the fact that according to Jesus' own commentary on the parable the terrain on which the two kinds of plants are growing side by side is the *world* and not the Church. The medieval sacralists had always used this parable to justify the inclusive Church and Calvin did not correct this faulty exegesis.

Manifestly Calvin was being pulled in two directions,ˣ caught in the same dilemma that troubled Luther, the dilemma of a believers' Church and an all-inclusive Church. He can settle for neither because he will not let go of the other. Because of this he could not live in peace with those who assailed conductual-averagism.

Luther likewise. He too wished to preserve the inclusive Church, even if that implied a latitudinarian attitude as to conduct. With the Anabaptists in mind, Luther said:

> When they look at us and see the offensive defects with which Satan distorts our churches then they deny that we are a Church and they are unable to lift themselves over this. In like manner were the Donatists minded. They put under discipline those who had relapsed and forbade them their Churches . . . . In the same way have the Manicheans and others behaved — as though the Church were already in glory and not in the flesh. Men ought not to dispute about the Church that way . . . whatever remains of sin this verily offends these spiritual Donatists . . . but it does not offend God, seeing that for the sake of faith in Christ He excuses it and forgives.[25]

ˣThe resulting ambiguity in Calvin's doctrine of the Church was, of course, the result of his monistic attempt to combine the Church of medieval sacralism with the Church of the New Testament. One could also say that it resulted from Calvin's attempt to combine the Church of the Old Testament with the Church of the New. In all events, one finds himself agreeing with Arthur Cushman McGiffert as he asserts that "Calvin's doctrine of the Church was a composite of many diverse and inconsistent elements, and, because of this, confusion concerning the meaning, place, and the purpose of the Church has since his day reigned almost everywhere in the Reformed wing of Protestantism." (Cf. Mc-Giffert's "Calvin's Theory of the Church," in *Essays in Modern Theology and Related Subjects,* p. 225.) It was the Reformers' muddled doctrine of the Church that drove away the Stepchildren and caused the Second Front to shape up.

Luther also tried to meet the New Testament's ideal, that of a believers' Church, with the formula of an *ecclesiola in ecclesia*, a little Church of true believers, apart from, but not separate from, the Church of the masses. Early in his career, in 1523, before the Second Front had formed, Luther wrote to his friend, Nicolas Hausmann, "My intention is, in days to come, not to admit any when communion is held save such as have been interrogated and who have given acceptable answers as to their personal faith. The rest we are going to exclude." (If Luther had acted on this insight consistently there would in all likelihood never have been a Second Front.) In his *Deutsche Messe*, composed in 1526, Luther wrote that:

> They who seriously want to be Christians and want to confess the Gospel in word and deed, these ought to inscribe their names in a book and assemble in a house by themselves for purposes of prayer, the reading of Scripture, the administration of baptism, the reception of the sacrament and to engage in other Christian activities . . . but I neither can nor may as yet set up such a congregation; for I do not as yet have the people for it. If however the time comes that I must do it, so that I cannot with a good conscience refrain from it then I am ready to do my part.[26]

At this point Luther was haunted by the same fear that had led to the creation of "Christian sacralism" many centuries earlier, the fear that to organize a believers' Church would terminate civil quiet and occasion civil commotion.[y] This the Stepchildren later threw in his teeth, asserting that he was by his own admission not sufficiently *khun* (that is, *bold*) to do what his better insights dictated.[27] It was in these private gatherings, in these meetings of the believers' Church, that Luther saw a chance to introduce the discipline required by

---

[y]When in Hesse, where Anabaptist pressures were particularly strong, the leaders of the Reform there gave evidence that they were thinking of meeting the Anabaptist threat by introducing discipline into the Lutheran Churches of Hesse, Luther wrote to them: "Euren Eifer für Christum und die chrictliche Zucht habe ich mit sehr grosser Freude erfahren; aber in dieser so trüben Zeit, die auch noch nicht genugsam geeignet ist, Zucht anzunehmen, möchte ich nicht wagen, zu einer so plötzlichen Neuerung zu rathen. Man musz fürwahr die Bauern lassen ein wenig versaufen, und einem trunkenen Mann soll ein Fuder Heu weichen." (Cf. *Werke*, St. Louis edition, Vol. XXIb, col. 1827.)

the New Testament. But he was dead set against any such
discipline in the Church of the masses. When he heard that
at Zwickau (where Restitutionist influence was strong) such
discipline in the Church of the mass was contemplated he
warned:

> . . . such reprimanding of specified persons is not in place
> except in the gathering of the Christians . . . , in a public
> preaching where Christians and non-Christians alike sit to-
> gether, as is the case in our churches, there the rebuke is to
> be general . . . no one being delineated in particular. For
> it is a general preaching and general it must remain, where
> no one is shamed before the rest or made to blush, until they
> have drawn apart and have come into the separate gathering
> where in orderly fashion petition, punishment, and admonition,
> may take place.[28]

This adds up to an inclusive Church in which there is no
discipline, plus a believers' Church in which there is — a
palpably impossible combination! Manifestly Luther was trying
to eat his cake and have it, was trying to do the things the
Second Front wanted done without undoing the things it wanted
undone.

Nowhere did Luther show more plainly how he was torn
between the two alternatives of a believers' Church versus an
everybody-embracing one than he did when, in 1526, Caspar
Schwenkfeld called on him. Schwenkfeld reports on the conversation:

> I talked at length with him about the Church of the future,
> how this was the only way in which the genuine Christians
> could be separated from the false and that otherwise the
> situation was hopeless. He knew all right that the ban must
> always accompany the Gospel and that where it is not in-
> stituted there things could not improve but only get worse and
> worse, for it is apparent how it goes everywhere . . . everyone
> wants to boast of being a Christian. To this he replied that
> he was greatly grieved at it that no one was showing any
> moral improvement. With the future Church, he said, he had
> not as yet had much experience, although he was minded to
> make a roster, listing the Christians, wanted their behavior
> scrutinized, and was thinking of preaching to these in the
> cloister, a chaplain addressing the rest of the *Pfarr* of the
> Church . . . ; I kept asking about the ban but he refused

to reply. I pointed to 2 Peter 2, where we read about "spots
and blemishes . . . feasting with you:" I asked him what
"believing with one heart and one mind" might be. To all
this he replied, "Yes, Caspar dear, genuine Christians are not
yet too common, I'd love to see two of them together, I don't
know where I could find so much as one."[29]

Here was a man keenly aware of the evil situation he had
inherited, that of the everybody-embracing Church. He was
especially aware of the incongruity when he was standing before the Sacrament. In his *Gründonnerstag* sermon, preached
in 1523, he had said that to administer the elements to every
comer, good and bad alike, was "not very unlike chucking it
down the gullet of a sow." And he fought, in word at least,
against the inherited evil of asking no questions of would-be
communicants. But this Luther was lost in the shuffle. The
exodus of the Stepchildren resulted in the abandonment of
the fond ambition of having some day a believers' church
kept that way by the exercise of discipline. Luther never —
even in his thinking, to say nothing about putting it into
practice — abandoned the inclusive Church; and that put his
fancy idea about *ecclesiola in ecclesia* into cold storage.

When the Stepchildren worked out in practice the ideals
which Luther had once cherished but which had seemed too
formidable for him, he became the more impatient with them.
His pupil, Justus Menius, spoke disapprovingly of the very
practice Luther had hoped to adopt but had not. He chided
the Anabaptists because "before they celebrate the Lord's
Supper it is their custom to exercise discipline first; and those
who have conducted themselves in a disorderly fashion . . .
as well as those who have recanted under pressure, are required before they are again admitted to the Sacrament to
repent of their specified sin, to the end that the brotherhood
may by all means be pure and without defect."[30]

We see then that the wavering attitude toward Church
discipline that came to expression in the camp of the Reformers
caused the radicals to abandon the ship; and that, when these
went ahead with the matter, the Reformers stiffened their opposition. It took years and years for the Reformers to consider
the idea a second time, and then the fact that they had once
opposed the Stepchildren in the matter stood in their way.

As late as 1569 there was still opposition to the introduction
of discipline in some Protestant circles and that because the
practice had come to be known as an Anabaptist excess.   In
the same year, the men of Zürich "reject the Bann and excommunication from the Lord's Supper, citing their dealings
with the Anabaptists, who considered this to be a prerequisite
of a true church. Where a heathen government functioned, the
Bann may have been needful, but this discipline . . . brings
about divisions and nourishes Pharisaism. Therefore the Lord's
Supper must be accessible to all comers."*

We see then that the difference of opinion that existed
concerning the kind of discipline that should be exercised in
Christ's Church was but a facet of the difference of opinion as
to the delineation of the Church. For men who think of the
Church as "including all in a given locality," discipline as it
had been distorted ever since Constantine was right and proper;
for those who thought of the Church as a society of believers,
some very radical changes were in order. The spokesman for
the Reformed camp put it very neatly and concisely at the Disputation held at Emden in the year 1578:

> Our view of the Church of God is diverse from that of "the
> men" [a very derogatory appellation]; they exclude the office
> of the magistrate from the Church and they refuse to ascribe
> to the civil power any punitive function in the Church of God.
> But we, in keeping with the Word of God include the office
> of the magistracy in the church of God. For this reason they
> say that in the Church punishment over and above that of
> excommunication shall not and may not be employed. To the
> question whether a minister and a Church are bound by the
> Word of God to admonish the civil government to pursue the
> heretic and put him to death we say yes, but they say no.[31]

We see then that, although there were in the early utterances
of the Reformers hints that they might introduce Church discipline after the style of the New Testament, this came to

---

*These sentiments indicate that in the Protestant camp the Constan-
tinian change was still looked upon as an advance upon earlier times.
The idea of a "larger fulfillment," of which we spoke earlier, was still
part of their thinking. The acquisition of the "other arm" had rendered
Church discipline in its New Testament delineation obsolete; so the men
in the Reformed camp were still implying.

nought in the battle against the Anabaptists. When it re-entered the stream of Reformation thought it could with justice be called an Anabaptist heritage. This situation has led a recent investigator to assert, with specific reference to Anabaptism:

> Although Calvin was hostile to most of its ideas it supplied Calvinism with the ingredient of the concept of the Church as a community of convinced believers in which a rigorous discipline and holiness of living were prominent requirements for membership.[32]

It is apparent then that the Reformers were not minded to discard the Constantinian formula; they sought to reform the Church on the last of "Christian sacralism"; this restrained them from launching a full-scale attack upon conductual-averagism; it likewise kept them from re-instituting Church discipline according to the New Testament blue-print. The liquidation of Servetus is of and by itself enough to point this up. The Reformers sought to construe the New Testament Church after the lineaments of the Old Testament,[a] thus reversing the forward movement of God's affairs in history by an atavistic stroke which coincided with the Constantinian change.

In this whole area the Stepchildren blazed a new trail, by repudiating the Constantinian change, by reinstituting the Church of believers with conductual distinctiveness, by driving away the sword function out of the Church, by re-introducing Church discipline in which excommunication is the ultimate penalty. This program earned for them the incriminating appellative of *Catharer*.

---

[a] Cornelius Krahn has written, with a fine insight: "Im Alten Testament wurzelend kann Calvin mit ruhigem Gewissen bei der Anwendung des Bannes auch der Todesstraffe beipflichten, während für Menno nach Christus Moses ausgedient hat und jetzt nur noch 'christliche' Mittel zur Säuberung der Gemeinde geboten sind." (Cf. Krahn's biography of Menno Simons, p. 117.) This unique insight as to the preliminary character of the Old Testament is one of the many features of the Anabaptist vision that was not derived from 1517, but dates back to pre-Reformation dissent against "Christian sacralism." The Waldensians, for example, were wont to speak of the Old Testament as *ley velha* and of the New Testament regime as *ley novella;* and they pointed to the fact that the *ley novella* "does not kill the sinner as did the Law of Moses but compassionately leads him to repentance; both the *ley velha* and the *ley novella* are from God but given for diverse objectives."

4 Sacramentschwärmer

*So then faith cometh by
hearing . . . .* Romans 10:17

THE STEPCHILDREN OF THE REFORMATION WERE FREQUENTLY
given the spiteful name of *Sacramentschwärmer*, or, more
simply, "Sacramentarians." It is with this term of reproach
that we shall be engaged in this chapter — or, more correctly,
with the aspect of the clash between the Stepchildren and the
Reformers which earned them this name. We shall see that
this clash was but another feature of the basic difference of
conviction as to the delineation of the Christian Church.

Primitive Christianity had had as its primary stock in trade
the preaching of the Gospel. It had preached the Good News
to all and had then baptized those who responded believingly
to it, so that there were "added daily to the Church such as
should be saved" (Acts 2:47).

This was a great innovation. The pre-Christian world had
known nothing like it. In the pre-Christian world there was
no religious dialog between "those within" and "those without."
All were in the same category; how could there be dialog?
In so far as there was speech at all it was in the form of the
monolog.

The early Church was convinced that it had heard a voice
from the beyond, a speech that ran counter to the speech of
man, specifically counter to his speech on the religious level of
life. It was a controverting speech, one that said *no* to man's
yes, and *yes* to man's *no*. And with this controverting speech
it sought the ear of all whom it could reach. At the heart of
this controverting speech was the *skandalon* of the Cross, God's
fiercest *no* to man's *yes*, His most emphatic *yes* to man's *no*.

132

The early Church considered the act of faith to consist, in the first place, in saying *yes* to God's *yes* and *no* to His *no*; it looked upon the moment of salvation as that moment when the hearer of the Word begins to speak in the idiom of that Word, God's controverting speech to man. In the authentic Christian tradition, the Christian man is the man who has been led to say Amen to the controverting voice from the beyond.[a]

And these amen-sayers, these men and women who chime in with the controverting speech of God, by that very act become just as controversial as is the oracle of God. Small wonder that it has been said that the true Christian is one who stands in tension with the world as it exists apart from the redeeming act of God. This is his calling; and in this he rejoices. For it is each time a reminder of his own metamorphosis and a proof of its genuineness. He knows how serious it is "if all men speak well of you" — for that implies that his *yes* is not as yet God's *yes* and his *no* not yet God's *no* — and he knows the joy of "having been counted worthy to suffer shame for his name" (Acts 5:41).

The ethnic world, that is, the world without benefit of the redemptive revelation of the Judeo-Christian heritage, had no speech from the beyond — for the quite sufficient reason that it had no recognized beyond. It did not have the terminology of *the Maker* and *the made;* much less did it have the concept of the Fall, the event that made the controverting speech of God necessary. Needless to say, it did not have, and could not have,

---

[a]The question has been raised in our times, and discussed with considerable ardor, whether it is with "Proposition" that the Church confronts the world or with "Person." Related to this question is the question whether the Church has a "propositional" confession. It must be granted that the New Testament knows nothing of a non-propositional faith; nor of a non-propositional revelation. The historic Christian faith has looked upon the act of faith as *credere* from one point of view and *fidere* from another point of view; the former one does vis-à-vis Proposition and the latter one does vis-à-vis Person. Actually therefore this is not a matter of *entweder-oder;* it is a matter of both-and. There can be no encounter with person except through the medium of speech. One must be *Schriftgläubig* before he can be *Christgläubig.* The Word-incarnate is not dissociable from the Word-inscripturated. In the light of this, our assertion, that the main stock in trade of authentic Christianity was the Word, must be seen.

the dialog of the *yes*-sayers and the *no*-sayers. It knew only concensus on the themes of religion, not the two-way speech that the Christians demanded and thrived on.

Seeing how radical was early Christianity's concept of its preaching mission, and how novel and different, we must not be surprised to see this concept of the preaching mission assailed. We must not be surprised to witness an atavistic retrogression here, a return to things as they are apart from the voice from the beyond. Here, as much as at any other point, the Church will have to be on its guard to hold fast that which it has, for there are always spirits abroad that would like nothing better than to turn back the hands of the clock and go back to the unanimity of pre-Christian times.

The early Church's conception of its preaching mission with its corollary, the formation of two camps, is ill-suited to the sacralist ambition. This preaching eventuates in two camps, the camp of those who have begun to speak in the idiom of the speech from the beyond and the camp of those who continue to speak as men spoke before it came. But two camps are precisely what the sacralist does not want. He must have all men in one and the same visible receptacle,[b] and he looks to religion as a prime contributor to the achievement of the

---

[b]Authentic Christianity's firm conviction that at the terminal point of history there are two camps, the "saved" and the "lost," was embarrassing to sacralists. Men who think in terms of one category in the *here* find it hard to live with the idea of two categories *there*. It seems that the concept of purgatory found its way into the world of "Christian sacralism" so readily because it offered a convenient way out of the embarrassment. It opened up the possibility of *one* category even in the beyond. It gave men accustomed to thinking of saints and sinners as undifferentiable here a chance to think of them as undifferentiable also in the hereafter. In this light the idea of purgatory is an elongation of sacralistic thinking. And it is not at all surprising to find the "heretics" hostile to the idea of purgatory. Generally speaking, they rejected it forthrightly. But they found still another way of combatting the idea of a single receptacle at the terminal point, by means of the concept of "the sleep of the soul," the idea that at death the souls of men enter into a state of complete lethargy, until the judgment day, when they are revived and go to their respective destinations. This notion of the "sleep of the soul," technically called Psychopannychism, was, as George H. Williams points out in his recent book on the Radical Reformation, a common feature of "heresy." It recurred, as did so many of the features of medieval dissent, in the camp of the Anabaptists.

homogeneous society. Therefore it must not surprise anyone that with the coming of "Christian sacralism" a heavy hand was laid upon the Word and the preaching thereof. It was but natural that something else should come in the place of the preaching technique. One could even predict what that something else would be, namely, transaction, manipulation, act, *ritus*.

For sacral society is act-bound society. In sacral society religion is rite, act entered into by all. And as such this act is then a device whereby the tribe is bound together. The Navajo medicine-man conducts an act; he makes the sand painting, and in it the tribe is bound together. And so it is in sacral society everywhere. The place and function of religion in a sacral society is such that there is virtually no room for personal religion; so much is religion a matter of society as a whole that it becomes hard to fit the private practice of religion into it. Plato has written this in his *Laws*:

> Let this then be the law. No one shall possess shrines of the gods in private houses, and he who is found to possess them and to perform any sacred rite not publicly authorized, shall be informed against in the ear of the guardians of the law; and let these issue orders that he is to carry his private rites to the public temples; and if he does not obey, let such a penalty be inflicted as to make him comply. And if a person be proven guilty of an impiety, not merely from childish levity but such as grown-up men may be guilty of, let him be punished with death.

Not only is private religion hard to control, but private devotions are, as this heathen thinker sees things, essentially a-social. To be religious in private is to deflect religion from its most important function, that of tying the tribe together. That is why Plato pleads for laws that render non-public religious ritual illicit.

It will be observed that for Plato religion is rite, as it is for all who write from a pre-Christian point of view. Plato is not worried about any words spoken, any message brought. It is not for such activity that he wants laws' enacted, but for ritual, act. For him religion is act. And act loses its point if done in private. This is typical of ethnic thinking in the matter.

Knowing the pre-Christian evaluation of religious act, we will not be surprised to find adherents of "Christian sacralism" everywhere and always ready to take up arms when they hear of non-public sacrament; a baptism applied merely to *some* and a sacramental table spread only for *an element* in society make the sacralist think the end of the world has come.[c] (We shall see that the Stepchildren were the victims of this sacralist thinking.)

It was therefore inevitable that with the coming of "Christian sacralism" preaching was crowded aside by act. In the place of salvation by believing response to the preached Word came salvation by act, by sacramental manipulation. The two have been in competition with each other ever since.[d]

The proponents of "Christian sacralism" in their search for act did not have to be altogether inventive. The authentic Christian tradition already had its acts. These needed only to be appropriated and magnified.

There was the *Agape* or love-feast, the Lord's Supper, a solemn performance intended to keep alive in the memory of Christ's followers the event of the suffering and death of Christ, as well as to remind them of the fact that He would come again. Moreover it was also a communion, a ritual in which the unity of the body and the Head was eloquently portrayed (as well as the unity that exists between member and member), set forth by the very human act of eating from

---

[c]This throws an interesting light upon the fact that at the end of Zwingli's reformatory career in Zürich no one was eligible for public office who did not go to the Lord's Supper (although it was added that this "was not to involve his honor"); attendance at Church had become obligatory. To make this coercion really effective it was further forbidden to attend mass in a neighboring town, a privilege granted in earlier times. (Cf. Farner, *op. cit.*, p. 125.)

[d]In sacramental churches preaching atrophies; in preaching churches the sacraments are secondary. Attempts have been made to combine the two "means of grace," but one or the other is always *primus inter pares*. No Church has been able to achieve in practice the equality to which it in theory holds. As the one increases the other decreases. Just now we witness a heightening of Sacrament in many Protestant Churches; this could be illustrative of what we say; the Word has been discredited (we do not say rightly discredited); hence the Sacrament receives the attention which once went to the Word.

a common loaf and drinking from a common cup. This already existing institution needed only to be accomodated a bit to make it serve the purpose which *act* has regularly served in sacral society. (There was also the *act* of baptism — which, as we shall see in a later chapter, the drafters of "Christian sacralism" were also able to bend to their purpose.)

Nor did the proponents of "Christian sacralism" have to be altogether inventive as they adjusted the *Agape* to their program. There was a precedent by which they could go. The minds of men in those times were already acquainted with terms and institutions to which the *Agape* could be made to conform.

There is a lingering suspicion, frequently uttered in Protestant circles, to the effect that Roman Catholicism is a hybrid form, authentic Christianity crossed with the pagan faith of pre-Christian Rome. At no point is the hybrid character of this offspring of the Christian mother and the ethnic father more apparent than in the "mass," as the *Agape* came to be called after the Constantinian metamorphosis.

What was the ancient institution, to which the *Agape* could be made to conform as men drifted toward "Christian sacralism?"

It will be recalled that in the days of Decius every householder had been instructed to fill out a formulary reading as follows: "I, N.N., have always sacrificed to the gods, and now in your presence I have, in keeping with the directive, sacrificed . . . and have tasted of the sacrificial victim; and I request that you, a public servant, certify the same." This formulary was intended to do two things. On the one hand it was part of a frantic effort to infuse new life into the dying religion of ancient Rome; on the other hand it was a device whereby each individual Christian could be located and taken in hand.

It would be most gratifying if we could know more about the evolution of the rite which is here described, the item about "tasting the sacrificial victim." That it was a feature of the practices associated with the cult of the so-called "mystery religions" is quite apparent. In these mystery religions (the only religious forms that had any vitality in those final days of pagan Rome), one partook of deity by ingesting a morsel of a sacrificial victim.[e] By such ingesting, something of the *élan* of the god was said to be infused into the devotee, in a transaction known as a *mysterion* — the word that has given us the expression "mystery religion." This word *mysterion* was by the Latins rendered *sacramentum* — the direct antecedent of our word "sacrament."

The important thing to notice, for our present purpose, is that in the formulary of Decius we have an attempt to procure religious homogeneity by the use of *sacramentum*.[f] It must also be observed that *mysterion* or the *sacramentum* intended to bring about religious uniformity in the scheme of Decius, was a *sacrifice*, something done on an altar.

It did not require a great deal of ingenuity for the fashioners of "Christian sacralism" to realize that with a few adroit alterations the *Agape* could be put in the place of the *sacramentum* and then serve the function which Decius had in mind, namely, the function of providing the monolithic society. A few alterations, a gather here and a tuck there, and the love-feast was all ready, ready to perform the function in the new sacralism which the pagan *sacramentum* had performed in the old.

The first thing that had to be done was to appropriate the pagan word *sacramentum* (recall that it occurs nowhere in the Scriptures) and to let it replace the word *Agape* of the authentic tradition. This was a clever stroke; every Roman citizen knew what a *sacramentum* was, and what it was supposed to do and achieve; he needed only to hear the word to know the theology, that of "tasting the sacrificial victim," a transaction signifying the participants' solidarity with the society of which he was a part.

A second thing that had to be done was to move the table out and the altar in. This would automatically make of the officiating minister a *sacrificateur*, a sacrificer, a priest; and this would as automatically change the viands, the bread and the

---

[e]It seems that in John 6:53-56 we have Christian truth stated in terminology borrowed from contemporary mystery religions.

[f]That the word *sacrament* is of ethnic origin is of course not open to question. The religion of pagan Rome was a sacramental religion. In 1 Corinthians 10:20f., Paul points out that it is incongruous to participate in the heathen sacrament and also in the Christian *Agape* or "table of the Lord."

wine that had stood on the table of the *Agape*, into the flesh and the blood of "the sacrificial victim."

A third thing that needed to be done was to eliminate as much as possible the "Take, eat" of the original ritual. This "Take, eat" was far too reminiscent of the voluntaryism that was so much a part of the authentic Christian vision; it portrayed too manifestly that in regard to the good things of the Christian faith there is always the take it or leave it. The determinative act of taking had to be eliminated and in its place had to come an act of imparting. Instead of a ritual in which the *partaking* was the central idea, there came a ritual in which the *imparting* was the central thing. The Constantinian change therefore made the "Take, eat" obsolete. Henceforth the *sacrificateur* would lay a morsel of "the sacrificial victim" upon the tongue of the recipient. All the recipient had to do in the new order was to let his mouth hang open — which requires less of an act on his part than to keep it shut.

With these changes the love-feast was suitable to the rôle in the new sacralism which the pagan *sacramentum* had played in the old sacralism.

It is not at all surprising that all through medieval times and on into Reformation times, and beyond them, *Corpus Christianum* was thought of as a thing held together by "sacrament."ᵍ That is what the function of the *sacramentum* had been in the days of the old sacralism; and that was the function of the "sacrament" in the new sacralism.

As we have already intimated, and as we shall see in some detail in a later chapter, the fashioners of "Christian sacralism" laid a hand also upon the lustration that was a part of the Christian heritage, made of it also a sacralism-serving thing. Moreover, the Constantinian change led to the creation of

----

ᵍAugustine taught, and all adherents of "Christian sacralism" repeated after him, that society cannot hang together unless it be bound by a common religion. And he taught that it is in the Sacrament that the cohesive power of religion resides. Calvin in his day endorsed much of this, saying, in Institutes IV, 14:19, that "Men cannot be welded together in any name of religion, whether true or false, unless they be bound in some partnership of signs or visible sacraments." It was the Anabaptists' assault upon the sacraments as binders of society that made them so odious in the sight of the Reformers.

several brand new sacraments — all of them very handy instruments for him who would bring into being, and keep it there, some "Christian" version of the pre-Christian monolithic, non-composite society.

When the Constantinian change was complete the technique of salvation by Sacrament had effectively replaced the older technique of salvation by the preached Word. The *predicateur* had been replaced by the *sacrificateur*. All through medieval times and on to the eve of the Reformation, the typical priest of the Empire-Church was a stranger to the word. (Luther discovered the Bible — after he had already for some time worn the cloth. The same thing is true of Menno Simons and of countless others.) The priest of whom this was not true, if indeed there was such, was a rare exception. The typical priest knew the ins and outs of the technique of salvation by sacramental manipulation; he was a novice in the technique of salvation by response to the preached Word.

The logic of salvation by sacramental manipulation leads straight to the idea of *ex opere operato*, the name given to the view that the transaction to which the Sacrament points is "done in the doing." It is the innate power of the Sacrament as the conveyor of grace that assures the mediation of salvation, this rather than the state or the attitude of the dispenser — or of the recipient, for that matter.[h] Small wonder that with those who resisted the Constantinian formula, the attitude of the recipient remained the one thing that mattered. Small wonder also that among those who deplored the Constantinian change, it was said that a priest who lives in sin is not competent to

---

[h]How essentially medieval Luther could be at times in regard to the sacrament, how dangerously close he sometimes walked along the brink of *ex opere operato*, may be gathered from these his words: "Wie könnte man die Taufe höher schänden und lästern, denn dasz es keine wahrhaftige gute Taufe sein sollte, die einem ungläubigen gegeben wirt? . . . Darum, dasz ich nicht glaubte, so sollte die Taufe nichts sein? . . . Was könnte doch der Teufel Aergeres und Lästerlicheres lehren oder predigen? Noch sind die Wiedertäufer und Rottengeister mit dieser Lehre erfüllt. Aber ich setze, das ein Jude die Tauf annähme (wie es oft pflegt zu geschehen) und glaubte nicht, so wollest du sagen: Die Taufe ist nicht recht denn er glaubt nicht? Das hiesze nicht allein mit der Vernunft genarrt, sondern auch Gott gelästert und geschändet" (*Werke*, St. Louis ed., VII, 990).

convey salvation and that the recipient must believe in order
to receive the good thing symbolized in the Sacrament.

The idea of salvation by sacramental manipulation also leads
straight to the idea of transubstantiation and the notion that
the officiating priests "makes" (this is the word that was in
common use in medieval times) the body and the blood of
Christ, "makes" them as he utters the words "Hoc est enim
corpus meum"[1] (for this is my body). To take the place of
the "sacrificial victim" of the pre-Christian *sacramentum,* the
elements of the Supper had to be made to cease being what
they were, bread and wine, and begin to exist as another
substance, flesh and blood. Hence the *sacrificateur* was em-
powered to transubstantiate.

Sacramentalism also leads to sacerdotalism. If salvation comes
by sacramental manipulation, then the manipulator becomes extremely important; in fact, he becomes indispensable. The
Church was extremely jealous of the priestly office, understandably so; for in it was lodged a great potential toward
the realization and the perpetuation of "Christian sacralism."
The Church created the "sacrament of Orders," an act whereby
power to transubstantiate was allegedly transferred from the
officiating priest to the head of the one being ordained. In this
way the Church had its company of trusted officials, its hard
core of "card-carrying party members," who strictly speaking
constitute the *ecclesia.*[1] By this, sacerdotalism revisionism was
effectively precluded. By it the masses were effectively defranchised. Only he really "runs" who has been "sent" — and
the Church saw to it that she "sent" only those whom she
could trust.

In this ordination procedure the important thing was not the
candidate's status as a believer and a converted man; the im-

[1]Medieval man, unable to understand the Church's jargon (it was all
done in Latin) did know this much, that at the sound of the words
"Hoc est enim corpus meum" something pretty mysterious was allegedly
taking place. So he began to refer to any mysterious going-on as
another case of *hocus-pocus* — that is what the words of the priest had
sounded like.

[1]In Roman Catholic theology the Church is, to speak strictly, the
teaching Church, the *ecclesia docens,* the ordained ones; it is only in
some loose sense that the *hearing* Church, the *ecclesia audiens* is included
in the concept *Church.*

portant thing was apostolic succession, an unbroken line of empowerment, a pedigree that ran back without a hiatus, supposedly all the way back to the Apostles. It was this that made the priest.

Such predication as accompanied the sacramental manipulation was done in Latin — even though to the common man this was unintelligible. In a system of salvation by sacramental manipulation this is no difficulty; it poses a difficulty, an insuperable one, only to the man who thinks in terms of salvation by believing response to the preached Word. The Latin was the official language of the Empire; for that reason it was the prescribed language of the Empire-Church.

We see then that the eclipse of the Word, the usurpation of of its place by the Sacrament modeled after the pre-Christian *sacramentum*, the heavy emphasis upon the manipulator, transubstantiation, the doctrine of *ex opere operato*, partiality toward the Latin language in the Church's activities — are all of them related phenomena. They are so many developments inherent in the Constantinian change; they are so many props of "Christian sacralism."

It is therefore not at all surprising that in the vision of the "heretics" there was a negative attitude toward this whole complex of ideas and institutions. In fact, a chorus of protest resounds across the ages, contesting all that feeds the idea of salvation by sacramental manipulation, and sustaining all that which belongs with the formula of salvation by believing response to the preached Word.[x]

Let us pick out a few voices in this chorus. In the year 1025 some "heretics" were located in the vicinity of Liège, where they had migrated in order to escape the wrath of the

---

[x]Those who adhered to the idea that salvation is by sacramental manipulation came to be known as Sacramentalists, and those who opposed this idea and held to the formula that salvation comes by believing response to the preached Word came, by a strange quirk of language, to be known as Sacramentarians. In this way, two words that have the same meaning etymologically came to stand for two radically different ideologies. In our further usage, a Sacramentalist will be one who has the high view of the Sacrament that came in with the Constantinian change, whereas a Sacramentarian will be a person who had a correspondingly low view of the Sacrament, giving it a place below that of the Word. The Sacramentarians were also called *Sacramentschwärmer*.

"fallen" Church, coming as they said from Italy. Fleeing from Liège they came to Arras, where they were arrested, just as they were taking to the road once more to escape the inquisitor. During their trial they asserted that "The mystery of baptism and of the body of the Lord is nothing." (The reader will recall that "mystery" and "sacrament" are synonymous.) They said that "There are no sacraments in the holy Church by which one can attain unto salvation."[l] Their faith, we are told, consisted in "leaving the world behind, keeping from fleshly lusts, earning their livelihood by the work of their hands, doing harm to no one, showing charity — if this right-eousness is observed, say they, then the work of baptism is nothing; if the truth is falsified, then baptism does not help unto salvation."[m] This was Sacramentarianism, pure and simple, a flat denial of salvation by sacramental manipulation, uttered with the insinuation that the "Truth" had gone into eclipse in the camp of the Sacramental Church, a loss that no amount of sacrament could make good.

These views were already old in 1025. In that same year Berengarius, a "heretic" who tried to sit it out within the prevailing Church, taught that "the body of the Lord is not

[l]The medieval "heretic" was decidedly Word-oriented. So thoroughly versed in the New Testament Scriptures were the "evangelical Cathars" (who after 1179 were generally called Waldensians) that Walter Mapes, a well-equipped son of the Catholic Church, said at Rome that he dreaded a disputation with them in the area of the Word. In one of the Waldensian tracts, the Word is called "salvation for the soul of the poor, a tonic for the weak, food for the hungry, teaching for the true, comfort unto the chastened, the cessation of slander and the acquisition of virtue." In another of these literary remains of these "heretics," the so-called *Cantica,* we read that "Even as they who are assailed by the enemy flee to a strong tower so do the assailed saints betake themselves to the Holy Scripture. There thy find weapons against heresies, armor against the assaults of the devil, the assaults of the flesh, the glory of the world."

[m]In all likelihood the word "truth" stands here for "the Word" or "Scriptures." We know that the Restitutionist "heretics" stood for the idea that the Scriptures are the sole rule of faith and conduct. We read, in a medieval inquisitor's delineation of the "heretic" that one of their "errors" is that "They scorn all that whereof they read not in the Gospel . . . ." (Cf. Coulton, *Inquisition and Liberty,* p. 190, quoting.) The fact that this inquisitor was himself an ex-heretic makes this testi-mony all the more significant; he had lived with the "heretic."

so much the actual body as a shadow and figure of the Lord's body." In so teaching, said the outraged Church, "he seeks to introduce ancient heresies into modern times."[1] (It may be observed, in passing, that the Stepchildren of Reformation times counted this Berengarius among those who "had a good beginning in the truth.")

This Sacramentarianism was never absent from the medieval scene. In the year 1112, we find, the Church locked horns with "persons who deny that the substance of the bread and of the wine which is blest by the priest at the altar is actually changed into the body and blood of Christ."[2] (These Sacramentarians are also said to have held "that the sacrament of baptism does not help little ones unto salvation.")

In the early part of the twelfth century there was a veritable avalanche of Sacramentarianism in Flanders, that fertile mother of generation upon generation of "heresy." In the vicinity of Antwerp the "heretic" Tanchelm arose, who "dared to agitate against the sacraments of the Church"[n] and who said openly that "It is nothing that the priests make on the altar." He warned his followers against the sin of "gazing on the sacramental body and blood of the Lord." This was indeed Sacramentarianism. It was also Restitutionism; for Tanchelm held that "only with him and his following does the true Church exist." So great was the following of this early Sacramentarian that almost the whole bishopric of Utrecht followed him and would certainly have defected from the fold of the "fallen" Church had it not been for the fact that the Church's trouble-shooter,

[n]Although the enraged Church gave currency to many bizarre and even ugly tales about this Tanchelm, so that it has become difficult to distinguish the true from the false, it is certain that he maintained that the Church gathered around him was the only true Church (he was therefore a Restitutionist); also, that he rejected the whole sacerdotal system of the prevailing Church and its system of salvation-conveying Sacraments. Like so many "heretics" before him and after him, he frowned on auricular confession, saying that one ought to confess in the ear of God and not in that of a mortal man. We find with him the formula, almost a constant with the medieval "heretics," that "In quacumque hora peccator ingemuerit, salvus erit, nec recordabar amplius peccatorum ejus, dicit Dominus." (In the very same hour in which the sinner sighs he is saved, neither will I make mention of his sins anymore, saith the Lord.) In this view of things the sacrament as well as the *sacerdos* become quite dispensable.

Norbertus, managed to get things somewhat straightened out. Norbertus was no doubt aided by the fact that one dark night as Tanchelm was crossing the Schelde River (so a faithful son of the "fallen" Church informs us), "a faithful cleric, driven by a pious zeal, bashed him in the head so that he died" (the original has *in cerebro percussit*).[3]

Tanchelm's ideas could not be so easily dispatched however. Half a century later, in 1163, a band of Restitutionists were burned at Cologne, "followers of Tanchelm," whose errors were:

> that they consider all men who are not of their sect to be heretics and infidels; that they spurn the sacraments of the true Church and say that they only have the true faith and that all others are worldly men and under condemnation. They say that the body and blood of the Lord is nothing, ridiculing the Mass and calling it by awful names, for which reason they do not patronize it . . . . They deride the Confessional, saying that one ought to lay bare his heart to God and not to any man. They contemn indulgences and penances, quoting the prophet to the effect that "in the hour in which the sinner sighs he is saved; nor will I make mention of his sins anymore, saith the Lord."[4]

Plainly we are concerned here with folk who were both Sacramentarians and Restitutionists.

In 1516, on the very eve of the Reformation, a man writing about this Tanchelm asserted that at Tanchelm's death his "heresy" had been "sown by the devil in various places, most of all in Bohemia, Thuringia, and Alsace — where to this day those who believe thus have by no means ceased to be." There were heavy deposits of such anti-Sacramentalism in all parts of Europe prior to the Reformation and it is from these areas that the people came whom Luther had in mind when he spoke of those "who in earlier times had been suppressed by the tyranny of anti-Christ." Of these deposits C. A. Cornelius, the first to attempt an inductive study of Anabaptism and himself a Catholic, was thinking when he said: "To Luther came others who, before his activity, had already abandoned the doctrine of the official Church, men who were encouraged by his activity to give expression to their ideas and to organize them into systems."[5] It was of these deposits that Zwingli was thinking when he reminded his fellow Reformer, Luther, in

1527, that "There have been men, not a few, who have known the sum and substance of the evangelical religion quite as well as you; however, out of all Israel no one took the chances involved in stepping forth to do battle, for all feared yon mighty Goliath, standing there in the fearful weight of his weapons and in challenging stance."[6]

It may be said with confidence that in the centuries that went before 1517 there never was absent from the scene a murmuring against the Sacramentalism that had swept in with the Constantinian change. One could not live out the span of an average human life without experiencing at first-hand that not all people believed in the so-called miracle of the mass.

Each successive wave of protest against the order that had begun with the Constantinian change no doubt bore the impress of its own times; but every eruption of "heresy" was like every other eruption in the matter of salvation by sacramental manipulation. During the frightful times of the Black Death, for instance, "heresy" reflected the times. It was not typical of "heresy" in other, more normal, times; it was probably not as evangelical, but it was just as anti-sacramental as any other wave of dissent. The "heretics" of that age "did not kneel before the holy sacrament when it was raised aloft and sacrificed in the holy mass." Nor did they "doff their hats" as the custom was, to greet the host. That this was a matter of great import is apparent from the fact that the custom arose to specify that at one's burial one's hat was not to be removed — a final gesture telling the world that the one who was being laid away had never made himself guilty of the idolatry involved in bowing to a morsel of bread. How serious this was may be measured by the fact that the bishop of Utrecht, Jan van Arkel, forbade, "upon pain of excommunication, to any priest under our jurisdiction to officiate at a burial of any corpse wearing a hat, or bearing the staff,° or any other item of the attire of the Flagellantes.[7]

°Manifestly these Flagellantes were also *Stäbler,* staff-carriers, of whom we spoke in an earlier chapter. It seems that whenever and wherever men grew critical of the "fallen" Church one of the first things to come under fire was her involvement in the sword-function. This in turn made the critics of this involvement inclined to carry a staff by way of contrast.

What was said of some "heretics" apprehended at Trier in the thirteenth century could be predicated of countless other eruptions of dissent:

> Many of them are well-versed in Scripture, which they possess in Teutonic translation; others repeat baptism; others do not believe in the body of the Lord; others say that the body of the Lord can be constituted by any man or woman, ordained or otherwise, in any dish or goblet and at any place; others hold that extreme unction is not necessary; others minimize the pontificate and the priesthood; others say that the prayers for the dead do not help; others neglect the feasts and work on the Church's festivals and eat meat in lent.[8]

This may sound like a series of loose and disjunct items but they are not that. Rather are they so many features of rebellion against the "fallen" Church's fallenness. The Church knew very well that "heretics are like Samson's foxes; they may present diverse faces but at the tail they are all joined together." And when she said this, she added dolefully that the commonality consisted in this, that they "have an aversion to the [Catholic] Church."

The Waldensians, too, were Sacramentarians.[ᴘ] They began their own celebration of the Lord's Supper with the prayer, "We beseech Thee Lord, thou who hast thyself borne our sins and our iniquities because of thy mercy . . . ." — a theology in which there is no impanation, no transubstantiation, no consubstantiation, not even an unusual and specific presence. One of their leaders, Martin Houska of Bohemia, spoke disdainfully of "kneeling before that morsel of bread?" Such transubstantiation as there is, said these Sacramentarians, takes place "not in the hands of the priest but in the heart of him who receives it worthily."

ᴘAnastasius Veluanus, that intriguing evangelical of early Reformation times in Holland (he assumed this name because after he had recanted under torture he returned to his Restitutionist convictions, dropping his real name, which was Versteeg, and assuming, in an area where he was not heretofore known, the name Anastasius Veluanus, the "Resurrected One from the Veluwe," his native province), tells us, as he speaks of the denial of transubstantiation: "Dese menong is oick gewest by den waldensen van den iar elffhondert und LXX bis noch toe." (This view was adhered to by the Waldensians, from the year 1170 to the present time.)

It was, of course, frightfully dangerous to be a Sacramentarian. To be one required of one to be absent whenever the mass was celebrated — the mass, around which the whole religious cult revolved, and on which the continuation of "Christian sacralism" depended. One could hardly be a Sacramentarian and so remain away and then continue unknown; many a "heretic" was spotted in this way. One can readily understand that all sorts of schemes were invented by the Sacramentarians to get around this difficulty. We read of one who, when it was time to "gaze adoringly," was found to have in his eye-sockets the two halves of the outer husk of the fruit of the walnut tree — a trick that earned him banishment for life. So much a principle was it with this man that to "gaze adoringly" on a morsel of bread was plain and simple idolatry, that he sought to ease his conscience by holding before his closed eyes the most opaque thing he could find.ᵠ Another medieval Sacramentarian fell into the clutches of the inquisitor when it was noticed that whenever it was time to "gaze adoringly" he absented himself to heed a call of nature. Sometimes the Sacramentarian would hold the wafer on his tongue — until he had the chance to spit it into his handkerchief or into a thicket.ʳ

What irked the Church particularly was that Sacramentarianism posed a threat to the monolithic society, the very end for

ᵠHe was banished "L jaer uuten lande van Vlanderen, omme diewille dat thelich sacrament lijdende up de strate hy in derisie ende versmaetheden van dien gheset heeft twee . . . noodscalen in zijne ooghen ende eenen in zijnen mont ende also knielende voor tzelve heleghe Sacrament, dat zaken zijn van quaden exempele, niet te lijdene zonder pugnicie." (See *Corpus*, II, 279f.)

ʳThis practical solution to a very difficult problem seems to have been bequeathed from one eruption of Restitutionism to the next. We find the followers of Tanchelm doing it and it became a part of the legacy of the Stepchildren. (This usage indicates that the "heretics" sometimes attended mass feignedly, for purposes of survival, a policy that has misled some investigators to conclude that these "heretics" were still "good Catholics.") We find one of the Anabaptists, Georg Leurle of Weilheim, saying during his trial in 1530, that "Die Kindertaufe, das sacrament des altars und die Messe und Ohrenbiechte seien nichts, die Mönche und Pfaffen seien nichts als Blindenführer," and acknowledging that he had "auch einmal das Sakrament empfangen und es in seinen Hut blasen wöllen, a strategy that didn't work in his case "weil es ihm zu rasch hinabgerütscht sei." He had swallowed it involuntarily.

which its own Sacramentalism had been devised. The Church was not driven by theological concerns in the first place; nor even for the salvation of men; its prime consideration was the threat which the Sacramentarians posed to its dream of *Corpus Christianum*. In the words of William of Newburgh, the heretics "when questioned one by one of the articles of the faith answer correctly as to the substance of the Physician on high, but perversely as to medication by which He deigns to heal human infirmity, namely the Holy Sacraments. They solemnly renounce baptism, the eucharist, and matrimony• and dare wickedly to derogate from the Catholic unity supported by these props."[9] This shows us precisely where the shoe pinched. The "heretics" were orthodox as to sin and grace, but they were intolerably unorthodox as to salvation by sacramental manipulation — which the Church had devised as "props" for "Christian sacralism."

Nowhere, as we have already said, was Sacramentarianism more a part of the very soil than it was in Flanders.ᵗ Here there were in existence, a century before Luther, underground anti-Catholic Churches — "Hussite Churches," as they were called in those days. They had all the features of what we would today call Protestant congregations — their own ordained men, catechism classes for prospective confessions of faith. They even maintained a kind of presbyterial organization, for they recognized and admitted to their pulpits ministers of their persuasion who pastored sister congregations. How many

•Throughout medieval times it was rumored that the "heretics" entertained very unorthodox ideas and practices in regard to marriage. They would have nothing to do, of course, with marriage *as a sacrament.* When they cohabited nevertheless the Church conveniently accused them of flouting the institution of marriage as such, an accusation that we do not need to take seriously. The Stepchildren had to hear these same charges, charges which we likewise must not take too seriously. (Which, of course, is not to say that there were not some wierd ideas as to marriage entertained at the lunatic fringe of Anabaptism.)

ᵗIt is an interesting fact that George H. Williams, although belonging to the school of thought, generally speaking, that sees in the rise of Anabaptism the fruitage of 1517, does say of the southern Low Countries that here Anabaptism drew from older movements (see p. 398 of his *The Radical Reformation*). In this he is, of course, on the right track. It seems to us that what Williams grants at this point and for this area must be granted for all other areas.

such churches there were we shall never know; were it not
for the fact that a few were liquidated we would not know
about them at all, so secret were they. One was betrayed by
an undercover spy who posed as a convert, in 1423. The
minister, Ghillebert Thulin (the name is also spelled Thurin),
was jailed because he was from Valenciennes and so under the
jurisdiction of Douai. The local pastor, Jehan de Hiellin, was
sentenced to life imprisonment but escaped, only to be re-
captured as he made his way in flight to Germany. It is
reported that the central feature of the doctrine of these
occult Churches was "that the substance of the bread and the
wine continue materially the same after consecration."[10]

Medieval Sacramentarianism commonly went hand in hand
with a rejection of the Church's sacerdotalism. As Herbert
Grundmann has said, "The heretics challenged the legitimacy
of the churchly ordination and on the basis of their own
insights constructed a rival church, one composed of 'good
Christians.' "[11] The leaders among these "heretics" were selected
because of their spiritual qualities; it was these qualities that
made them to be promoted to the rank of "elders," or whatever it was they were called. Sometimes this policy was singled
out as the outstanding characteristic of the "heretic"; Alanus of
Lille for example, a loyal son of the prevailing Church, defined
a heretic as "one who asserts that merit achieves more toward
consecration and the giving of the benediction and the binding
and the loosing than does the ordination or official status."
Alanus added that the "heretics," by pursuing this policy, "go
greatly against the Church and show themselves averse to
her."

The "heretics" countered the Church's sacerdotalism with
laicism, that is, with lay performance of all the things the
ordained cleric did. There were frequent occurrences of lay
administration of the Lord's Supper, lay shriving too, lay

---

[11]The expression "good Christians" points to the assault by the "heretics" upon the conductual averagism that prevailed in "Christendom."
For their insistence upon "a walk worthy of the calling," they were called
by such names as "bons gens," "bons garcons," "bons valets," etc. A
"heretic" burned on the eve of the Reformation was popularly called
"de rechtvaerdige Jan," "honest John," no doubt because he too lived
an exemplary life.

marriages, lay burials. But this laicism came to expression most commonly in the form of lay preaching. This emphasis on lay preaching is not surprising in view of the fact that the "heretics" believed in the formula of salvation by believing response to the preached Word. They had only a secondary interest in the many ritual performances that priests engage in; their primary interest was in the Word.

Small wonder that the Church turned her heavy artillery upon this lay preaching. We read of one directive after the other aimed at the suppression of this practice, so dangerous to the Church's pretention. We read, in a directive issuing from Trier in 1277: "We command, firmly and strictly, that preaching is not to be permitted to the untaught, such as the Beghards or Conversi, or any other . . . , in villages or streets . . . ."[11] From Verona, in 1184: "Since some folk under a kind of piety joined to a denial of the apostolic dictum 'How shall they preach unless they be sent!'ᵛ sustain their right to preach, therefore we place under anathema all who whether forbidden or unbidden . . . make bold, whether in private or in public, to preach."[12]

Just as the Church's sacerdotalism was joined with a partiality toward the Latin, so was there in the camp of the Sacramentarian "heretics" a partiality toward the vernacular. The Church left no stone unturned in an effort to keep the Bible in the vernacular out of the hands of men. In 1203, for instance, the bishop of Liège (where "heresy" was endemic) decreed that "All books containing the Scriptures in Romance or Teutonic tongue are to be delivered into the hands of the bishop, who will then return those which in his judgment should be given back." The Council of Bézieres, held in 1233-

---

ᵛWith this stereotyped formula, that no one is to preach who has not been "sent" (and only she "sent," assisted in this by the civil power) the Church sought to exercise complete thought-control; and she succeeded, too, to a frightening extent. Those who preached without being so "sent" were said to "run of themselves." Naturally this included every "heretic." The "fallen" Church did not wait to see *what* such a one taught; it was enough that he taught "unsent." By the time the Reformation had come full circle the Reformers were saying the same things that the earlier sacralists had said. We hear Zwingli, for example, asserting that "neman sol leeren, weder der gesendt wirdt" (no one is to teach except those who have been sent). (Cf. *Werke,* IV, 383.)

34, forbade the Bible in the vernacular to lay persons. So also the Council of Terracona in 1234. In 1369 the Emperor (Charles IV, who because of his menial subordination to the papacy was nick-named *Pfaffenkaiser Karl*) issued an edict (dictated to him in the papal palace at Lucca) prohibiting all books in German treating of the Holy Scriptures "especially since to lay-folk of either sex it is by canonical usage forbidden to use books of the Sacred Scriptures in the vernacular."

The Church's fulminations were all in vain. Hand-copied exemplars of the Scriptures in the vernacular continued to be made and used. When printing from movable type came into use, a veritable flood of Scripture in the vernacular poured across the land. According to Ludwig Keller (who had a good chance to know since he was a professional librarian) there were twenty-five editions of the Gospels prior to 1518; the Psalms had been done thirteen times; parts of the New Testament times without number, all in the vulgar tongue.

Since it was frightfully dangerous to possess such a copy of the Word, the "heretics" played it safe by storing the Word in a place to which the inquisitor had no access, namely, in human memory. One finds it almost impossible to believe what an inquisitor, Etienne de Bourbon, a Dominican monk who had spent his life running down "heretics," tells us about this:

> They know the apostles creed excellently in the vulgar tongue; they learn by heart the Gospels and the New Testament, in the vernacular and repeat them aloud to one another . . . . I have seen a youthful cow-herd who had lived but one year in the home of a Waldensian heretic who had attended so diligently to all that he heard that he had memorized within that year forty Sunday Gospels not counting those of the feast days . . . . I have seen some lay-folk so steeped in their doctrine that they could repeat by heart great portions of the Evangelists, such as Matthew and Luke, especially all that is said in them of Christ's teaching and sayings, so that they could repeat them without a halt and with hardly a word wrong here or there."[13]

Sometimes we find this vernacularism closely joined to the laicism that marked the "heretic." We read:

> They say that the Holy Scripture hath the same effect in the vulgar tongue that it hath in Latin; for this reason they cele-

brate [the Lord's Supper] in the vulgar tongue and give the
sacrament . . . . They read the Gospels and the Epistles in
the vernacular, explaining and applying them in their own
favor and contrary to the statutes of the Roman Church . . . .
They teach that every saint is a priest."

The extent to which the faith of the "heretics" was centered
around the preached Word may be gathered from a passage
that occurs in one of the Waldensian tracts, the *Alcuns volon
ligar* ("Some Desire to Read"):

The priests cause the people to perish of hunger and thirst
to hear the Word of God . . . , not only do they themselves
refuse to hear and receive the Word of God but . . . they,
in order that it may not be preached make laws and orders
as it pleases them, just so the preaching of the Word is
obstructed. The City of Sodom will be pardoned before these."

So averse was the "fallen" Church to the Word that it
actually implied that those who became intimate with the
Book deserved to die; it bent the passage in Exodus to its
purpose, the passage that provides that "every beast that
touches the mountain shall be thrust through with a dart."
When in Reformation times the Bible in the Spanish vernacular
was put on the market a leading cleric of the prevailing Church
actually said that in the event the King would let the Word
be preached he and his colleagues would run him out of his
realm! Indeed, salvation by believing response to the preached
Word and salvation by sacramental manipulation lay in mortal
combat with each other all through medieval times.

There was then a lengthy tradition of anti-sacramentalism
when Luther began his reformatory endeavor. It is also apparent that this anti-sacramentalism was not an unrelated
phenomenon, but was intimately related to the rest of the
Restitutionist vision. It would be quite unrealistic to imagine
that all this agitation had not conditioned men and made
them ripe for action.

Whether it was because the Reformers were themselves
conditioned by these ancient rebellions against the Sacramentalism that had so long served the cause of "Christian sacralism,"
or whether they in an understandable desire to have a following went out of their way to cater to men so conditioned,

or whether it was due to their fresh examination of the New
Testament, the fact seems to be that, at the outset, the Reformers spoke, at times at least, in the idiom of the ancient
protest.ʷ Bucer seems to have preached in Sacramentarian
vein at the outset; for when the Second Front had been opened,
those who had regrouped there said of him: "Bucer has for
years preached the sacrament correctly and properly; now
however he has gone back on this and preaches a different
view." Bucer had cast the die for neo-Constantinianism; and
this made him retrench in the matter of the Sacrament.

It seems that Luther also expressed himself, early in his
career, in a way that cheered the hearts of the heirs of the
old anti-Sacramentalism. The Waldensians at any rate thought
they had heard him say that "the body of the Lord is not
actually present in the Lord's Supper." Luther's earliest followers stood very close to the ancient Sacramentarians. Hendrik Voes and Johannes Esch, who were burned at Brussels
in 1523 and who were looked upon by Luther as the first
martyrs for his Reform, although themselves ordained men,
taught that "all men are priests in God's sight." They doubted
seriously "whether there is a difference between a *sacerdos* and
a *laicus* in the matter of the consecration of the Eucharist and
whether such consecration is the prerogative of the priesthood."
They said that "Lay people are priests, as much as those who
have been ordained by the bishop; we do not understand it
that way that the bishop bestows a new ability to consecrate."
We can agree with Professor Pijper, the man who in our times
has edited the hearings of these Antwerp martyrs, when he
says: "These views remind me of the teachings of the
Waldensians."

There can be no doubt, however, that when the Reformation
had crystallized in the pattern of neo-Constantinianism it was
all over with this conciliatory attitude toward Sacramentarianism. In its final version, Reformation theology attempted a

---

ʷThere is large truth in the assertion made by a recent writer that,
"It must be admitted that not only Zwingli but also other Swiss and
South German Reformers originally held views similar to the Anabap-
tists'" (Wilhelm Hadorn, *Die Reformation in der Deutschen Schweiz*,
p. 104.) There is no need to confine this remark to the Swiss and the
South German Reformers. It holds for other areas as well.

combination of the formula of salvation by sacramental manipulation with the formula of salvation by believing response to the preached Word. This swing to the right precipitated the exodus of those adherents who had been too much under the influence of the ancient anti-Sacramentalism to go along with this retrenchment. They withdrew, regrouped, and opened the Second Front.

Here the ancient Sacramentarianism lived on, unabated and undiminished.ˣ Although the believers of the Second Front came to be called Anabaptists, they could with equal propriety have been called Sacramentarians. One finds it impossible to say which was more definitive of the Stepchildren, their deviating views as to baptism, or their deviating views as to the other sacrament. Sometimes whole groups of them were sentenced for their Sacramentarianism, with not a word said about unacceptable views concerning baptism. Anabaptists were simply Sacramentarians who had been rebaptized. The name "rebaptized Sacramentarians" actually occurs in the sources. One can understand why Cornelius Krahn should say that "certain basic elements of the Anabaptist movement . . . of the Netherlandsʸ . . . grew out of the Sacramentarian move-

---

ˣHow thorougly opposed to the Sacramentalism of the sacralists the Stepchildren were is apparent from the writings of such a man as Balthasar Hübmaier. He wrote that "the third error" of the prevailing view was that the water of baptism and the elements of the Supper had been transformed into "sacraments" ("Das wir das Tauffwasser eben wie auch brot und wein des altars haben ein Sacrament gehaissen und es dar fur gehalten haben." He said, moreover, "Mezs ist nit ein opffer, sunder ein widergedechtnyss des todts Christi; derhalb sie weder für tod noch für lebendig mag uff geopffert werden." With a play on the word they called the mass a *missbrauch* and lamented the day when "des herren nachtmal im missbrauch und opffer verwandlet ward." ("Mass" is *mis* in Low German; hence the play on *Missbrauch*.)

ʸThe Dutch expert in things Anabaptist, Van der Zijpp, has said in a similar vein that "The so-called Sacramentarians or evangelicals in the Netherlands, the number of whom must have been large in many towns, are known to have been averse to Roman Catholic doctrine and practice . . . . Why did the majority of these now decide for Anabaptism? No satisfying answer has been found." As we see it, no answer is needed, seeing that no problem exists. These people were inclined to an ancient insight, had been conditioned by pre-Reformation Restitutionist agitation, before, during, and after, their alleged "decision for Anabaptism."

ment . . . ."[14] There is no reason however to single out the
Netherlands, for what can be predicated of this area can be
predicated of any other area in which Anabaptism erupted.
Wiedertäufer and *Sacramentschwärmer* are Restitutionists
looked at from slightly different angles.

It was typically Anabaptist to say that "Christ is not really
in flesh and blood in the holy sacrament of the altar or con-
secrated host of the mass. This is an idol and the mass is an
abomination or disgusting thing in the sight of God. One
commits idolatry when one listens to the mass or adores the
sacrament of the altar." The Anabaptists would have nothing
to do with salvation by sacramental manipulation; nor would
they have anything to do with "gazing adoringly." One of them,
Sauermilch by name, spoke quite derogatively of the Sacrament
of the prevailing Church, calling it "an other God, called by
them the *Sauberment*," a pun that yields its meaning when we
render *Sauberment* as "sorceryment."[15]

Nor were the Anabaptists in any sense tolerant of the
sacerdotalism of the prevailing system. They had their own
leaders, men whom they called "elders"; but they did not
recognize any wide discontinuity that separates the lay-man
from the cleric. In fact, they were content to practice laicism
whenever it was necessary. We read, at any rate, of the earliest
Anabaptists in the Wassenberg area, that they baptized in
unhallowed precincts and by the hands of laymen: "Diederich
Jurgens baptized a child with his own hands, *buissen*[16] *der
kercken*" (outside the Church, or, without the Church's
knowledge).

Nor were the Stepchildren at all concerned about apostolic
succession. They were not interested in any continuity with the
Church of the past; for them that Church was a "fallen"
creature. Not some reformation of this "fallen" creature was
their objective but a new beginning, a Restitution. They were
not interested in carrying coals from a fire that had been
smouldering and smoking for so many centuries; they were
out to kindle a new blaze.

Needless to say, the Anabaptists were confirmed vernacular-
ists. For them the Latin tongue was not a hallowed tongue.
Hardly a line was written by them in that medium and what
they did write in that language was for the outside, for ex-

port, as it were. They spoke the words of baptism in the vulgar tongue, preached and prayed in it. Their Bibles were in the common language.ᵃ

The Reformers by and large did not go along with the anit-Sacramentalism of the Stepchildren. In the early days, it is true, they had often expressed themselves in a way very similar to that of the later Stepchildren; those were the days when Luther was still toying with the possibility of having some day a Church of believers;ᵇ those were the days when Zwingli challenged the idea that the mass had a sacrificial dimension; those were the days in which Bucer talked about the sacrament in a way that was quite acceptable to the Sacramentarians. But that phase went by. The Reformers, after the exodus of the radicals had drained away the more ardent foes of the old Sacramentalism, veered to the right. They began to espouse views that resembled those of the earlier "Christian sacralism." Not all of them went equally far in that direction; Luther went farther than did Zwingli; but all of them took up a position critical of the Sacramentarians. Calvin drifted farther toward the old sacramentalism than the sons of the native Protestantism of the Low Countries liked, so that these cautioned him against a view behind which the Ubiquitists (i.e., the Lutherans) could hide.ᵇ Far to the right are the Episcopalians, among whom, especially among those

ᵃThe thoroughgoing vernacularism of the Stepchildren may be seen in the words of one of their leaders, Balthasar Hübmaier: "Der todt des herren soll nach eins yeglichen lands zungen gepredigt werden . . . . Es ist viel besser, ein eynigen versz eins Psalmen nach eyns yeden Lands sprach dem volck zu vertolmetschen, dann fünff ganz Psalmen in frembder sprach syngen und nit von der kyrchen verstanden werden" (*Quellen IX*, p. 73).

ᵇIn May of 1522 Luther expressed the hope that "We who at the present are wellnigh heathen under a Christian name, may yet organize a Christian assembly." (Cf. Karl Holl, *Gesammelte Aufsätze zur Kirchengeschichte*, p. 359.) The irony of the situation is that when two years later the radicals set out to do that very thing, Luther turned on them with sore displeasure. The difference between the two programs was that, whereas the Stepchildren were willing to let go of *Corpus Christianum* in order to attain unto the believers' Church, Luther and the rest of the Reformers were not thus willing.

ᵇHow dangerously close to *ex opere operato* the Reformers could sometimes come may be gathered from the following. The Anabaptist, Hans Braun, said that he "didn't like what he saw here" [he was a recent that are "High Church," we find a sacramentalism that is hardly distinguishable from the sacramentalism of the Catholic tradition, for which reason they are also known as "English Catholics."

As we have said in passing, the Reformation left undecided the question whether salvation is by believing response to the Word or is by sacramental manipulation. There is a tendency to believe the former without rejecting the latter. Sometimes it would seem that the sacrament is the thing that really matters, as for instance when a person "under discipline" is forbidden to take a place at the Lord's Table, with nothing said about participation in the other means of grace.[c] Most Protestant churches would permit a layman to preach, would even applaud such a venture; but most Protestant churches would raise an eyebrow at the report of lay administration of baptism. Protestant seminaries allow their senior students to "preach" (some do insist on the quotation marks) but not to administer the Lord's Supper (not even with quotation marks). It is only in the churches that trace their ancestry back to the Stepchildren that salvation by sacramental manipulation has been consistently repudiated.[d]

---

refugee from other parts] "dann es gehen huren und buben zum sacrament." His opponents said, in criticism of his criticism: "gleich als wolt er sagen, diselben dörfften des sacraments nit, so sie es doch am meisten bedorffen; dan je kräncker einer ist, je nötter jm der artzt thut." (Cf. *Quellen VIII*, p. 442.) As if the mere reception of the elements could do the impenitent sinner any good!

[c]It is interesting to note that among the Bohemian Brethren, with whom there was such a fine Church order that the Reformers were deeply jealous, a member who was "placed under discipline" was denied not only the sacrament but also attendance at the preaching of the Word. Here was an attempt at least to keep the one "means of grace" from crowding the other one aside.

[d]It is an interesting and significant fact that among the Protestant Churches wherever the formula of salvation by believing response to the preached Word has been recovered, there *establishment* and the view that somehow society and Church are coextensive have gone in eclipse. Conversely, among Churches that still hold to establishment, there preaching is atrophied. There is almost no preaching in High Church areas of Episcopalianism; it is here that we get the closest to "Christian sacralism." Conversely, Fundamentalist Churches are very nearly a-sacramental; it is here that we find the most wholesale repudiation of "Christian sacralism."

In this connection it is perhaps useful to point out that although the Stepchildren plainly owed a debt to earlier Sacramentarians they were often loath to acknowledge the fact. Apart from the fact that in their vision institutional continuity was not important, this loathness can be easily explained. The medieval world had heaped so much of opprobrium on the "heretic" that it was highly undiplomatic to acknowledge indebtedness to these "children of hell," as they had been denominated.

To this day we find a certain hesitation, even on the part of Christians who plainly owe a debt to the pre-Reformation "heretics," to acknowledge the fact. The time has come to desist from this. The time is coming, if it is not already here, when people will be proud to acknowledge that they stand in a tradition that leads back to the medieval "heretic."

The "heretics" were folk "of whom the world was not worthy." An integral part of their total vision was that salvation comes by believing response to the preached Word rather than by sacramental manipulation. In a word, they took at face value the New Testament doctrine that "Faith cometh by hearing and hearing by the Word of God" (Romans 10:17). They asked the question, in all seriousness, "How shall they call on him in whom they have not believed? and how shall they believe in him of whom they have not heard? and how shall they hear without a preacher?" Because they believed that salvation comes by way of believing response to the preached Word, they opposed any and all forms of Sacramentalism. It was this that earned for them the derogatory name of *Sacramentschwärmer*.

5 *Winckler*

> *Come ye apart into a desert place* . . . . Matt. 6:31

ANOTHER TERM OF REPROACH WITH WHICH THE REFORMERS regularly belabored their Stepchildren was the derogatory name *Winckler*. It is with the name and the issue involved in it that we shall be engaged in this chapter.

The word *Winckler* is derived from the German word *Winckel* (modern spelling *Winkel*) meaning a corner or an out-of-the-way place. *Winckler* are consequently people who gather in some corner or secluded place, for purposes of religious exercises. Such gatherings came to be known as *Winckelpredigten,* Winckel-preachings.[a]

Very prominent in the word *Winckler,* and its derivatives, is the idea of illicit, clandestine, unauthorized. In English-speaking areas, the word *hedge* has undergone a closely similar evolution. It meant first of all a fence-row; then, as an adjective, it came to mean illicit, unauthorized. A *hedge*-priest in medieval England was a man who performed the functions of a clergyman without waiting to get a license. (Such hedge-priests were plentiful enough.) The Dutch word *haag* has had a similar development. It means basically a hedge; but came presently to· stand for illicit. The *hagepreken* (hedge-preachings) that took place in the fields of Flanders on the eve of the Eighty Years' War were called by that name not because there were

---

[a]That the *Winckler*-gatherings came to be known as *Wincklerpredigten* is mute testimony to the fact that among the people who staged these unauthorized gatherings the reading and the expounding of the Scriptures was paramount, the main dish on the menu.

hedges there but because these gatherings were formed without license from the civil powers. The *hagepreken* were *Winckel-predigten*, unauthorized, unscheduled gatherings for religious purposes.

We encounter a related word in the sources, the word *Winckelehe*, a word that deserves mention here because it too was thrown at the Stepchildren.[b] A *Winckelehe* is a

[b]The Anabaptists suffered great hardship because their marriages were looked upon as *Winckelehe*, illegal cohabitations. This is the final chapter in a long story. In pre-Christian thinking the marriage ceremony lies very close to the center of the religious cult, as do the rest of the things that have to do with the vital statistics. The primitive Christian Church did not take over this pre-Christian emphasis upon the marriage ceremony; it honored marriage and did all it could to restore to it the dignity it deserves. But it did not consider it a specifically religious, certainly not a redemptive, institution. This secularization of marriage on the part of the early Christians drew the ire of the pagan world. We find the pagan Celsus upbraiding the Christians for this, in these words, written about the year 180: "One has to do one of two things; if you think it beneath your dignity to serve those who sustain the world [the reference is to the gods] then men and women may no longer marry, may no longer rear children, nor do any other thing in this life; they can then only retire from the scene, without leaving any progeny . . . , However, if you marry anyway and rear children, enjoy the fruits and participate in life . . . then you must give the appropriate honor to those to whom these things belong [i.e., the gods], you have to perform the religious duties . . . , lest you give the impression that you are ungrateful toward them. For it is not right to participate in the things that belong to the gods without paying something for it." It is hardly necessary to point out that this whole philosophy of marriage became incorporated in the vision of "Christian sacralism." We need only to remind ourselves that the medieval "heretics" repudiated this whole sacralization of marriage, a policy that thereupon earned them the accusation that they were "against marriage." Nor will it come as a surprise that, after the Reformers had completed their swing to the right, the old medieval concept of marriage was incorporated in their views. Marriage in the old Reformed Church Orders is an ecclesiastical affair. And it speaks for itself that the Stepchildren refused to go along with this. They made their vows before their own clergymen — and so laid themselves open to the charge of *Winckelehe*. The noise of the Second Front in regard to marriage can be heard in the notorious Groninger Edict of 1601. This Edict (It may be consulted in the Knuttel Collection, No. 1172, of which the University of Michigan has a copy), drawn up and promoted by the Reformed pastors of the City of Groningen, contains also this item: "All who cohabit as man and

marriage performed in an out-of-the-way place and performed
by someone *unsent* by the prevailing Church and its partner,
the State.

As such, *Winckelpredigten* (and *Winckel*-marriages, for that
matter) are an integral part of Restitutionist vision and practice.
Nor is this at all strange or surprising. Let us trace the developments of which *Winckler*-activities are the result and
outcome.

In pre-Christian society, that is, in sacral society, the religious cult is a public affair.[c] It belongs to the tribe or the
Volk; and the chieftain of the tribe, or the ruler of the *Volk*,
is automatically in charge. So also in the Roman society in
the midst of which Christianity was laid down. Rome's temples
were public buildings and that which transpired in them was
every Roman's business. In Roman society, the Church and
the State were fused (to use the two terms is virtually to
commit an anachronism, for they were in actuality as yet
undifferentiated; perhaps we had better say "the religious and
the secular," although that, too, would be something of an
anachronism). As a consequence, and most naturally, the rituals
of religion were public; and the temples were public places,
as public as the post office is with us.

The vision of the primitive Christian Church called for a
new kind of religious gathering. It conceived of its assemblies
as events espoused by believers and in that sense non-public.
To its society only they belonged who had been admitted.
To its gatherings others were permitted to come, even urged
to come, as spectators, or *auditores* as they were called,

---

wife without the benefit of law shall be required to have themselves
married in accordance with the Church Order, within one month, or
face punishment as fornicators . . . . All who have themselves married
[the original uses a derogatory expression here: "sich copuleren laten"]
outside a Reformed Church . . . shall be punished as the case may
require." Although there is, of course, not the slightest New Testament
warrant for such ecclesiasticalization of marriage, one encounters remnants of it among Reformed constituencies that have not quite sloughed
off their "Christian sacralism."

[c]The reader will recall that Plato wanted to have laws passed whereby
private rites of religion were prohibited. See the passage from Plato's *Laws*
quoted in the previous chapter, p. 135.

listeners, candidates; but the meeting as such was the property of those who *belonged*.

Significantly, the early Christians had not so much as thought of asking permission, or license, to meet. Just as the Master had gathered, and His disciples, so they met — without permission granted, or even asked, or, for that matter, thought of.

They followed this procedure intuitively — implied as it was in their basic assumptions. This policy was dictated not so much by the probability that the request would be refused anyway as by the conviction that to act otherwise was to act out of character. To meet under government auspices would be to bring strange fire upon the altar, would be to go against one of the new faith's most basic insights. The early Christians met in non-public places for principial reasons. Early Christianity conceived of society in any given situation to be a composite thing, consisting of some who glory in the Cross and some who stumble over it; and in a composite society, a cult that is common is by definition precluded.

It was this novel way of doing things that irked the Roman citizen, this a-sacral way of carrying on. Few things were censured so frequently and rebuked so vigorously in the early Christians as the fact that they held their meetings off by themselves. To the Roman citizen this looked like the sheerest sedition; here was the public cult of the official religion that was supposed to hold Roman society together; and then off there in an out-of-the-way place the meetings of the Christians! They were up to no good.

> At their nocturnal gatherings, their solemn feasts and barbarous meals the bond of union is not the sacred rite but crime. It is a people that lurks in the dark and shuns the light, silent in public places, talkative in caves . . . . Why do they make such an effort to conceal whatever it is that they worship? Honorable acts welcome publicity; only crimes delight in secrecy. Why have they no altars, no temples, no well-known images? Why do they never speak in public, never meet freely, unless it be that the hidden object of their worship is either criminal or disgraceful? . . . and these abominable secret haunts where these impious wretches hold their meetings are increasing in number all over the world! These execrable conspirators must be utterly rooted out.[1]

When in the Constantinian change Christianity was made the official religion of the empire, the rôles were changed; Christianity came out of the catacombs and began to parade in public. After all, it was now related to the empire in the same way that the ethnic faith had been related to it in earlier times. The cult of Christianity was now made a public affair — under the direct supervision of the civil ruler. Very soon pretentious Church buildings, built with public funds, began to be built, often on the very site where there had been a shrine to pagan deity in earlier times.

In view of the fact that not all Christians were able to accept the Constantinian change, there were those who continued to meet in the old way. There is reason to believe that in order to escape the wrath of the proponents of the new sacralism, they sometimes attended the public gatherings, feignedly be it said, only to slip over to the off-the-record gathering where their real religious loyalties were fed.

Needless to say, the Constantinians were at once aware of the seriousness of this non-conformist behavior. They prevailed upon the civil power to deal severely with these *Winckler*. Following the pattern set in the older sacralism, which had led to the suppression of the Christian assemblies, so now under the terms of the new sacralism was the arm of the State turned against the non-conforming ones. Among the first *Winckler* were the Donatists. Against them and the *Winckler* gatherings, severe measures were taken. The death sentence was prescribed for anyone convicted of having participated in any conventicle or *Winckelpredigt*.[2]

Ever since, all through medieval times, there were *Winckler* — for there were always those for whom the Church of Christ consists of believing folk and of them only. Ever since, all through medieval days, there were those who made the life of the *Winckler* difficult — for there were always those for whom the Church embraces the total civilization.

Hilary of Poitiers, whom we have mentioned before, was aware of the disastrous sweep· of the Constantinian change and bemoaned it. This Hilary also had nostalgia for the days of the old esoteric meetings of the Christians. With a glance at the huge cathedral-like[d] edifices that were springing up to accomodate the new public cult he said sadly: "We do wrong in venerating the Church of God in roofs and structures. Is it doubtful that the Antichrist will sit there? Safer to me the mountains and the woods, the lakes and the caves and the whirlpools; for in these, either hidden by them or sunken in them, did the prophets prophesy."

There was very good reason why the Church made war on the *Winckler*. They posed a threat to *Corpus Christianum* and were an assault upon the sacralist formula. As Herbert Grundmann puts it, "The Church never once let up on the idea that unauthorized religious discourse by an uncommissioned preacher was heretical." Because of this sensitivity the Church was incessantly on the warpath against the *Winckler*.

Workshops, especially places where weavers plied their trade, were often the scene of *Wincklerpredigten*. As early as 1157 the Church was already alert to the dangers inherent in the weavers' gatherings. The Council of Rheims, which met in that year, issued a very stringent warning against "a very impure sect of Manicheans[e] and vile weavers who often flee from place to place and change their names, leading captive silly women laden with sin . . . ."[f] A little later, orders

---

[d]The cathedral is best described as the architectural embodiment of "Christian sacralism," as towering above the city square it casts its shadow across the path of every person dwelling in its vicinity. It is not surprising to see Hilary somewhat less than completely happy at the sight of the pretentious buildings, erected at public expense. We shall see that this dislike for the cathedral became a part of the heritage of the medieval "heretic"; also, that it recurred in the vision of the Stepchildren.

[e]By this time the word *Manichean*, for a long time used synonymously with the word *Cathar*, had manifestly already become a common noun, designating the "heretic" in general.

[f]The reference here is to 2 Timothy 3:6, where we read about people who "creep into houses, and lead captive silly women." The medieval Church applied these words to the "heretic." "Creeping into houses" was then interpreted to refer to the "heretics'" practice of invading a parish assigned to a specified priest. Anselm of Laon offered this exegesis of the passage as early as the year 1117, saying: "ex his enim sunt, qui penetrant domos et captivas ducunt mulierculas oneratis peccatis . . . , illi penetrant domos, qui ingrediuntur domos illorum, quorum regimen animarum eos non pertinent . . . ."

were given to brand these weaver "heretics" on the forehead
and to banish them from the realm. They would be given
a chance to clear themselves by trial by fire; if a red-hot iron
burned them they were guilty, if it left them unscathed they
were innocent.

These weaver — "heretics" were arch-*Winckler*. In his
Sermons Against Heretics, Eckebertus speaks of them as people
"called *Cathars* in our German tongue, *Piphles* in Flemish, and
Texerants in Romance, because they are weavers." They are
folk, Eckebertus tells us, "who say that the true service of
Christ and the true faith are to be found nowhere but in
their conventicles, which they hold in cellars and weaving
establishments and similar subterranean places." So also that
medieval woman with her very keen nose for "heresy," Hildegarde van Bingen, who said that to find the "heretic" one
should look "in subterranean dwellings in which weavers and
tanners work." Still another, Saint Bernard, in his *Sermons
on the Song of Solomon,* complained that the moment a priest
leaves his parish, the people, young and old, "flock to the
weavers' conventicles to attend the worship services there."
An ancient chronicle says in connection with a "heretic" who
was burned at Kamerijk in Flanders in the twelfth century,
". . . of this sect many remain in certain cities until the present
time; their name derives from the weavers' trade."

We cannot hope in the nature of things to know very
precisely the content of the sermons preached in the *Winckler*
gatherings. They were held in secret, and for reasons of safety
little or nothing of what they preached was put in writing.
We would expect it to be pretty much the same, however, as
that bill of fare to which the Restitutionists generally rallied.
The very fact that these meetings were held in competition
with the authorized gatherings is enough to establish this.

This weaver tradition reached right into Reformation times,
as did the weavers' *Winckelpredigten.* In 1522 a fraternity
existed at Saint Gall in Switzerland, the members of which
called themselves "Christian Brethren." Many of them were
weavers and the meetings were held in the weavers' guild
house. Here the *Liebesmahle* (i.e. the love-feasts, namely the
Lord's Supper of the "heretics") were held. Zwingli himself
was intimate with these *Winckler,* having partaken of the

Supper with them in 1522 — before the rift had occurred which
opened up the Second Front.ᵉ

As late as 1566 the association of weaver and "heretic" was
still vivid in men's minds. We read that the city of Leyden
was predisposed to heresy "because of the many linen weavers
there, who are everywhere infected with this scourge."

We have already touched upon the fact that with the
Constantinian change came the building of pretentious buildings to house the now public cult of the new religion. We
have also seen that men like Hilary of Poitiers deplored the
development. Men of Restitutionist convictions commonly disliked these edifices, architectural embodiments of sacralism that
they were, and are. We read of medieval "heretics" who
"scoff at a church of masonry, looking upon it as a mere barn
and calling it in their vernacular a 'stone house.' Nor do they
admit that God dwells there and that prayers made in it
are more meritorious than those uttered in a chamber." So
much was the choice between the two kinds of gatherings a
matter of principle with the Restitutionists, that one of the
things required of a convert to the reinstituted church was the
promise not to go again into a stone-pile, a *cumulus lapidum*.

We find this same appraisal of the buildings that housed the
public cult with the men of the Second Front. One of them,
Georg Zaunring, said, "The Christian Church is His living
temple wherein He dwells and wherein He abides; Oh brethren,
in that, and not in any stone houses." The Anabaptists, at
least at times, required the promise of their converts: "in kain
stainhaufen mer ze geen," not to go again into any stone pile.[3]

The reason for the church's vehemence in regard to the
Winckler was not concern for theological correctness. By her
own repeated declaration the theological content of the menu

ᵉIt is more than likely that the kind of gatherings to which Balthasar
Hübmaier referred in the following passage were *Winckler*-gatherings,
already *old* in 1524: "Nach dem ein alter brauch von der zeyt der
Aposteln her reychet, so schwer sachen ynfallen, den glauben betreffende,
das als dann etlich, welchen das Göttlich wort zu reden bevolhen, sich
Christenlicher meynung versamlen, die geschrifften conferieren und
erwegen, uff das in weydung der Christenlich schäflin nach ynnhalt des
worts Gottes einhelligklichen fürgefaren werde. Dise versammlung hat
man vor zeytten Synodus, aber yetzt Capitula oder Bruderschafften
geheyssen." (Cf. *Quellen IX*," p. 72.)

served in the *Wincklerpredigten* was quite all right. What the Church had against these gatherings was that they were a standing threat to a sacral order. They were a standing threat to her darling, the sacrament of Orders, a "sacrament" which provided the legal framework for the suppression of everything except the authorized cult. The essence of this kind of "heresy" cannot be put in theological terms; the essence of it was its anti-sacralism.

Only so can we understand how that one pope after the other issued directives aimed at the liquidation of the *Winckler.*

Innocent III, addressing his subordinates in Metz in the year 1199, the Metz that already then had a bad record for "heresy," said:

> Our brother, the bishop of Metz, tells us that in his diocese and in your city a great many lay-folk, both men and women, . . . have had French translations made of the Gospels, the Epistles of Paul, the Psalms . . . and other books, which they read together and preach from in their clandestine conventicles, vilifying those who do not attend, and resisting to their face the priests who would instruct them, arguing that they find in their books much better instruction. Now it is doubtlessly true that the desire to know the Scriptures and to exhort men to follow these is not reprehensible . . . but what is to be condemned is the holding of secret assemblies . . . , arrogating to oneself the right to preach, jeering at the ignorance of the priests.[h] For the Scriptures are of such profundity that not only the simple and the illiterate but even the learned ones cannot attain to a knowledge of it, so that it is enjoined in the Law of God that every beast that touches the holy mountain shall be thrust through with a dart . . . , since in the church the doctors are charged with the preaching therefore no one may usurp this office.[4]

[h]The "heretic" was so much better versed in the Scriptures than were the regular clergy that Saint Louis advised men not to debate with a "heretic" but rather to "thrust the sword into the man's belly as far as it will go" (Coulton, *Inquisition and Liberty,* p. 81 quoting). Let us hope that this bit of advice, so quite out of keeping with what we know of the personality of St. Louis, was not seriously meant. It does indicate however that the "heretics" were formidable opponents in the matter of knowledge of the Scriptures. As we have already pointed out, Walter Mapes, a well-equipped churchman, said that he dreaded a debate with the "heretic."

This had been said before, long before. But it had not helped. That is why Innocent had to repeat the orders. His predecessor, Lucius III, had sought in 1184 to squelch the *Winckler,* but to no avail. He had placed under perpetual anathema, everlasting damnation, "all *Catharos, Patarinos* and those who falsely style themselves Poor Men of Lyons, *Passaginos, Josepinos, Arnaldistos* — and any and all who, whether against orders or without orders . . . make bold to preach in private or in public."[5] (It will not have escaped the notice of the reader that in the pope's way of thinking "heretics" can be clubbed together and disposed of in one and the same edict. They were indeed so many consecutive eruptions of one and the same thing — rebellion against the Constantinian order. The "Poor Men of Lyons," otherwise called the Waldensians, who were then, according to the usual way of thinking, but five years old, are of a piece with *Catharos, Paterinos, Passaginos, Josepinos, Arnaldistos,* etc., etc.).

This too had been said earlier. But it had not helped. An earlier pope had blustered in very nearly the same words. Alexander III had at the Council of Tours, which sat in 1163, decreed that:

> . . . no one shall, under pain of everlasting anathema give residence to the heretics that have drifted over from Toulouse and Gascogne, nor buy from them or sell to them, so that they may be compelled to repent. He who ignores this directive will be hit by the same anathema. The magistrates are to cast them in prison after having stripped them of their belongings. Their clandestine assemblies must be rigidly prevented.[6]

Such bitterness as is revealed here, such a reckless policy of extermination, points to a grievance of long standing. Such rigor, so early, suggests a quarrel of long standing. How long? The record of occurrences that long ago becomes sketchy and tenuous, but it is not hazardous to suppose that *Wincklerism* had troubled the Church ever since the launching of the Constantinian venture; legislation aimed at the suppression of *Winckelpredigten* dates back to that moment. The Codes of Justinian, as we have indicated, provide for capital punishment for him who stages a clandestine assembly.

Wincklerism was old in medieval times. William of Saint Amour, writing in the thirteenth century, as he expatiates on "The Dangers of Modern Times," speaks of "false teachers who preach unsent; no matter how learned and how saintly they be, even if they perform signs and wonders, unless they are properly elected by the Church they are not sent ones."

The Host in Chaucer's *The Canterbury Tales* says "I smell a Loller [a Lollard] in the wind." One may say that hardly a breeze ever blew in those times in which one could not detect the presence of a "Loller."[1] Hedge-priests were everywhere. There was nary a forest whose depths had not been the scene of some kind of illicit religious gatherings, hardly a cave that had not witnessed a *Wincklerpredigt*, scarcely a barn or warehouse or deserted mill that had not shielded some nocturnal gathering for *Winckler* purposes.

Not only were *Winckler* gatherings old and wide-spread; they were also amazingly popular. Of the *Winckler* it may certainly be said that "the common people heard them gladly." In the century of the Black Death the *Wincklerpredigten* were patronized more voluminously than were the authorized services of the Church. We read in a fifteenth-century chronicle, preserved in the city library at Brugge, that:

> In the year 1349 . . . a sect came up called the Cross-brethren. They wore a cross before and behind and came out of Germany and were headed for Brabant. Behind this sect walked many assembled folk . . . . They had many points of unorthodoxy; for they did not adore the holy sacrament as it was raised aloft at the mass, nor did they show reverence to the priesthood . . . . In 1350 there was a great indulgence

---

[1]The etymological derivation of the word *Lollard* is uncertain. The most likely guess is that it is from a Flemish word, *lollen*, to sing softly and soothingly. This is the more likely in view of the fact that Lollardy is of Flemish origin (the name occurred in Flanders a full century before Wiclif, with whom the Lollards are *usually* associated). We know that "heretics" frequently sang their "heresy" into men's hearts. The reason for this is quite apparent; it was relatively safe to *sing* deviating views, for one could always say, if the hand of the inquisitor were laid upon him, that he had picked up the ditty unthinkingly, and so escape. In all events Lollards were "heretics" who *sang* the ideas contained in the *Winckelpredigten*. The place of *song* as a vehicle for the dissemination of dissent deserves a thorough investigation, the "hymnody of heresy."

at Rome and many went to Rome to be absolved. Well they
might; for many were in the ban of the pope because of the
Cross-brothers and the Lollards, persons who had fed them or
had conversed with them.

So popular were these dissenters (the reader will have observed
that their "heresy" also contained the items of Sacramentarianism and anti-sacerdotalism) that as the pope, Clement VI, put
it, "They bid fair to thrust the Church backward into the
destruction . . . men saying that their songs and sermons were
worth more than those of the Church." So popular were these
Flagellantes and their unauthorized rites that even the rulers
flouted the thunderings of the pope. At Mechelen the authorities
provided not only straw to bed them down but also beer,
wine, and bread, at public expense. Ghent paid the rent for
wagons supplied for their convenience.

As always it was not the theological conviction of these
"heretics" that bothered the Church[1] but rather the threat
posed for the sacralist way of life. And deep down, again as
always, lay the notion that unity at the shrine is the prerequisite to peace on the square. "Since we are informed,"
so reads the papal instruction, "that of late certain folk have
again come up of themselves, and, without the consent of the
holy catholic church, have held meetings and gatherings . . .
a matter contrary to the God of heaven, against the holy
church and the Christian faith, contrary to the person of
every good man, a matter out of which much turmoil and
civil disquiet is likely to come . . . . Therefore we give orders
that no man, whosoever he may be . . . shall sustain, lodge,
supply with food or water, in any way whatsoever, nor con-

---

[1]Although the Flagellantes were like the "heretics" of other and less
anguished times in that they were a revolt against the easy-going everybody-
embracing Church, they were unlike other eruptions of rebellion against
the medieval order in that they were not as evangelically oriented. In
fact, the whole idea of flagellation is decidedly un-evangelical. This
wave of Restitutionism carries the mark of the times, the times of the
Black Death, as do most movements in history. The rise of Flagellantism
does reflect a widely felt conviction that the prevailing Church and its
technique of salvation was inadequate. Criticism of the Church's conductual-averagism was very prominent in the Flagellantes' protest. Contemporary testimony informs us that the Flagellantes did bring about
a great many conversions.

verse with these or allow themselves to be converted to their fellowship by them — on pain of ten years' banishment."[7] Here we hear the words of a man who, like the Constantine of old, is concerned with the religious uniformity because in his sacralist way of thinking it is the *sine qua non* of tranquility on the streets. He is against the *Wincklerpredigt* because of the threat it poses to the sacralist scheme of things.

From the above it will be apparent that it was far from easy to be a *Winckler*. In fact, it was frightfully hard. If you cannot buy or sell, if it is virtually suicidal for anyone to give you food or drink or any other comfort, then you are in a bad way indeed; you have been read out of the society of men; open season has been declared on you. Small wonder that men of *Winckler* habits were tempted to attend the activities of the fallen Church feignedly and then to patronize the *Winckler* gatherings as a means to express their real religious selves. This duplicity was very common. It came to be known as Nicodemitism,[x] a name derived, of course, from the Biblical character who was one thing in the daylight and another thing at night.

The Church knew all about the Nicodemite practices of the *Winckler* as early as 1145. In that year action was taken against certain "heretics" that had been located near Liège. For purposes of identification we shall recite the entire description:

> In this heresy there are distinct levels; it has its auditors who are being initiated into error; it has its believers who are already deceived; it has its clergy and   priests and prelates, just as we have them. The wicked blasphemies of this heresy are that they say that in baptism sins are not remitted; they

---

[x]It was common practice among medieval "heretics" to frequent the services of the prevailing Church often enough to escape detection and the Church's vengeance. This policy has led many investigators astray. It has been alleged, for example, that the Waldensians remained "good Catholics" — because they allowed themselves to be seen once in a while in the gatherings of the Catholics. But this does not at all imply that they were as yet not estranged; it only goes to show that they were prudent. What kind of "good Catholics" the "heretics" were may be gathered from the fact that one of them was heard to mutter as he entered the cathedral, "Caverne des brigandes, que dieu te confonde!" (Den of robbers, may God confound you!).

consider the sacrament of the body and blood of Christ to
be foolishness; that by the imposition of the pontiff's hand
nothing is conferred; that no one receives the Holy Spirit unless good works are in evidence . . . . They preach that the
entire Catholic Church is found with them; they say that the
oath is a crime. And . . . they partake of our sacraments,
fraudulently, so that their wickedness may be hid.[8]

Here we have a full-orbed Restitutionist Church, with complete structurization; here is articulate Sacramentarianism; here
is Catharism, with its conviction that faith without works is
dead; here is the Restitutionist view that the prevailing Church
is a fallen creature and that the true Church is with the "heretics"; here is the customary Restitutionist rejection of the oath.
And sandwiched in between these familiar items we find
mentioned the Nicodemite practice of participating in the
authorized Church's sacraments, at least going through the
motions, for the sake of survival.

In the same decade Saint Eckebertus complained similarly
of *Winckler* with Nicodemite habits: "When they come to hear
mass or to gaze on the Eucharist they do it all in make-believe
fashion, so that their infidelity may not be noticed."[9]

Of all the pre-Reformation Restitutionists none were greater
Winckler than were the Waldensians. They held illicit gatherings everywhere, in season and out, from the Mediterranean to
the Baltic. Posing frequently as wayfarers or peddlers, they
would recite a section of Scripture and if it seemed not too evidently unsafe to do so they appended a brief homily. Such
preaching, associated as it was with a personal godliness that
even enemies acknowledged, was extremely effective. As a result Europe was shot through with converts and semi-converts
to the Restitutionist religion. The Dean of Notre Dame in
Arras was reciting stark naked truth when he asserted, a century
before the Reformation, that "one third of Christendom if not
more has attended illicit Waldensian conventicles and is at heart
Waldensian."[10]

People who conducted the *Winckelpredigten* had to be con-
tinually on the move. So great was the risk that usually the
personal name of the preacher was not divulged, not even to
those who were presumably on the "heretic's" side. He would
come from nowhere, speak his piece, and disappear as uncere-

moniously as he had come. By the time the Church had been apprised of his presence the man was already out of reach.

This policy of coming and going earned for the "heretic" several unsavory names. One was *Truand,* a word related to our "truant," chosen in view of the fact that they were constantly not in the expected place. Another name that derived from the *Winckler* way of coming and going was *Leufer,* runner, a word that soon picked up the idea of running on one's own, running without being sent. This name was heard in the noise that issued from the Second Front in the days of the Reformation, especially to designate the man who runs unsent, unsent by the office which alone sends men.

In an effort to suppress the *Winckler* activities, the Church decreed that every cleric must be bound to a parish. Every man was to have his area beyond which he was not to go and into which no one else, least of all a roving *Winckler,* was allowed to go. We have already noted that the Church drafted 2 Timothy 3:6 (the passage that speaks of "creeping into houses") to enforce its rule, for to "creep into houses" was, so it was said, to invade another man's parish.[1]

Just as in pre-Constantinian times the Christians were taunted for holding meetings in private, so were the "heretics" reproached for their conventicles. Quoting the Scriptural passage about "Their sound is gone out through all the earth," their foes contended that the very secrecy of these gatherings proved that these *Winckler* were not the good shepherds of which Jesus spoke when he said "The good shepherd giveth his life for the sheep." When the Waldensian pastors fled for their lives, the inquisitors

---

[1]This whole medieval notion, that there are parishes in the which only a specific person is allowed to read the Scriptures and expound them, is without any basis in the New Testament. Jesus and His disciples observed no such regulations, came and went as they saw fit, a fact to which the Stepchildren, when rebuked for holding *Wincklerpredigten,* were not slow to point. Calvin, no doubt chagrined by the fact that the practice of the Stepchildren in this matter was close indeed to that of the Apostles, asserted that this was a matter of aping the Apostles rather than emulating them. The passage reads: "Ilz estoyent au paravant en celle resverie, que c'estoit contre Dieu qu'un pasteur fust deputé a certain lieu; mais vouloyent que tous ceux qui seroyent en l'estat courussent d'un coste à l'autre, contrefaisans les Apostres comme singes et non pas comme vrays imitateurs."

chided them for leaving: "Why didst thou not persist with thy sheep in Thuringia, the Mark, Bohemia, and Moravia . . . . Why comest thou not into Austria and Hungary . . . ? Thou appearest nowhere, thou fleest ever, and leavest the simple poor in their tribulation. I say boldly that if thy doctrine were true, it would be easy for thee to spread it in every place. Now, forger, thou must hide thy false coin with greater caution!"[11] We shall hear very similar charges leveled against the believers of the Second Front.

In spite of the Church's efforts to stamp them out, the *Winckler* meetings went on unabated. After all, men in underground activity have ways of coming and going that baffle their enemies. They can meet, and come away, covering their tracks so adroitly that their pursuers are baffled. Frustrated and bewildered, the Church ascribed the elusiveness of the "heretic" to a league with the devil, inventing the most grotesque stories. In the words of a dignified cleric, the Dean of Notre Dame at Arras:

> When the Waldensians wish to go to their conventicle they first rub an ointment on their palms . . . as well as on a stick, an ointment supplied to them by the devil. Then they straddle this stick and fly to whatever place they wish to go, over cities and forests and lakes . . . . They congregate about tables decked with wine and bread.[m] Devils in the form of billy-goats, or dogs or apes are present; sometimes in the form of a man . . . . They worship these, kissing the billy-goat's *derriere*, with candles in their hands . . . . Then they tread on the cross, spitting on it in despite of Jesus Christ and the holy Trinity. Then they present their buttocks to the sky,[n] in derision of God . . . .[12]

[m] The reference is of course to the communion table as spread by the "heretics." So much had an altar usurped the place of the Table of the Lord of authentic Christianity that when this cleric saw a table with bread and wine on it he didn't recognize it for what it was!

[n] This item about "buttocks to the sky" may have had its origin in the fact that the "heretics" knelt when they prayed, with their cheeks pressed to the earth (we read the accusation: "praying according to their manner and rite, bowed on bent knees"; Coulton, *Inquisition and Liberty*, p. 195). This posture of prayer, assumed in semi or total darkness, for reasons of safety, there being always the danger of a spying inquisitor looking on, looked to the uninitiated like a matter of "presenting their buttocks to the sky." The accusation seems to have been something of a cliché, a feature of the stereotyped image of the

Since the Reformers became enmeshed in the toils of a new "Christian sacralism" a collision with the Waldensians for their *Wincklerism* and Nicodemitism was inevitable in their day. There was no reason for conflict concerning conduct — for the Waldensians' conduct was exemplary; but conflict touching *Wincklerism* was inevitable, not so much because of the duplicity involved as because of the fact that *Wincklerism* was an obstacle to the creation of a sacral order in the Protestant signature. To the Waldensians of Austria, the Reformers wrote: "Your purity of doctrine and of life pleases us greatly;° What displeases us however is the hiding of the truth and your failure to confess openly, and, that in order to escape persecution you frequent the papist temples."

William Farel expressed displeasure likewise with the Waldensians' *Wicklerism*. Although he went on preaching tours to these "brethren of the Piedmont," as he affectionately called them, he began to rebuke them for failing to try for a public cult. In 1537 a letter of such rebuke was put in print. This material was at once translated into English and German, so that all might know what is the duty of those who have embraced the evangelical faith but live in a papist society. Six years later Viret addressed himself to the same fault. He too urged that a better way must be found than to meet in

---

"heretic"; for we read in a medieval poem that "Twee bagynen, twee bogaerden, drie susteren ende twee lollaerden, dese dienen God al met den aerse." (Cf. *Nederlandsch Kluchtspel*, 2, 51, 51 in Verwys en Verdam.)

°Some writers, especially those of Lutheran orientation, with whom to be evangelical is to follow Luther's one-sided emphasis on the forensic item of justification by faith, have contended that the pre-Reformation "heretics" lacked an evangelical quality. On their premises this is no doubt true; but, as Professor Ebrard has it, "if one recognizes it as evangelical Christianity when salvation is said to depend on a man's personal attitude of heart toward Christ and not on some relationship to a priesthood, and where the Scriptures are taken to be the highest and only ultimate authority, then he will ascribe the evangelical quality to such . . . , in the fullest possible sense." (Cf. Ebrard, *Dogmengeschichte*, II, 323.) The present quotation indicates that the Reformers did not hesitate to ascribe to the Waldensians an orthodox evangelical quality, both as to doctrine and as to the conduct or practice.

Winckler fashion; specifically, a public cult in the signature of the Reformed theology must be initiated.

John Calvin took up the matter of the evangelical and the *Winckler* type of gathering, in a tract written in 1543. He too lectured the *Winckler* for their failure to agitate for a public cult. When those for whom this was intended said he was asking too much, Calvin came back with a second tract, written in 1544. Both these tracts were printed in Latin translations in 1549. Appended to Calvin's two tracts were excerpts from the writings of Melanchthon, Bucer, Peter Martyr, and two supplementary letters by Calvin himself. A Dutch translation of this anti-*Winckler* material seems to have been prepared early. Valerand Poullain concerned himself with the matter, writing from Strasbourg on November 28, 1544. All told, it is quite apparent that the argument for the creation of a Reformed public cult to take the place of the Catholic public cult was very much in men's minds in the early decades of the Reformation. No doubt all this writing served to steer the Reformation into the neo-Constantinian way into which it went.

The heart of Calvin's rebuke of the *Wincklerpredigten* addressed itself quite apparently to the fact that as long as men were satisfied with them there would never be a public cult in the signature of the Reform. For him the real issue had not been joined unless and until the sacralism of the medieval order had been replaced by a sacralism in the signature of the Reform. He wrote: "If all those whom our Lord has enlightened would with one accord have the fortitude to die and leave all behind rather than to profane themselves with the wicked superstitions then He would help them with a means not recognized now." And what is that means, one that will really put the Reform across? Calvin spells it out: "Then he will convert the hearts of Princes and their lieutenants, to the casting down of idolatries and the restoration of the true service and worship of God."[13] What he is saying is that if the evangelicals will on the one hand remain away from the erstwhile public cult and on the other hand initiate a rival public cult, then the hand of the rulers will be forced, as it were, to make the Reform their business. That this is the direction into which the Reform did actually go, in all the lands into which Calvin's writings went, needs hardly be said.[p]

The identity of Calvin's neo-Nicodemites has never been settled among the historians. We venture to suggest that they were Restitutionists in general and Waldensians in particular. It is significant that in a letter dated. 1532 (before all the polemical writings aimed at the Nicodemites therefore) we are informed that certain Waldensians were attracted to the reform in Geneva (the first French Bible published there was paid for by the Waldensians of the Piedmont). In the letter mentioned, they refer to themselves as "Lovers of the Gospel in Payerne," and say that they are glad that in Geneva "men have left the doctrines of men and have accepted the Word of God" and they, calling themselves "the little flock of Jesus Christ" (typically Restitutionist language), express the hope that "many nycodemysans may declare and manifest themselves."[14]

By no means were all in the Waldensian camp ready to go along with Geneva, however. The younger barbes,[q] who had come under the spell of Geneva, were ready to do Geneva's bidding; but the idea ran into resistance from the side of the older barbes. To resolve matters a Synod was held at Chianforan, near Angrogne, in the Piedmont. William Farel was on hand to see that things went the Reformers' way. The amalgamation of the two groups was made contingent upon capitulation to

[p]Calvin's agitation for the initiation of a public cult in the Reformed signature was not without effect. In the Low Countries, where the influence of Calvin begins around the year 1550, the first bid for the establishment of a public cult came with the so-called Chanteries, nighttime singings of the Genevan Psalms in Tournay and Valenciennes (then a part of the Pays-bas) in the fall of 1561, by a procession of many hundreds of people. Against these demonstrations, the nature of which the Regent understood only too well, very severe measures were taken. The next effort to bring into being a public cult of Protestant stamp were the hagepreken of 1566. They were the prelude to the Eighty Years' War.

[q]The Waldensians referred to their spiritual leaders as barbes, a word that means uncle in Provençal, the language in which most of the Waldensian tracts were written. The word was chosen, so it would seem, in order to contrast with the Roman Catholic custom of calling the spiritual leaders fathers. It is significant that, in some areas at least, the Anabaptists, who in so many ways fell heir to Waldensian teachings, referred to their leaders as Ohm, uncle!

Geneva in the matter of the public cult. This was to ask quite
a little, for the sacralist ideology was altogether foreign to the
Waldensian tradition. Other points discussed dealt with "the
right of the sword," the permissibility of the oath, exclusion of
false brethren by the ban — all of them well-known items in
the Restitutionist vision. The Waldensians confessed that "many
Waldensians motivated by weakness or fear of persecution
present their children to the priests of the Catholic Church
and go to mass even though their hearts condemn these things."

To the older *barbes* integration with the civil government
was treason, a compromise at the point where their ancestors
had fought so long and so hard. They walked out in protest
when the younger leaders gave evidence of a readiness to comply.
A delegation of the old guard went to the various centers of
Waldensianism to lick their wounds, first to Strasbourg and then
to Bohemia and Moravia.

The concessions wrung from the Waldensians at Chianforan
did not yield much fruit. That part of the Waldensian camp
that was not absorbed into the Reformed camp continued as
heretofore.[r] The Waldensian Church which did not amalgamate
with the Reform never sought or accepted the hand of any
prince or ruler. It continues to this day in the Restitutionist
tradition, a free church that has never tried to be anything but
"a church based on personal faith." It has never sponsored a
public cult.

Prior to 1545, the year Calvin's tracts were written, the Reform in Flanders had been sustained by Churches "under the
Cross," that is, without government sanction. By 1560 neo-
Constantinianism was making its bid for the Flemish soul. The
year 1545 marks the beginning of the defeat of Restitutionism
in these parts; at about this time it was becoming apparent that

---

[r]It has been suggested that the amalgamation of French-speaking
Restitutionism and the French-speaking Reform movement headed off
the development of a French-speaking Anabaptism. It is a noteworthy
fact that although Waldensianism was prevalent, perhaps equally prevalent, in French-speaking and German-speaking areas, Anabaptism erupted
only in the latter — where Waldensianism seems to have become extinct
at about the time of the opening of the Second Front. Chianforan would
then explain what became of the Waldensian heritage in French-speaking
areas.

the future was to be in the signature of neo-Constantinianism
rather than in that of Restitutionism. The Year of Wonders, as
1566 came to be known, saw the neo-sacralism, for which the
writings of Calvin had cleared the way, firmly in control, with
nobles and consistories in league with each other. In that
year — there is some reason to think that it was in 1565 —
there was an occult Synod held, at which a prominent issue
was the matter of the public cult. The *hagepreken* of 1566
were the implementation of the decision to try for a public cult
in the signature of Calvinism. At this point begins the Eighty
Years' War, a war in which the ancient sacralism was challenged
by the new — with final victory for the new in the year 1648.

When the Reformation crystallized in a Constantinian pattern,
it left a sizable residual of Restitutionism — which we have
come to know as the Second Front. It need hardly be said
that here the *Winckler* way of doing things remained in vogue.
Wincklerism was an integral part of the Anabaptist conviction;
and the slur of "*Winckler*" was heard repeatedly at the Second
Front.

Sometimes the sole charge was that of having had part in a
Wincklerpredigt. Rudolph Förster and Ulrich Bold were expelled from Basel "for having preached in *Winckels* . . . which
is contrary to the Christian Church and the ordinances." Sometimes the sole measures taken to eliminate the opposition offered
by the Second Front was to forbid their *Winckelpredigten*. The
Kirchenrat of the Palatinate, an area that was officially Reformed, advised its constituents "to obstruct with all diligence
every unauthorized conventicle in houses and forests; for no
matter how sound the preaching may be and the reading, such
unauthorized conventicles have not only the quality of schism
on the ecclesiastical level but also of sedition on the civil level
and give occasion to every manner of disobedience and vice.
They are in no case to be tolerated."[15]

One of the proof-texts which the men of the Reformed camp
used, to put the Anabaptist *Winckler* in a bad light, was John
18:20, "I spake boldly unto the world . . . in secret have I said
nothing," and they obligingly translated this latter phrase with
"in winckeln hette er nüt geleret."[16]

Few matters contributed as much to the tension that developed
between the two camps as did the matter of the *call*. The Re-

formers continued in the ancient tradition that one is not lawfully in office as a minister of the Gospel unless he has been
commissioned by the magistrate∗ — which of course implies that
he who "runs" without being so sent is a *Winckler*. As a matter
of fact, the definition officially given of the *Winckler* is as
follows: "*Winckler* are people who without call or commission
by the magistracy put themselves forward to preach, likewise
those who preach in unusual and improper places."[17] This was
written in 1528, when the Second Front was just shaping up,
and reflects the thinking of every one of the Reformers.

Nor was this mere theory. Any man who engaged in the
activity of a *Winckler*, so defined, was subject to arrest. Many
an Anabaptist was put in jail for no other reason than that he
had preached without such a call or authorization. We shall
quote a few examples. On November 12, 1531, the mayor of a
little place called Bacha informed his superior, Landgrave Philip,
that on the previous night "as the gates of the city were being
closed we conducted a search at places that were suspect and
we found Melchior Rink (whom they call 'The Greek')ᵗ with
twelve others . . . gathered together; we learned that they had
preached, specifically on the passage at the end of Mark,ᵘ where
Jesus Christ our Savior instituted baptism, explaining it in the
way customary with their sect."[18] Similarly we find some Anabaptists in jail on March 15, 1537; no other reason is specified
for their detention than this: "We apprehended them in the house
of a citizen named Herman Guel, and found that they had
preached . . . . The Constable arrested them and took them

∗At the Disputation held at Emden in 1578 the Reformed clergymen
who had been commissioned to refute the Anabaptists argued mightily
that "Wy hebben gheene macht om Predickers te beroepen ofte aen te
nemen; maer dat coemt toe der Overicheyt." The deposition of a minister
was said to be the prerogative of the magistrate likewise: "Die afsettinghe
en is niet by my, noch by den Dienaren, maer by der Overicheit ende
by der Ghemeynte die hem aenghenomen ende inden Dienst bevesticht
hebben." (Cf. the *Protocol*, fol. 233.) Needless to say, the Anabaptist
leaders would have nothing to do with the curious tenet of "Christian
sacralism" that to be legally called, one must have been called by
the magistrate.

ᵗMelchior Rinck was known as "The Greek" because of his great
proficiency in the Greek language and literature.

ᵘMark 16:15f. was a favorite passage with the Stepchildren because
in it believing goes before baptizing.

prisoner. We are herewith delivering them into your hands."[19]

The reader will recall that the notorious Groninger Edict, drawn up by the Reformed clergymen of that city in 1601, provides heavy fines for any and all who conduct or attend *Winckelpredigten*. It provides heavy fines for any who allow their premises to be used for *Winckler*-gatherings.

Here was a head-on collision. On the one hand were the Reformers who insisted that a man must have a commission from the magistrate and is a *Winckler* if he preaches without such a commission; on the other hand were their Stepchildren who were just as insistent that the magistrate has nothing to do with these matters and that he who so kowtows to the civil ruler is by that token a hireling. Among the "errors" of the Anabaptists were therefore listed the following points:

> 1) that anyone who has a true faith may preach, even if no one has commissioned him; for Christ has empowered any and every man to preach when He said 'Go, teach all nations' Mth. 28; 2) a call issuing from men has no valor and he who is called that way is the flunky of a ruler and a men-pleaser; 3) Luther, Oecolampadius, and all who teach as they do, are false prophets, men who lead people astray, devil-servers; 4) all who go to hear them, believe what they teach, believe and do improperly, and are not in God's but in Satan's congregation.[20]

In this the Anabaptists were in dead earnest. The Church that had allowed itself to become identified with the State was to them a fallen Church, and all who made their peace with this fallenness were serving under the flag of the enemy. They therefore refused to listen to any preaching except that of the *Winckler* — or, as they were also called, the *Leufer*.[v]

Philip of Hesse, although he was one of the most liberal and progressive men of his day, a man far ahead of his times also in the matter of policy in regard to the Anabaptists, nevertheless shared with the Reformers the view that *Winckler* are intolerable. He gave orders, in 1531, that "whoever violates the preaching office . . . by assuming it uncalled, shall be banished forever upon pain of capital punishment if ever he returns."[21]

---

[v]At the trial of certain Anabaptists, held in 1533, it was reported that "Sie horen auch keine underweisung dan wie sie von den leufern under-richtet sein" (*Quellen Hesse*, p. 71).

In the very next sentence Philip reveals the deeper reason for such rigor as well as the reason why banishment seemed to be the appropriate punishment. He put it this way: "Since such a man places himself outside the Christian community [*dweil er sich der christlichen gemeine enteussert*] he can not be tolerated any longer in the secular community [*soll er auch under der zeitlichen gemeine nicht geduldet*]." This was only consistent sacralism; if the religious community and the secular community coincide, then a man's exodus from the former implies his expulsion from the latter. "His house, his homestead, his fields and his meadows and property appertaining thereto, are to be sold and shall be put in the same category as those of a Jew with whom also there is no inheritance right."

Not only did the neo-Constantinianism of the Reformers in their final phase dictate such rigor against the *Winckler;* it also resorted to compulsory attendance at the public cult. Nineteen persons, we read, ". . . have been ordered, singly and corporately, on the Saturday before, to be in Church on Sunday morning, at Herde, to listen to Christian instruction in the points in which they err, propounded by the pastor of Hersfelt as His Royal Highness' legate." Manifestly the men were just a bit too grown-up for such measures, for not one of them appeared. "Not one of them has obediently put in his appearance however; they afterwards gave as their reasons, that God does not dwell in temples made with hands."[22]

The *Winckler,* who constituted the Second Front, pointed with considerable glee to the passage which Luther had written (in the days before the Restitutionists had consolidated their forces), in which he stated his ambition to assemble the true believers "behind closed doors." When interviewed about "gathering in fields and forests, unoccupied terrain or private homes," they shot back, "One of your own prophets, Martin Luther, wrote about that kind of meeting (in a booklet entitled *Deutsche Messe*), saying that men ought to gather behind closed doors [*in einem versperten haus*] to treat of the Word and ordinances of God — but added 'I am not courageous enough to make a beginning [*Ich bin noch net kun solches anzufangen*] lest it be looked upon as a faction-fomenting business.' "[23]

Luther's extreme dislike of the Restitutionists' *Winckelpredigten* may have been in part due to the fact that, in speaking thus of him, the Stepchildren were unpleasantly right. He had indeed advocated meetings behind closed doors, in groups in which only true believers were acceptable. He had been careful not to suggest that these non-public gatherings were to replace the public cult — a thing that would be considered intolerably radical. No, he had intended these meetings to supplement the pattern dictated by sacralism. That nothing came of his fine plan is, of course, not surprising — the combination of a Church of believers with a Church "embracing all in a given locality" is intrinsically impossible. And he had indeed said that he was not ready to organize such gatherings because he realized that it would be interpreted to be seditious. There was not much he could say to those who now threw his own earlier words in his teeth. Perhaps, as we have said, this was in part the cause for his bitterness toward the *Winckler*.

In any event, Luther wrote, in 1530, that:

> *Winckelpredigten* are in no case to be tolerated . . . . These are the thieves and murderers of whom Christ spoke in John 7, persons who invade another man's parish and who usurp another man's office, a matter not bidden them but rather forbidden. And a citizen is obliged, if and when such a *Winckelschleicher*ʷ comes to him, before he listens to him or lets him teach, to inform his civil magistrate as well as the pastor whose parishioner he is. If he fails to do this then let him know that he behaves like one unfaithful to his magistrate and that he acts contrary to his oath, and, as a despiser of the pastor whom he is supposed to respect, acts against God. Moreover he is thereby himself guilty and has become a thief and a rogue along with the *Schleicher* . . . . They must neither be tolerated nor listened to, even though they seek to teach the pure Gospel, yes, even if they are angelic and simon-pure Gabriels from heavenˣ . . . . Therefore let everyone ponder this, that if he wants to preach or teach let him exhibit the call or the commission that drives him to it or else let him keep his mouth shut. If he refuses this then let the magistrate

---

ʷThe German word *Schleicher* designates one who enters surreptitiously; a *Winckelschleicher* is then a person who slips into the parish of a publicly-appointed clergyman with the intention of holding a *Winckelpredigt* there.

ˣHere we have, as so frequently, a left-handed testimony to the theological correctness of the content of the *Winckler's* message.

consign the scamp into the hands of his proper master —
whose name is *Meister Hans*.[24]

"Meister Hans" is a euphemism for the hangman!

All told, it would seem to be quite apparent that when the
Reformers called their Stepchildren *Winckler*, they were throwing after them an already old name, because an old practice was
being looked at from an old point of view, that of "Christian
sacralism." We therefore find ourselves agreeing with T. W.
Röhrich as he writes: "The sects that in Reformation times
delineated themselves so sharply had their historical basis in
the earlier parties, such as the Friends of God, . . . the *Winckler*."
There is a deep, if half-hidden, truth in the confession made by
an imprisoned Anabaptist who said, "We have lain hidden in
the bosom of the catholics."[25] This they had done as Nicodemites,
of course. Anabaptism had been cryptic before it moved out
into the open in response to the Reformers' swing to the right.
Even after it had moved out into the open, Nicodemite practices
continued. Menno Simons had to rebuke the practice in his day.[26]
Nicodemite practices were part of the legacy of Restitutionism,
and the Anabaptists resorted to them almost spontaneously.[y]

Wherever the neo-Constantinianism of the Reformers went,
there the *Wincklerpredigt* was assailed;[z] and wherever the influence of the Stepchildren was felt, there it was defended as
right and proper and as the only right and proper kind of cult.
The argument was even carried to the shores of the New World.

Roger Williams complained that "Prelatists, Presbyterians, In-
dependents, have all struggled to 'sit down under the shadow
of that arm of flesh' [the civil ruler] but that the Separatists

---

[y]The Anabaptist, Hans Cluber, when asked why he participated in
the mass, even though he did not believe in the so-called miracle of
the mass, replied: "Etzlich nemens irer guter halben, das sie davon nit
verjagt werden" (*Quellen Hesse*, p. 87f.).

[z]We find the words *"loopers"* and *"sluipers"* used in the minutes of
the Classes of the Reformed Churches of Flanders, around 1580, as
derogatory appellations for persons who preached without due ordination.
Especially one Michiel de Klerck seems to have given the authorities
some trouble in this matter. The Classis sent Philippus de Witte, the
burgomaster (who was also an elder) to confer with de Klerck. The
upshot was that he was categorically forbidden to continue in his
evangelistic efforts. (See H. Q. Janssen, *De Kerkhervorming in Vlaanderen*,
I, 378f.)

alone could make a fair plea for the purity of Christ, in whose
cause Barrow, Greenwood and Penry had been hanged." These
men had ostensibly done battle for the old Second Front insight
that "the true Church of Christ cannot exist where it is inter-
twined with the secular power." And for this doctrine they had
been liquidated. For these martyrs, the Church consisted of
believing men and women and of them only, whereas in the
minds of those who put them to death the Church contained all
in a given political unit. It was a matter of the composite society
versus the noncomposite society. It was a difference of conviction
as to whether the Church of Christ is *Corpus Christianum or
Corpus Christi*. It was ever the question of the rightness or the
wrongness of "Christian sacralism."

Such a man as John Wesley was caught on the horns of the
same dilemma on which the Reformers had been caught; only
he chose the other alternative. When he was under fire for
holding gatherings of the *Winckler* type he replied vigorously:

> You ask how it is that I assemble Christians who are none
> of my charge, to sing psalms, and hear the Scriptures ex-
> pounded? And you think it hard to justify doing this in
> other men's parishes, upon catholic principles . . . . I think it
> not hard to justify . . . . God in Scripture commands me, ac-
> cording to my power, to instruct the ignorant, reform the
> wicked, confirm the virtuous. Man forbids me to do this in
> an other man's parish; that is, in effect to do it at all, seeing
> I have now no parish of my own, nor probably ever shall.
> Whom then shall I hear, God or man? If it be just to obey
> man rather than God, judge ye. A dispensation is committed
> to me and woe is me if I preach not the Gospel.[27]

John Robinson, whose parishioners were to have much to do
with the transfer of the ideas of the Second Front to the shores
of the New World, had also addressed himself to the question
as to how the Church of Christ is to be delineated. And he had
identified himself with the view of the Second Front. Consequently the usual hardships had devolved upon him. Wrote he,
for the benefit of the Constantinians who opposed him:

> As for the gathering of a church . . . I tell you that in what
> place soever, by what means soever, whether by preaching
> the Gospell . . . or by reading, conference, or any other means
> of publishing it, two or three faithful people do arise, separate

> themselves from the world into fellowship of the gospell . . .
> they are a true Church truely gathered, though never so weak,
> a house and temple of God, rightly founded upon the doctrine
> of the Apostles and Prophets, Christ himself being the corner
> stone, against which the gates of hell shall not prevayl, nor your
> disgracefull invectives neyther.[28]

As the result of the pioneering by men who shared the vision
of the Second Front, it has come about that not only has the
Wincklerpredigt been made legitimate in these United States, but
the public cult has been ruled illegitimate. The First Amendment
sees to that, with its "Congress shall make no law establishing
religion, nor prohibit the free exercise thereof." The intention
of this oft-misinterpreted Amendment is not to enforce a-religion
or irreligion; it is to enforce impartiality in religious matters.
The First Amendment does not intend to say that the State is
not to "aid religion"; it intends to say that the State shall not aid *a*
religion above other religions; it intends to say that there is to
be no establishment of religion (which would be to aid *a* religion) nor the converse of establishment (which would be to
prevent the free exercise of the rest of the religions on the
scene). The First Amendment is not so much the fruitage of
the French Revolution as it is the legacy of Restitutionism.

All religious gatherings in these United States are *Winckler*
gatherings; they are all of them held off the streets and in non-
public locales. Even the Catholic gatherings are *Winckel-*
gatherings. We say "even the Catholic gatherings" because the
Catholic Church has never officially made its peace with the
American version of things; wherever it is able to do so it demands for its services the status of the public cult; it continues
to be less than satisfied with the idea of a composite society.

And yet, even Catholics in America are prepared to say that the
American experiment in Church-State relationships *works*, works
to the advantage of all parties, the Catholic Church included.
We point, for example, to the words of John Cogley who wrote:

> We have no Church-State problem in the classic sense. Our
> system of separation, it seems to me, is as close as any people
> can come to resolving the inescapable difficulties in trying to
> give to Caesar what is Caesar's and God what is God's . . . .
> It works. The rights of the Church are scrupulously observed
> in the American courts; the needs of the State are recognized

and honored by the Church. I cannot think of any place on
earth where it is easier for a man to fulfill his religious duties
than in the United States — to give God what is His. Nor
can I think of a place where the State asks so little of what
the religious man cannot give. When it does, the religious man
can make a conscientious appeal and the State will listen. I
said . . . it works. Where is the Church in a healthier condition?[29]

The benefits that accrue from the repudiation of "Christian
sacralism" may be observed on every hand. Protestants share
in them quite as much as Catholics do. If such repudiation
works, works to the *genuine welfare* of the Church, then this is
strong proof that it is right in principle. A candid examination
of the New Testament also enforces the conviction that it is right
in the Biblical light.

Which is to say that history has endorsed the views set forth
in the New Testament, views for the defence of which the
Stepchildren of the Reformation were pejoratively styled
Winckler.

6 *Wiedertäufer*

*The answer of a good con-
science toward God . . .*
I Peter 3:21

ANOTHER ONE OF THE TERMS OF REPROACH HEARD AT THE
Second Front was *Wiedertäufer*, a word meaning Anabaptists,
which in turn means rebaptizers. The name points to the
Stepchildren's practice of baptizing all who joined their congregations, even though these had been baptized already in
the inclusive Church, a practice which to their enemies looked
like rebaptism.

The sources single out no man as the originator of sixteenth-
century rebaptism. In the words of Josef Beck, "From whom
the idea of rebaptism issued, of this the sources say not a
word."[1]

This requires an explanation. To rebaptize is to do an extremely radical thing — how radical we shall have occasion to
see. How so radical a practice sprang up anonymously is passing
strange — if it is assumed, as the vogue is, that Anabaptism was
simply the product of the sixteenth century.

But this silence as to who must be credited with the idea
becomes wholly explicable once it is realized that what was
known as Anabaptism in Reformation times was in no sense a
new thing. Neither the name nor the practice was new. Nor
was the philosophy that lay behind the practice in any sense
new. The Anabaptists did not initiate a new school of thought;
they merely re-stated an ancient ideology — in the idiom of the
sixteenth century to be sure, but ancient nevertheless. No
one is credited with having invented the Anabaptism of the
sixteenth century for the sufficient reason that no one did.

189

Rebaptizing is as old as Constantinianism. There were Anabaptists, called by that name, in the fourth century. The Codes of Theodosius already prescribed very severe penalty, capital punishment, for anyone who was convicted of having rebaptized.[2] In fact, the first Anabaptist martyrs of Reformation times were put to death under the terms of these ancient Codes.

The very rigor practiced against Anabaptists requires our attention. To rebaptize was considered a capital crime. One gets the impression that this rigor was not born of solicitude for theological orthodoxy.

The fact is that the Codes were as severe as they were because much more was at stake than mere theological correctness. What was at stake was Constantinianism itself. We who have lived for some time now in the climate of societal compositism will find it hard to understand how a position and a practice which in our times do not so much as raise an eyebrow should in former times have called down such wrath. To understand this rigor one must in his mind reconstruct the world of "Christian sacralism" and the place which baptism, more specifically infant baptism, had come to occupy in it.

In an earlier chapter we saw that those who promoted the Constantinian change had seized upon the Christian *Agape*, had made it over so that it might do for the new sacralism what the pagan *sacramentum* had done for the old; we saw that the "mass" was the Christian *Agape* after it had picked up the overtones of the old pagan *sacramentum*. The Christian Supper had been changed into a sacralism-serving thing. Very similarly was the already existing institution of infant baptism laid hold of, subjected to a similarly motivated change, in order that it too might serve the cause of "Christian sacralism." Men took the existing institution and made of it a "christening," that is, a · ritual whereby every child in the Empire was taken and "made a Christian of" — before he had any voice in the matter. Since every child so "christened" was considered to be a "Christian" ever after, this was a highly useful institution, one that would see the sacralist ambition very far toward fulfillment. This fact, and this fact alone, will explain why protagonists of "Christian sacralism" have always been ferocious enemies of all who challenged "christening." It was not so much a concern for the salvation of men's souls that dictated the baptism policy;

it was rather a socio-political consideration. The protagonists of "Christian sacralism" were interested in "christening" because they were interested in the same thing in which Constantine had been interested, namely, a binder to give coherence to society. When Charlemagne, for example, prescribed the death penalty for any man who refused to submit to Christian baptism, he did this for political, not religious, reasons. For the sacralist the "christening" of everyone in the realm is a thing of utmost importance, for in that way a homogeneous society is made possible.

We shall illustrate, with an example from history, that it was not in the first place a passion for theological correctness, nor even for the salvation of infants, that made the magistrates interested in "christening," but rather its sacralism-promoting potential. From the many possible examples, we choose that of Margaret of Parma. When in 1567 she had reduced the city of Valenciennes, her first concern was to liquidate the "heretical" preachers and her second concern was to see to the restoration of "christening." She had asserted that "assuming that the King should allow two religions — a thing I cannot believe he would do — then I would still refuse to be party to such a plan; then I would rather let myself be torn into quarters!" With the capitulation of the ill-fated city she was in position to stamp out the idea of permitting more than one religion. And so she decreed: "Newly born infants shall upon birth be carried to the parish church in plain sight, to be baptized — under pain of very heavy and rigorous correction for the parents if they have them baptized in another way. Capital punishment is decreed for the parents and for him who officiates at such other baptisms."[3]

Here we have a magistrate who is fanatically committed to the sacralist premise that all citizens must adhere to one and the same religion; she would rather die a violent death than be party to societal compositism. Her rigorous policy in regard to the baptism of infants finds its explanation in this her commitment to the sacralist formula.

So great a stake did the proponents of Constantinianism have in the institution known as "christening" that they frequently resorted to *Zwangtaufe*, that is, baptism performed against the wishes of the persons involved. Actually, when

Charlemagne decreed that "any who refuse baptism shall be put to death," he was already practicing *Zwangtaufe*. The agents of the "fallen" Church practiced forced baptisms in outright fashion very commonly. We have already referred to the fact that the "missionary" to the Flemish countryside, Amandus by name, met with so much opposition that he had to pick himself out of the Schelde repeatedly. It has been suggested that this treatment was a case of *Zwangtaufe* for *Zwangtaufe*.

So great a stake did the sacralists have in "christening" that a great many Jews were in medieval times baptized against their wishes. At times in medieval Portugal and Spain as many as eighty percent of the Jews had been subjected to the indignity of *Zwangtaufe*. As we shall point out in its proper place instances of *Zwangtaufe* occurred in Reformation times and right up to relatively recent times. It is the concomitant of Constantinianism.

Although infant baptism had occurred, more or less sporadically, in pre-Constantinian times, "christening" dates from the inauguration of "Christian sacralism." For the fashioners of the new order, infant baptism was too valuable to leave unexploited; in a matter of decades it had become almost universal practice. It was inevitable that those who were not kindly disposed toward the Constantinian change should launch an assault upon baptism in its new form.

The Donatists were the original Anabaptists. Constantine and his collaborators within the Church, convinced as they were that there can be no peace in the market place unless there is concord at the shrine, had begun to bring about the baptism of the rank and file. Thereupon the Donatists began to say that baptism administered by an everybody-embracing Church is not Christian baptism but a sorry surrogate. They therefore felt called upon to administer real baptism to those who joined their fellowship, even if these had already been subjected to the lustration of the "fallen" Church. This was by their opponents derisively referred to as rebaptism. In their eyes rebaptism was frightful procedure. If one's baptism is a sign of one's citizenship in "Christendom," then a second baptism is a badge of disloyalty to that "Christendom." And so legislation was drawn up with a view to the liquidation of those who obstructed the development of "Christendom." There is a whole chapter in the ancient codes with the healing "ne sanctum baptisma iteretur" (that baptism is not to be repeated); and in these codes the death penalty is prescribed for the original Anabaptists.

Mentioned in the same context is also the infraction of conducting a conventicle or, as we have called it, a *Winckelpredigt*. It, too, was to be punished by death. These two infractions, that of the *Wiedertäufer* and that of the *Winckler*, are in this ancient legislation clubbed together; this will not surprise us once we have grasped the real issue. Both are assaults upon the idea of a Church "including all in a given locality"; both have as their objective the recovery of a Church "based on personal faith." Both are assaults upon *Corpus Christianum*, carried out in the interest of *Corpus Christi*.

Donatism was successfully suppressed. But that does not mean that the vision of Donatism was eliminated. It proved to be impossible to stamp out the conviction that lay at the heart of the Donatist rebellion. We continue to hear the overtones of Donatism all through medieval times. There were always those for whom the Church was a body of believing men and women rather than the christened masses. Occasionally, even the word "Donatist" was heard, up to modern times.*

In the year of our Lord 1050, for example, action was taken against certain "heretics" with whom one point of "heresy" was that "they overthrow infant baptism." Moreover, it is said in the same breath that in so doing "they introduce ancient heresy."[4] A century later we find the pope, Lucius III, assailing "heretics" who "touching baptism . . . do not hesitate to think or teach otherwise than the holy Church of Rome teaches and practices."[5]

Men who were critical of the latitudinarianism of the everybody-embracing Church were sure to criticize its baptism; in the light of the New Testament its "christening" procedures laid it wide open to criticism. Even among "heretics" who

---

*When the Brownists attacked establishmentism in England, they were dubbed "a Donatist sect." (Cf. George Peabody Gooch, *The History of English Democratic Ideas in the Seventeenth Century*, p. 85.) Late in the nineteenth century those who advocated a Free Church in Germany, as opposed to the *Landeskirche*, were likewise called "Donatisten."

tried to operate within the Church, the Church's baptism frequently was under attack. We see this in the case of one "Brother Michael" who was burned at Florence in 1389. Although he wore the cloth of the prevailing Church, his heart was the heart of a "heretic." He seems to have had around him a contingent of disciples, members of his *ecclesiola in ecclesia;* we owe the story to one of these. In the course of his trial, such remarks as the following were thrown at him: "So the Church has remained among you!" "O, you who say that we are not baptized, nor true Christians!" "Thou art not among heathen folk!" Manifestly "Brother Michael" was quite close to the Restitutionist vision, even though he continued outward connection with the Church. Nor was he far removed from Anabaptism; for anyone who challenges the validity of the Church's "christening" needs to go but one step farther to be a full-fledged rebaptizer. The logic of the situation requires that step. One cannot remain content with a baptism which he considers invalid; he must re-baptize, if he takes baptism at all seriously.[6]

It is well known that Pierre de Bruys, who lived in the twelfth century, attacked the christening customs of the prevailing Church. He taught that no one should be baptized until he had reached the age of discretion. He assailed "christening" not only, but also practiced rebaptism. The word, of course, he did not use (no Anabaptist has ever been at peace with that word); but the Petrobrusians, as Pierre's followers were called, declared: "We wait until the proper time has come, after a man is ready to know his God and believe in Him; we do not, as they accuse us, rebaptize him who may be said never to have been baptized before."

This was Restitutionism plain and simple. What was unique in this eruption of Restitutionism was that it was attempted inside the everybody-embracing Church. Evidently de Bruys was faced with the same dilemma in which we saw Martin Luther involved, that of the Church as a society of believers versus the Church as a society embracing all in a given locality. Like Luther, he apparently toyed with the possibility of creating a believers' Church without abandoning the inclusive Church — an impossible combination of mutually exclusive concepts. The consistent thing to do was to leave the everybody-embracing Church and reinstitute a Church of believers. Not *ecclesiola in ecclesia* but Restitutionism was the effective solution of the problem posed by "Christian sacralism."

That solution was tried — often enough in medieval times, and consistently, too. We read, for example, of a large contingent of "heretics" burned at Trier in 1231. They had their own ecclesiastical set-up, even a bishop or general supervisor. They had all the tell-tale features of Restitutionism — they were well at home in the New Testament, which they possessed in the vernacular; they did not believe in the body of the Lord — that is, they were opposed to transubstantiation; they said that a priest living in sin was incompetent to officiate at the Sacrament; they believed that any man or woman can administer the Sacrament, out of any bowl or chalice and at any place; they said that extreme unction and prayer for the dead are superfluous; they minimized the sacrament of Orders. And, attached to this list of items of "heresy" — all of them well-known features of anti-Constantinianism[b] — we find that these "heretics" also "repeat baptism."[7]

Not only did the complex of ideas that lie behind the practice of rebaptizing come to expression throughout medieval times and as parts of the Restitutionist vision, but this feature was sometimes considered the central point in it. Peter the Venerable, a trusted son of the Empire-Church, declared that "the first point made by the heretic is that children below the age of intelligence cannot be saved by baptism." The argument here is exactly that which we shall hear from the lips of the Anabaptists of Reformation times; the sole difference is that, whereas the Anabaptists said it in German, it is here couched in medieval Latin.

We have it on good authority that the Waldensians, those heirs of the ancient Anabaptists and forerunners of the new, practiced rebaptism. A fourteenth-century manuscript preserved

---

[b]These "heretics" were accused of being a bizarre cat-cult. The association of cats and heretics is common; the reason for this is not altogether clear. The most promising guess is that the word *Kathar* was in the popular mind associated with *Kater*, tom-cat. In this way the cat may have become associated with magic, for heretics were commonly accused of necromancy. This may also explain why a female heretic was often called a *Tibbe*, a female cat (cf. our "tabby-cat").

at Strasbourg informs us that the Waldensians "have themselves
rebaptized by their own clergy." That this was indeed the
custom among the Waldensians was known to Luther, who
said of them:

> These brethren hold to the idea that every man must believe
> for himself and on the basis of his own faith receive baptism
> and that otherwise baptism or the sacrament is useless. So
> far they believe and speak correctly. But when they proceed
> then to baptize little children nevertheless . . . that is to make
> sport of holy baptism . . . . It cannot help them that children
> are baptized on their future faith . . . for faith must be on
> hand *before* and *in* baptism, otherwise the child is not delivered
> from the devil and from sin . . . . Therefore need would re-
> quire that the Waldensians would have themselves rebaptized
> just as they baptize those who come to them from us.[8]

Here we have rebaptism going hand in hand with the practice
of infant baptism. What the Waldensians had against "christening" was not the infancy of the recipient but the Constantinian
overtones of the ritual. Therefore they rebaptized converts from
the prevailing Church and practiced infant baptism in the case
of their own little ones.

In another place Luther reported similarly about the Anabaptism of the Waldensians. It was in 1522 that he wrote of
them: "They baptize little ones . . . and rebaptize those who
come to them from us."

Here again is proof that early anti-pedobaptism was not
based on a distinguishing view as to the accessibility of child
life to the grace of God but was based rather on an aversion
to "christening," that is, to baptism with sacralist overtones.
This early Anabaptism was not so much a matter of anti-pedobaptism as a matter of anti-Constantinianism.

It is significant that, in some instances at least, the Anabaptism of the sixteenth century did not in its earliest mani-
festations assail infant baptism as such but rather the "christening" of the fallen Church. We read that in the earliest days
of Anabaptism in the Wassenberg area, infant baptism was not
as such repudiated; what was repudiated was the "christening"
ritual. In connection with one of the earliest evidences of
Anabaptist stirrings in these parts we read: "a child was baptized

in a dwelling, by Hendrick van Hoengen, in Godert Reinhart's house . . . it will become one year old this summer . . . . Diederich Jurgens baptized a child, with his own hands."[9] Here we encounter a clean break with the Empire-Church, a gathering in a private home, where the sacrament of baptism was administered by an unordained man. This is Restitutionism of the first water. Yet it goes hand in hand with the baptism of a child less than a year old.

Among the Bohemian Brethren it was likewise customary to rebaptize converts from "Christendom"; but here also the point was not anti-pedobaptism but anti-Constantinianism, for the Brethren did practice infant baptism in the case of children born to "believing parents," that is, to parents who were members of the Church of the Brethren, of the *Unitas Fratrum*.[c]

We see then that rebaptism did not necessarily go hand in hand with a rejection of pedobaptism. It is said that Michael Sattler, one of the first to lose his life for the cause of Restitutionism, was at the first rather kindly disposed toward infant baptism. This less than vehement attitude toward it was manifested at various other sectors of the Second Front. What was opposed, we may therefore say, was not so much pedobaptism as such but "christening." The outright rejection of infant baptism came when it became apparent that the Reformation was heading in a neo-Constantinian direction. Not until the Reformers began to embrace the old institution of "christening" did the Anabaptists by way of reaction make a clean sweep of the board. Prior to that point there had been considerable give and take on both sides.

As long as the Reformers were still riding the fence, as long as they tried to live with their dilemma, they were, to put

---

[c]Bartholomäus von Usingen, one-time teacher of Martin Luther, considered the Anabaptists to have descended from the "Picards" of Bohemia. In a letter preserved in the City Library at Hamburg (cited by Ludwig Keller in his *Die Anfänge der Reformation und die Ketzerschule*, p. 234) he wrote "quia autem hoc tempore de Picardismo exierunt quos Anabaptistas vel Catabaptismas ab iterata tinctione vocant." It is perhaps too sweeping to say that "Anabaptism came forth from Picardism"; but it is altogether likely that the Anabaptists owed their ideas about baptism to earlier eruptions of Restitutionist dissent. An ideological continuity between the two rebellions against the medieval order is plainly present.

it mildly, far from being fanatic proponents of infant baptism.[d] They *became* such. And their development in that direction dates from the moment when those who came to be dealt with as Stepchildren had made it plain that for them there was no dilemma. It was then that the Reformers became emphatic supporters of the other horn of the dilemma. And with that the contest was on, with each side throwing in all that it had.

This sequence is most clearly traceable in the case of Huldreich Zwingli, on whose doorstep infant Anabaptism was born. Early in his career as a Reformer he was, to put it too mildly, rather lukewarm toward the baptism of little ones. He confessed in those early days: "Nothing grieves me more than that at the present I have to baptize children, for I know it ought not to be done."[10] This was plain talk. Here was a man who was deeply aware that the renewal of the Church called for a radical break with "christening." He knew that this was pretty central in the Reform, so central that it weighed more heavily on him than any other matter.

We cannot help asking why Zwingli, if he was so sure that "christening" was wrong, did not let it be known that he was desisting. To answer this question, one must remember that the civil rulers of the city were sacralists; they saw in sacrament the cement that bound society together; they would therefore be loath to part with the infant baptism. This meant that

---

[d] In the Reformed Church at Nordlingen, in the earliest times (in 1525, when the polarity between the Reformers and their Stepchildren had not yet reached a critical stage therefore), it was left to the parents whether they wished to have their children baptized or not. We read: "Wij doopen kinderen en volwassene perzoonen, en wij stooten die geene niet uit van de Kerke, die haare kinderen niet ter doop brengen, maar die alleenlijk door de oplegging der handen en 't gebed der Kerke, den Heere Christus werden aanbevoolen. Christus heeft geenen ouderdom te doopen belast, maar ook geene verbooden." On the usual assumption, namely that all who rallied to the Reform were children of 1517, it is quite impossible to explain the situation at Nordlingen. Here were people, members of the Reformed Church, who were far from enthusiastic supporters of infant baptism, with a sensitivity so pronounced that the leaders of the Reformed Church accommodated themselves to it. Whence this sensitivity? Certainly not from any of the Reformers in their final phase. We are obliged to look to pre-Reformation conditioning to explain this situation.

if Zwingli were to act on his insight he would immediately
come under their displeasure. This could imply the drying up
of the spring from which he drank, the loss of his stipend.
That it was this consideration that caused Zwingli to draw
back is quite apparent from the words with which this utterance
of his ends: "If however I were to terminate the practice then
I fear that I would lose my prebend."

On another occasion Zwingli wrote, "I leave baptism un-
touched, I call it neither right nor wrong; if we were to baptize
as Christ instituted it then we would not baptize any person
until he has reached the years of discretion; for I find it nowhere written that infant baptism is to be practiced . . . ." This
again is clear enough. Although Zwingli begins by saying that
he wishes to refrain from cutting the knot, he certainly gives
his opinion and expresses his conviction. It is that "christening"
has no foundation in Scripture and that the right baptism is
believers' baptism.

Again we are driven to ask why he then hesitated, why he
drew back from the course which he felt had Biblical warrant,
and why he continued in the way that lacked such warrant. To
find the answer to this question, one must remember that the
former course was frightfully radical. To propose to terminate
"christening" in a sacral society, which had for a millennium been
held together by it, was to propose a pretty radical thing. It
was very similar to reading some men out of society. That is why
Zwingli added: "However one must practice infant baptism so as
not to offend our fellow men."

At still another point, Zwingli spoke his mind on this matter
to his associates Hans Hager and Ruodi Feissenwasser. To
them he confessed: ". . . if we were to baptize in accord with
the command of Christ then we would not baptize anyone
until he has reached the age of discretion." This again is
altogether plain.

One is led to ask once more why this Reformer then dragged
his feet, why he allowed himself to be party to the perpetuation
of a practice which as he saw things lacked Biblical warrant.
And again Zwingli answers our question. It is again the matter
of offence. He adds specifically: "But on account of the possibility of offence I omit preaching this; it is better not to
preach it until the world is ready to take it."

It is quite apparent that what restrained Zwingli from introducing believers' baptism was the consideration that such a
baptism would tend to divide society — the one thing that
men of sacralist conviction cannot allow. Anything that results
in composite society is for the sacralist an intolerable evil. That
it was this that kept Zwingli back is altogether apparent.
Baptism, said he, is "a visible sign wherewith a man makes
himself responsible to God and makes this apparent to his
neighbor with the outward sign, without faction-making, otherwise it brings into being a sect and not one faith."[11] Zwingli,
like so many of his generation, was blissfully unaware that the
Church of Christ is by definition a sect.° They were mortally
afraid of everything that so much as smacked of *Rotterei* or
faction-making — forgetting that the Church of Christ as set
forth in the New Testament is by definition a *faction*, in any
given situation, a *party*, a segment of society — never the
totality.

Later on, when the Second Front had been opened and
Zwingli had turned his guns upon his erstwhile companions, now
known as Anabaptists, he was, of course, embarrassed by his
earlier utterances in regard to the baptism of infants. He
seems not to have kept his anti-christening ideas out of his
pulpit utterances quite as much as he had planned. The
Anabaptist leaders at any rate were not slow to accuse him
of doing an about face. And he in turn tried to whittle down
what he had said. Hübmaier, one of the captains in the Second
Front, scolded him: "You used to hold to the same ideas, wrote
and preached them from the pulpit openly; many hundreds
of people have heard it from your mouth. But now all who
say this of you are called liars. Yes, you say boldly that no
such ideas have ever entered your mind, and you go beyond
that, things of which I will hold my tongue just now."[12]

°The word *sect* is not from the Latin *secare, to cut,* as is often said,
erroneously; it is from *sequor,* of which the root idea is *follow.* This
etymology of the word *sect* was known to literate men in Reformation
times. We find, for example, in an order by Philip of Hesse concerning
the Anabaptists, that not only "ihre duces and redlinführer [literally
wheel-turners] sonder auch alle ihre sectatores und nachvolger" were
to be jailed. In this passage *sectatores* are followers, synonymous with
nachvolger. It should need no defense that a Christian is a *Nachvolger,*
a follower, a sectary, by definition.

Zwingli, understandably irked, replied: "After it had been rashly accepted that the sign testifies to the faith then men had to assail infant baptism. For, how could baptism testify to the faith in the case of little children, seeing they cannot believe. This error had misled also me some years ago and made me think it were better not to baptize little ones until they had grown up."[13] He had saved the day for himself; but it had cost him the concept of believers' baptism. He was now defending unbelievers' baptism, that is, a baptism that is proper even where faith is presumably *not* present.

In passing, it may be useful to recall that Luther went to the same extreme in his attempt to get away from the Anabaptist doctrine that baptism is in place only where faith is presumably present. With his customary rashness he cried out:

> How can baptism be more grievously reviled and disgraced than when we say that baptism given to an unbelieving man is not good and genuine baptism! . . . What, baptism rendered ineffective because I do not believe? . . . What more blasphemous and offensive doctrine could the devil himself invent and preach? And yet the Anabaptists and the *Rottengeister* are full up to their ears with this teaching. I put forth the following: Here is a Jew that accepts baptism, as happens often enough, but does not believe, would you then say that this was not real baptism, because he does not believe? That would be to think as a fool thinks not only, but to blaspheme and disgrace God moreover.[14]

If Zwingli emerges from his wrangle about infant baptism as something less than a paragon of courage, let it be recalled how frightful was the only other road open to him. Here was the Council of the city cautioning him (when the news had reached them that Zwingli was going roughshod over age-old institutions of "Christendom"), saying: "It becomes no one, and least of all a preacher, to call ancestral deliverances and ordinances superfluous, foolish, or vain . . . . By so doing the holy Church, the ancient fathers, the Councils, the pope, the cardinals, and bishops, etc., will be made to look ridiculous, will be disdained and eliminated." Lest one should think that it was a concern for theological correctness that motivated the Council, it should be noted that they added in the same breath, "And then there will spring up disobedience toward the magistracy, disunity, heresy, and the weakening and diminution of the Christian faith." To go squarely against this philosophy, so typically sacralist, was no small thing. It would be frightfully costly to go against it — how costly the Anabaptists were soon to learn.

On January 17, 1525 the Council at Zürich notified the public that there was to be no tampering with the sacralism-serving institution of "christening." All parents were in the same edict ordered to have their children baptized within a week, upon pain of banishment.[r] This precipitated the flight at once of the Anabaptist leaders: Reubli, Brötli, Hätzer, and Castelberg. Zwingli would have been among them if he had not swung to the right. A little later, in 1529, the Diet at Speier decreed that, "Every Anabaptist or rebaptized person, of either sex, is to be put to death, by fire, or by the sword, or by some other means."[g] Zwingli would have been in the direct path of this

[r]This became standard procedure in other cities. On February 8, 1535 the City Council at Strasbourg gave orders that not-yet-baptized children were to be presented for baptism within six weeks; to give this directive strictness, there was added: "Welcher sich aber das zu thun widern würde, den sollen sy den geordneten herrn geschriben geben, der gepür nach mit inen zu handlen" (*Quellen VIII*, p. 431).

It is interesting to note that those who failed to comply contended that the local pastors had taught that infant baptism was not obligatory — as was no doubt true. One said, "Die predicanten haben doch II jaren gepredigt, das man jnen die gewissen soll frei lassen, des wollen sie sich frei halten unnd warten, waz inen got daruber gebit" (*op. cit.*, p. 440f.). Another, who was a recent arrival in Strasbourg, said that "doctor Capito und Butzer in syner zukunfft [arrival] zu ime gesagt, wie der kindertauff in der schrifft nit gegrundt sei er soll auch noch in aim [einem] jar by inen fallen. Daruff hab er sich mit wib und kinder hie nidergelassen." Still another, Conrad Schretz, asserted that he "will sein kind nit tauffen lassen, dann die herren prediger habens hie offentlich gepredigt." And yet another, Christof Meisinger, contended that he too "will sein kind nit tauffen lassen, dann doctor Capito hat vor VI jaren zu jm und annderen gesagt, der kindertauff sei nit, er muss fallen."

[g]Speier was, of course, Catholic-controlled. The rigor practiced by the Catholics against the Anabaptists did not, however, exceed that of the Protestants. In 1534, for example, the Protestant city of Strasbourg decreed that no child was to be left unbaptized, and that children so left unbaptized would be baptized by the officers of the law. We read: "jeder bürger und einwohner dieser stadt sein kind nicht über die zeit der kindbett ungetauft lassen solle . . . , dann sonst werde ein rath taufen lassen, unt die ungehorsamen der gebühr nach straffen" (*Quellen VIII*, p. 399).

decree — if he had not veered from his erstwhile course. To go against such odds was to risk much. It was an assignment for which only radical men are normally equipped.

Zwingli had escaped — but at the cost of a return to the Constantinian formula, now on a provincial scale and with Swiss Protestantism rather than Roman Catholicism in the favored place. And as one after the other of his erstwhile associates went to the executioner, they could be heard to say acidly of Zwingli, "Today he preaches one thing and tomorrow he takes it all back again; to be specific, for years now he has preached that children must not be baptized, but now he tells us that they must be."[h]

Nor was Zwingli the only one who in his early days had desired the termination of "christening." Bucer had said on December 24 of 1524, as he spoke for the whole college of pastors at Strasbourg: "If someone wishes to wait with baptism . . . we would not for that reason separate from him nor condemn him; let everyone figure it out for himself. The Kingdom of God does not consist in eating or drinking, and therefore not in water baptism, but in righteousness and peace and joy in the Holy Ghost."[15] It was the rise of Anabaptism as a protest against the Reformers' indecision that made them the ardent protagonists of infant baptism that they became.

Luther was likewise embarrassed with "christening." But he was too well aware of the radicalness of a clean break with it to abandon the sacralism-feeding institution. Wrote he: "There

---

[h]"Hüt prediget er eins, morn widerrüfet ers, und namlich hat er prediget von jaren, dan man die kindlin nit tauffen solle, jetz aber sagt er, man sölle sy touffen." (*Quellen VI*, p. 53.) It seems that when the news of Zwingli's swing to the right reached the ears of his colleague Sebastian Hofmeister, he was deeply troubled. When the Anabaptist leader, Hübmeier, discussed Zwingli's change of front with Hofmeister, the latter replied, in writing (Hübmeier had the original in his possession so it seems, for he wrote "das urtayl hab ich sein aigne handschrifft"): "unser brüder Zwingli, so er ye wölle das die khindlin müssen getaufft werden, von dem zill irre und nit nach der warhait des Evangelii wandle. Warlich, ich hab nitt mügen gezwungen werden, das ich mein khindlen taufte. Demnach handlest du Christenlich, das du der rechte Tauff Christi, der lang dahinden gelegen ist, widerumb herfür furest. Wir wöllen solchs auch unnderstan . . ." (*Quellen IX*, p. 236). There was quite apparently considerable vaccillation among the Reformers, at the first, with regard to traditional "christening."

is not sufficient evidence from Scripture that one might justify the introduction of infant baptism at the time of the early Christians after the apostolic period . . . . But so much is evident, that no one may venture with a good conscience to reject or abandon infant baptism, which has for so long a time been practiced."[16]

Needless to say, this constitutes a violation of Luther's *sola Scriptura* doctrine; this is an un-Lutheran capitulation to *het historisch gewordene;* this takes us dangerously close to the Catholic position of "Scripture plus tradition." How came Luther to express himself in such an un-Lutheran way? The answer is that Luther was in a dilemma. To the extent that he was drifting toward a new version of "Christian sacralism," he had to come to the defence of "christening," even though he had to compromise his own doctrine of *sola Scriptura* in doing it.

The Reformer Oecolampadius felt himself similarly in a tough spot. He, too, had rallied to the support of a new "Christian sacralism"; and that required of him also that he rise to the defence of "christening." And he likewise felt that the data of the New Testament was inadequate, that he would have to take recourse to *het historisch gewordene.* To escape from the Anabaptist argument, this Reformer cried out, "I know only too well that you keep calling 'Scripture, Scripture!' as you clamor for clear words to prove our point . . . . But if Scripture taught us all things then there would be no need for the anointing to teach us all things."[17] Here is a Protestant who speaks in an idiom that is foreign to Protestantism. He is not opposing the Anabaptists on Scriptural grounds; for, by his own confession, he does not consider these grounds to be adequate. And yet he fights the Anabaptists bitterly. Why? Because he is unwilling to let go of "Christian sacralism." And it was this unwillingness that was the motivation of the agitation against the Stepchildren — who *had* let go of "Christian sacralism."

These Stepchildren were not in the dark as to what the motivation was for the Reformers' frantic defence of "christening." They knew that it was not exegesis nor theology, but rather the issue of the propriety of "Christendom." As one of them put it, "They fight for infant baptism not out of love for the children . . . but in order that they may uphold a false Christendom, which they all got by setting up such a baptism.

For Satan realizes that as soon as a fellowship of believers is set up, in which obedience to Christ is manifest, then his darkness cannot stand any longer before the light, for it then becomes apparent that his 'gospel' and his 'Christendom' are 'the abomination of desolation.' "[18]

It appears then that the Anabaptists turned their guns on the institution of "christening" because they had rejected the "Christendom" which this institution fed. And it appears that the Reformers read the riot act over these Anabaptists precisely because they themselves had cast in their lot with neo-Christendom, with "Christian sacralism" in Protestant format. The position which any given person took toward "Christendom" determined his attitude toward "christening"; the skirmish touching the propriety of infant baptism as it had been practiced for more than a millennium was but part of the battle concerning the delineation of Christ's Church.

In this light we can understand Felix Manz' otherwise dark saying, "More is involved in baptism, things on which I prefer not to enlarge just now."[19] We can understand also the note written down by the Clerk of Courts, "They don't want to hear of infant baptism nor allow it; but this will at the last put an end to the secular rule." This well-informed observer was convinced, sacralist that he was, that there must be a "christening" if there is to be rule and order; he saw right well that if the Stepchildren got their way Christendom would be a thing of the past — which for a sacralist implies the end of order. We begin to see why Felix Manz was drowned in the cold black waters of the Limmat.

We begin to see through Conrad Grebel's assertion that the medieval order "nienderth mit basz möchte nidergleit werdenn dann mit den kindertouff"[20] (can be laid low with nothing as well as with the termination of infant baptism), an assertion we find also on the lips of Grebel's colleague, Felix Manz.[21]

As the leaders among the Stepchildren spoke, so spoke also the followers. Hans Seckler said that "Infant baptism is a supporting pillar of the papal order and as long as it is not removed there can be no Christian congregation." (It must be observed here that in the eyes of the Stepchildren the "papal order" was repeating itself in the camp of the Protestants;

Seckler's words were directed against "Christian sacralism," whether of Catholic or Protestant quality.)

A simple peasant woman who had been gained for the Restitutionist vision put it this way, in 1528: "Long ago a man was not baptized until he was twelve years old and had come to years of discretion, when he was placed before the alternatives of being baptized or remaining a heathen. But in this way of doing so many remained heathen that the priests decided to baptize children when they were still young so that they would be and remain Christians."[22] One must have some difficulty with this peasant woman's representation of the rise of infant baptism; but one cannot quarrel with her delineation of the motivation behind the rise of "christening"; certainly not with her assertion that "christening" came into vogue along with an effort to secure a non-composite society.

We are in position now to understand how and why the Reformers supported *Zwangtaufe*, as support it they did. Even Philip of Hesse, a man from whom one would least expect it, was prevailed upon to order the children of the Stepchildren baptized, against the parents' wishes. We read in an instrument from his hand, dated February 19, 1541, addressed to his sub-ordinates at Kassel: "Our orders to you are . . . to have his children made partakers of baptism . . . . Have them baptized by virtue of your office."[23]

Apparently and understandably the Stepchildren were not greatly impressed by the high-handed technique of *Zwangtaufe*. The pastors at Hausbreitenbach and Friedwald at any rate reported, "There was an Anabaptist here, named Schwartzhaus, who had for years refused to have his child baptized, a child which the mayor had taken, along with Philip's little girl, and had had it baptized. Schwartzhaus informed some persons later that he had washed the filth off again [*den dregk wider abgeweschen*]."[24] If this is not sufficiently respectful language, let it be charged to those who by *Zwangtaufe* had robbed the rite of baptism of its dignity in the first place.

Sometimes the cases of *Zwangtaufe* are reported with all the pompous verbiage usually associated with the courts. We read, for example, of a case that occurred in 1577: "Michael Richter . . . has found his way into the sect and error of the Anabaptists, and in spite of the fact that his errors have been most faithfully pointed out and rebuked, he still refuses to have his child baptized. Therefore we have been obliged to baptize said child, the civil authorities approving; the more so since the child was critically ill.[1] Present at the baptism were these following witnesses: Wilhelm Baur . . . , members of the City Council. Also present was the Reverend Paul Grevenius, the pastor, and Johann Pfluck, the Dean of Neustadt. I, Michael Herolt, Dean of Altenstadt performed the rite."[25]

From the foregoing, one might draw the conclusion that these forced baptisms were done for humanitarian reasons at least in part; here was a child whose life expectancy was not good, and so men saw to it that the child was baptized. However, we ought not to let ourselves think that any love was wasted on the Stepchildren; the following is typical as to this matter. According to the testimony given before the Court at Stadeck in 1575, "There have indeed been Anabaptists among us in previous times; but they have all been exterminated by the magistracy — save two who were ill and who refused to recant and who died a lingering death [in prison], whom the preacher caused to be buried, not in the cemetery nor with Christian rites, but next to the cemetery."

One cheering item in an otherwise wholly sordid story concerning *Zwangtaufe* is the fact that the magistrates seem to have felt almost instinctively, that there was something strangely wrong about it. Those of the vicinity of Württemburg, at any rate, asked a committee of the clergy to set forth in writing how it was argued that a magistrate is duty bound to baptize children against the parents' wishes. In order that the opinion might reflect a broad enough base, a committee of four were picked, two Lutherans, one Reformed man, and one Roman Catholic. Naturally there were four reports, each expert arguing the matter in his own way. But the reports stated *quasi unanimiter* that "The Church and especially the magistrates are duty bound to have the child baptized against the parents' wishes."[26]

These reports, couched for the most part in ponderous Latin, also argued down an imaginary opponent who contended that,

[1] Apparently there were still people around in Protestant lands who felt that a child that dies unbaptized is lost, a notion for which there is no New Testament warrant, but is a very handy device for protagonists of "Christian sacralism."

since it was not customary to force-baptize the children of
Jewish parents, it was permissible to follow the same policy
in regard to the children of the Anabaptists. But the theologians
argued — this is very revealing — that these are not parallel
problems, seeing that Jewish children were not a part of
"Christendom," whereas the Anabaptists' children were! The
latter's parents were *apostates*; and in sacralistic thinking these
are dealt with very severely.

Manifestly the advice of the Württemburg theologians was
followed — until the acids of modernity had eroded away their
folly, or, until the civil powers cut themselves loose from the
apron-strings of the Church. As late as the year 1863, forced
baptisms occurred. We read of one performed with five police-
men present, as well as the midwife that had delivered the
child. It is reported that the local pastor, in an effort to
break down the father so that he would present the child for
baptism, actually told the man that he had been "informed
by the Holy Spirit that the child was not going to live." The
report does not say whether these prognostications, via this
preacher's private line to heaven, came true.

This then was the point at issue; the Stepchildren had repudiated "Christian sacralism" and this repudiation made them
reject "christening." As Henry Bullinger put it:

> From the beginning it was principally a matter of separation
> for the purpose of creating a divided church . . . , because they
> wished to abandon the Papists and the Evangelicals . . . and
> live in a new Baptist order, which they call the true, blessed,
> Christian church, therefore their leaders received baptism . . .
> as a sign of the separation.[27]

It was this charge that was uppermost in men's minds, that to
rebaptize was *Rotterey* (faction-making). If the Stepchildren
had been willing to leave "Christendom" intact, then their opponents would have been willing to go along with them in
many if not most ways. Zwingli's impatient cry was "Gond hin,
lebend zum aller christlichisten . . . , allein underlassend den
widertouff; denn man sicht offenlich, das ir üch damit rottend!
(Run along, live as Christian-like as you please . . . , only lay
off on the rebaptizings, for it is as plain as day that with it
you are making a faction!)[28]

Another charge that was constantly in the air was that the Stepchildren were bringing into being a *Sonderkirche*, a word that can perhaps be best translated with "a Church apart" (the *sonder* being related to our English *sunder*), apart from society, not identical with it, not coterminous with it. This was precisely where the shoe pinched; this the sacralist cannot allow; this the New Testament vision demands; this the Restitutionist is bent on having.

That this was the real issue becomes utterly clear from a statement made by Melanchthon, who said in a polemic against the Anabaptists:

> Now let every devout man consider what disruption would ensue if there should develop among us two categories, the baptized and the unbaptized! If baptism were to be discontinued for the greater part then an openly heathen mode of existence would come about — a thing for which the devil would like very much to have the way opened.[29]

For all his learning, and for all his acquaintance with the Scriptures, Melanchthon remained so caught up in the toils of "Christian sacralism" that he was unable to see that baptism is by definition a symbol of *unity* within the Church, but a symbol of *dividedness* in society.

The rejection of "Christendom" was the crux of the matter; this rather than a basic "dualism between nature and grace" as legend has it. If it is "dualism" to operate with the distinction of common grace and special grace, and therefore with the distinction of State and Church, if this makes one a "dualist," then the Stepchildren were, of course, dualists — but with a dualism that is inwrought in the New Testament. It must be said that he who shies away from this dualism is himself getting involved in a monism, a monism which the New Testament will not allow.

The rejection of the medieval monism led the Stepchildren to consider the Old Testament obsolete at this point. In this downgrading of the Old Testament, the Anabaptist vision was unique and in no sense simply "left-wing." As the late Dr. Harold Bender put it:

> Anabaptism was not fully conformant to Reformation Protestantism, in that it refused to place the Old Testament on a

parity with the New Testament, choosing rather to make the
new covenant of Christ supreme and relegating therefore the
Old Testament to the position of a preparatory instrument in
God's program. This important basic attitude toward the two
testaments has significant theological consequences, with its
bearing on the concept of the Church . . . , as well as on
ethical questions . . . . Baptism is not the counterpart of circumcision therefore.[30]

It was indeed a deep-seated conviction with the Stepchildren
that "We are not children of the Old Testament but of the New."

The Stepchildren complained loudly that the weapons which
the Reformers used in the battle at the Second Front were
weapons taken from the Old Testament arsenal. They looked
upon the policy of sliding from the Old Testament to the New
as a master evil, one from which all sorts of evils come. In
the words of Dirck Philips, one of the most influential thinkers
in the camp of the Anabaptists:

The false prophets cover and disguise their deceptive doctrines
by appealing to the letter of the Old Testament, which consists of types and shadows. For whatever they cannot defend
with New Testament Scriptures they try to establish by the
Old Testament, on the letter of the books of the prophets.
This has given rise to . . . many false religious forms. Yes,
it is from this fountain that the sacrilegious ceremonies and
pomp of the Church of Antichrist and the deplorable errors
of the seditious sects have come,[1] which in our day under
the guise of the Holy Gospel . . . have done much injury and
have caused great offence.[31]

Such demotion of the Old Testament occurred constantly in
Anabaptist witness. It may indeed be said, in the words of
Bender, that this is one of the earmarks of the Anabaptist
vision.

Those who opposed the Stepchildren extracted the last bit of
mileage out of this Anabaptist treatment of the Old Testament.
It gave them a chance to identify the Anabaptists with the
ancient dualists of Manichean type; and they kept accusing
them of holding "that Jesus Christ is at odds with the Father,"
a charge which the Stepchildren rejected with vigor. As Pieter

[1]The reference is to the Münsterites, who had indeed, as they grasped
the sword, looked to the Old Testament for Biblical warrant.

van Ceulen put it at the Colloquy held at Emden in 1578, "Christ is not at odds with His Father; but He does teach in all things that which is more complete." It would seem that the Reformers, in their haste to find the Stepchildren guilty of heresy at this point, were themselves led into error, the error of not appropriating the teaching, found so unmistakably present in the Epistle to the Hebrews for example, that the Old Testament is superseded by the New. One can go very far indeed in saying that there is discontinuity between the Old Testament and the New before one lands in error as great as that of the man who refuses to accept the discontinuity that the New Testament plainly teaches.

The clash between the Reformers and their Stepchildren came to its classical expression in the argument as to whether "baptism has come in the place of circumcision." The Stepchildren were inclined to deny any relationship between the old rite and the new; their opponents were inclined to overlook certain real differences between them.

It seems to the present writer that in this debate as to the relationship, if any, between circumcision and baptism, both sides at times over-stated their case. We do well to explore this matter a bit.

In their haste to do justice to the New Testament teaching on the matter, the Stepchildren overlooked the fact that the two rites do have things in common. Both are symbols of grace, one and the same grace; both signify cleansing; both incorporate the recipient into a fold; both lean heavily on the benefit of nurture. So one could go on. But one must add at once that the Reformers in their haste to establish continuity between the two rites overlooked the discontinuities. They seem not to have perceived that baptism has indeed "come in the place of circumcision" and for very good reasons. They seem hardly to have pondered the fact that if it happened under divine supervision that the ancient rite was dropped and a new rite adopted, this can only mean that the older rite was no longer adequate or tolerable in the new situation.

In all events, circumcision was bound by race, by peoplehood, or, more elegantly, by Volkstum. The happenstance of citizenship in the Jewish State entitled one to circumcision. The mutilation of circumcision was a sign of one's Jewishness —

just as non-mutilation was a sign of one's gentileness. In circumcision *Volk* and *Volk Gottes* were coextensive entities. In this the Old Testament rite was decidedly pre-Christian and sacralism-sustaining.

In the New Testament a *Volk Gottes* emerges that is not bounded in the old way. The boundaries of *Volk* are ignored and crossed and disregarded. This is the deep-seated meaning of the allegation that "in Christ there is neither Jew nor gentile." Few things are said as plainly in the New Testament, and as often, as that Christ's Church is not coextensive with any socio-political grouping or ethnic delineation, and that national boundaries are meaningless in it.

It was this novelty, introduced on the day of Pentecost, that put circumcision on the shelf, so making room for its successor, for baptism. Small wonder that circumcision was shelved; it had tribal overtones of which it could not be divested. A new *Volk Gottes* was envisioned, and a new badge was needed to mark the member of this new *Volk Gottes,* one that did not have the objectionable tribal overtones. This new badge was baptism.

And baptism was practiced in this its authentic thrust until the age of Constantine; and then it was *lost.* With the Con-stantinian change, baptism picked up the very overtones for which circumcision had been discarded: *Volk* and *Volk Gottes* were again given a common boundary. When "Christendom" was launched, things were forced back into the pre-Christian mold. Baptism became a new circumcision, now known as "christening." And this atavistic form occupied the stage all through medieval times — save of course in the camp of the "heretics." Here, in the camp of the "heretics," the suprana-tional quality of the New Testament Church remained alive in the minds of men. Small wonder that in this camp they baptized converts from "Christendom!"

Although the Reformers at first gave promise of seeking out the old paths again, the Reformation in its final thrust not only failed to expel the deformation known as "christening" but gave the ritual a new lease on life. When the Reformation was an accomplished fact, the map of Europe was covered with *Landeskirche,* sacralist units, smaller in format to be sure, and with an improved theology no doubt, but just as medieval as the old order had been. *Volk* and *Volk Gottes* were everywhere once again conceived of as one and the same thing. Nor did it alter matters appreciably when the former was referred to as the Church visible and the latter as the Church invisible,ᵏ — not any more than when the former was said to consist of *christians* and the latter of *Christians*.

The Reformers' delineation of the *Volk Gottes* commonly lacks the sophistication that the term has in the New Testament.¹ One looks in vain for a consistent awareness of the non-nationalness of the New Testament Church. One looks in vain for a careful observation of the fact that baptism marks the *Volk Gottes*, believers and their little ones, and not the *Volk* as such. Instead we read constantly that the *Volk Gottes* of the Old Testament and the *Volk Gottes* of the New are on the same plane, that of nationalhood. We hear Bucer, for example, in his rounds with the Anabaptist Jörg Schnabel, say:

> We have abundant command to accept the child. If we are to receive peoples into the fold then we have to receive them the way the people of Israel were received. And how is that? This way, 'I will be your God and the God of your seed'. I ask then whether the children are not a part of the *Volk* . . . . Our ground then is that just as the Jews were accepted so we and our children are accepted, by means of the sacrament of regeneration.³²

It is no wonder that the Anabaptists resisted this teaching. It finds no support in the New Testament. Saint Paul did not

---

ᵏIt was not until in Zwingli's thinking the ecclesiastical fellowship and the civil community had coalesced, when in the language of his admirer, Alfred Farner, "kirchliche und bürgerliche Gemeinde eins geworden sind," that the distinction of "ecclesia visibilis" and "ecclesia invisibilis" found their way into his utterances. Farner has located the exact moment when this change in Zwingli's thinking takes place: March of 1525, when in Zwingli's *Commentarius* — 'sich bei Zwingli Ansätze findet zu einer Wandlung im Kirchenbegriff . . . . Er führt ein dritte Bedeutung von 'Kirche' ein . . . . In diesem dritten Sinn wird 'Kirche' genommen für alle die sich zu Christus bekennen, auch für die Ungläubigen unter ihnen." Zwingli was prudent enough to realize that *this* Church is not in review in the Apostolic Creed, "neque de ista fit mentio in symbolo"; he should have added "neque in Scriptura," for the New Testament knows no such Church either.

¹Karl Barth has spoken of the Reformers' delineation of the *Volk Gottes* as a "theological Judaism" — with considerable justice, as it seems to us.

baptize the Thracians on this missionary journey and the Macedonians on the next. The Constantinians have set this pattern of receiving *Völker*, peoples — not the apostles, nor the primitive Church.[m]

Zwingli's delineation of the *Volk Gottes* is likewise devoid of the sophistication that marks the New Testament delineation of it. Hear him say to his Stepchildren:

> It is apparent to all who believe that the Christian covenant of the New Testament is the old covenant of Abraham save only for the fact that the Christ who was only promised to them has been made manifest to us . . . . This the figures and the types of the Old Testament make apparent. Of Isaac and Ishmael you find it recorded, in Galatians 4, that 'Esau was the first-born and was rejected; Jacob came in his place'. The intention of this is that a heathen *Volk* should after the rejection of the Jews come in their place as the *Volk Gottes*. Of the two wives of Jacob, Lea and Rachel (of whom it so happened that the former was fruitful but the latter less than

[m]Karl Barth has dwelt on this fact, saying that "the people of God as a congregation of Christ is no longer a fellowship with a *Volk* but with men taken out of families and *Völker*; the heathen now come into the spiritual Israel as beings born anew by the Spirit of God and not by tribes and families." Barth, who refers to Constantine as "Schöpfer des Systems der Christlichen Volkskirche," says that when the Church submitted to the Constantinian change she walked into the arms of "einer grossen Fiktion und Illusion, zu deutsch einer grossen Lüge." He thinks the Constantinian change led the Church to "open or secret betrayal of her holiness, her message, her witness," and he thinks the Church has paid, and must pay still further, a "heavy price for her error." Barth asks wistfully whether "now that *Christian Europe* returns with hellish laughter to its erstwhile wild freedom" the Church would not do well to admit that she represents a minority "so doing her environment a better service by being a sound Church." It is passing strange that Professor Berkouwer lets all this go in one ear and out the other, alleging that Barth's construction of things "geen aanspraak kan maken op serieus historisch onderzoek," and that it only confuses the issue to introduce the issue of "Corpus Christianum" into the discussion concerning infant baptism. Berkouwer calls Barth's argument "the least successful" he has undertaken. We shall leave it to the reader to determine who it is that has the historic record on his side, Barth or Berkouwer. (For details concerning the debate between the two theological stalwarts, the reader is referred to Berkouwer's book on *De Sacramenten* as well as his *Karl Barth en de Kinderdoop*, together with the works by Barth referred to in these two books.)

acceptable) the former stands for the rejected Jewish *Volk*; and Rachel, who finally became fruitful, signifies the heathen *Volk* which was to become an elect *Volk* to take the place of the Jews.[33]

Aside from the fact that this is intolerable allegorizing, done in order to escape out of the clutches of the Stepchildren (who ever heard of Esau being a type of the to-be-rejected Jewish *Volk* and Jacob a type of the to-be-accepted-in-their-place heathen *Volk;* not to say anything about the typology of Jacob's two wives, an allegory just as precarious), it is quite apparent that Zwingli failed to perceive that the New Testament *Volk Gottes* has a supranational quality.

Zwingli shows his hand still more plainly in the sequel where, referring to Hosea 2:23 and its statement about *Lo-ammi* (not my people), he says that "This word shows plainly that the church consisting of a gentile *Volk* has come in the place of the church consisting of the Jewish *Volk*." In connection with the saying that "Many shall come from the east and from the west" Zwingli actually glosses the word "many" with *"die menge,"* a word meaning "the whole mass." To what astounding lengths do theologians sometimes go in their ambition to find Biblical warrant for their own ideas — in this case the idea of "a Church including all in a given locality!"[n]

It is hardly necessary to point out that this was bound to irk the Stepchildren. They had discovered that the *Volk Gottes* of the New Testament is supranational, that the *Volk Gottes* of the New Testament consists of men and women drawn from every kindred, clime, and tongue. Their discovery made them averse to the "christening" they had inherited, the new cir-

---

[n]Reformed people who come to the New World from Europe seem to find it extremely difficult to accomodate themselves to the idea of a *Volk Gottes* that in no way coincides with the *Volk* as such. We shall illustrate. The Christian Reformed Church has received into its fellowship a great many Dutch immigrants of late, especially immigrants that have come to live in Canada. The idea of a Church that is partly in Canada and partly in the States seems to give these people great difficulty. There is a persistent attempt therefore to carve out, at the very least, a Provincial Synod the southern border of which would coincide with the degree of latitude that marks the border between the States and Canada. In this way *Volk* and *Volk Gottes* would be identified once more.

cumcision, whereby the supranational *Volk Gottes* was identified once more with *Volk* as such.

One final matter requires our attention. The reader will
recall that Bucer spoke of baptism as "the sacrament of regeneration." This is an expression that has Biblical warrant.
But as soon as baptism is made coextensive with infant baptism
this expression becomes somewhat difficult. Men have invented
the idea of baptismal regeneration to get away from the difficulty, also the concept of "presumed regeneration" in the case
of baptized little ones, an expression that has in turn given
rise to a great deal of bickering and dissension. No matter
how we turn it, the link between the baptism of an infant
and the regeneration of that infant is one that is far removed from experience, in time at least. The Stepchildren
sought to bind baptism and regeneration more closely together in experience. For them baptism was a high point in
the experience of a Christian. A favorite text with them was
1 Peter 3:21: "Whereunto baptism doth also now save us,
not the putting away of the filth of the flesh, but the answer of
a good conscience toward God." For them baptism bound
together all that God has done redemptively, *for* man and *in*
man; and they were inclined to stress the latter (just as their
opponents were inclined to stress the former). They felt that
when a man was properly placed under the water, this was
a pledge that he was not only right with God but that, by
going down into death and rising again in newness of life,
he was also, in principle at least, once more a being with
whom God was pleased. Needless to say, the moment of
their baptism was a high point in their total religious experience.

Anyone who has read in the New Testament will know that
in this the Stepchildren were on good New Testament ground.
Baptism does indeed signify a dying unto sin and a rising
again unto newness of life. But, strange though this may
sound, the Reformers disliked what the Stepchildren said in
this matter. So long had baptism and the language of baptism
dealt with things that lie far removed from conscious experience,
that when the Anabaptists contended that in the moment of
baptism they experienced "*grosse erkickung des gemüts,*" great
refreshing of soul, their opponents called this claim "*nur ein*

altwybisch und närrisch geplerr," old wives tales and the prattle of fools. For good measure Zwingli added:

> If they hold to this then they had better have themselves baptized not just once but over and over again, a thousand times. For if the baptism with water renewed and strengthened and comforted the soul then no one would withhold it from himself but would have himself baptized again and again, as often as he was assailed. Then the repeated lustrations or baptisms of the Old Testament would be re-introduced.[34]

We shall leave it to the theologically mature to decide whether the Stepchildren were not right as they sought to recover something of an existential dimension in the rite of baptism. Zwingli's doctrine at this point indicates that such recovery was highly needful.

At another point, Zwingli responded to the Stepchildren's claim that in baptism they experienced inner exhilaration by saying:

> Good news! Let's all go for a plunge in the Limmat! Let every pious Christian observe with what fabrications the old enemy comes now to trick us in order to divide us. He sees that otherwise the matter will make good headway; and so he has to divide us![35]

Manifestly Zwingli wanted the unity of *Corpus Christianum* preserved — cost what it may, even if it required a denial of the New Testament teaching that some have experienced salvation and some not, even if it required the patently apocryphal idea that all men in "Christendom" are regenerate, in some fashion at least.

Zwingli's "most unkindest cut of all" occurred when he said, "Let him who talks about 'going under' go under [the water]!" It may well have been this unkind word that inspired men to truss up Felix Manz so that he could not swim, and to send him thus bound to the bottom of the Limmat! Manz had talked about "going under" in baptism; well then let him have his fill of it! If such advice seems far from the spirit of Christ, as indeed it is, then let the reader ponder that *fallenness* bears frightful fruit, in churches as well as in the human race.

Robert Friedmann has said that "the main line of Protestant theology is a onesided interpretation of the Pauline teaching of justification by faith; although including this doctrine in its foundation, sixteenth-century Anabaptism shows definitely a different orientation." With the Reformers there is indeed an imbalance between the forensic and the moral, between salvation *as pardon* and salvation *as renewal*. Against this imbalance the Stepchildren braced themselves from the very first; and it was this different orientation that made them feel less than happy in the parade headed by Luther. This difference between the two parties came to expression very clearly in the doctrine of baptism. For the Reformers, baptism speaks principally of pardon; for their Stepchildren, it speaks as eloquently of renewal. Although there was nothing being said that the Reformers needed as badly to hear, they stopped their ears, as it were. Fortunately for us the old hymn has been written: "Be of sin the double cure, save from wrath and make me pure." In this hymn the imbalance of the Reformers has been overcome (significantly, this hymn does not emanate from the mainline stream of the continental Reformation).°

How the Stepchildren fought to rectify the imbalance of which we have spoken may be gathered from the words of one of them, Peter Tesch, who as he spoke for a band of Anabaptists incarcerated at Marburg put forth the following confession:

> We believe and confess from the heart that we and all the children of Adam are so corrupted by original sin that we and all men would be with justice condemned by God forever, we along with our and their good works. Also, that we receive forgiveness of sins, the Holy Spirit, freedom, and the new birth and salvation, only through the merits of our Lord Jesus Christ, when we truly and with the whole heart believe. This is that first righteous-making, which the Scriptures ascribe to faith in Christ, without any work or merit or contribution by man, yes, without his will, prayer or desire, solely through faith in the mercy and the grace of God in Christ Jesus. However, this faith must be engaged in all good works through love, which it is capable of doing, in Christ — all things

----

°A second hymn in which the imbalance of the Reformers is surmounted is that hymn in which it is said that "He breaks the power of cancelled sin . . . !" Here also a link is forged between *pardon* and *renewal*. Significantly, this hymn also does not stem from the mainline continental Reformation.

being possible and even light, which were previously unpleasant and arduous. Of this kind however there are, if we look carefully, but very few as yet, persons who have a true, a living, a potent and saving faith; Instead we see, by and large, a dead, barren faith and an empty imagination, in that men do not only omit to do the good but also perform the evil, voluntarily and freely. Therefore it will not help those who boast of such a faith, with which they put themselves at ease in the midst of all boldness, lasciviousness, and excess . . . . This is predicated of the bold, the audacious, the unfruitfully believing Christians (who in reality are unbelievers) and it is not applicable to the weak, the right-minded believers or the imperfect Christians, who can still slip and slide and fall, but who remain unrejected, seeing that they love the moral improvement in Christ. Therefore we think it necessary that in the sermons everywhere a faithful warning and admonition be given and that it be insisted on that even as the inability to do the good is in us by reason of original sin so the ability to do the good is present through faith in Jesus Christ, from God and of grace . . . , so that if one is somewhat faithful (which is much) so also will the greater that is needed unto salvation be given. In this way offensive men may have taken away from them the false excuse for their open blasphemy.[36]

We submit that this is not bad theology. In it we detect an emphasis that was greatly needed, in Reformation times and in any and every age. There is a world of truth in the assertion, heard to this day at the end of the worship service among the Amish, those descendants of the Stepchildren, that when salvation has come full circle there, in principle at least, "God is once more satisfied with us."[p] Of this baptism spoke to the

---

[p]No doubt there are dangers inherent in this representation, so dear to the heart of the Amish believer. The danger of Pharisaic self-congratulation, for example, is close at hand. However this is true of all of Christian truth. Each and every item can easily lead to abuse. Think of what men have made of the concept of salvation by grace apart from human merit! In Paul's day there were already people who said "Then let us sin for all we're worth." It must be remembered that Luther's idea of *simul justus ac peccator* is likewise open to grave misunderstanding and open error; it can lead to the monstrous notion that the believer, the saved man, is a sinner still *in the same sense* as heretofore. In fact, the concept of *sola fide* can become the occasion for frightful heresy, as men had already discovered when the Epistle of James was being written.

Stepchildren, "the answer of a good conscience toward God" (1 Peter 3:21). Realizing that in the traditional baptismal practice the language of inner renewal had quite died down, they went about to restore it.

It was the Stepchildren's agonized attempt to divest the institution of baptism of corruptions of long standing, and to return it to its pristine significance and signification, that earned for them the spiteful name of *Wiedertäufer.*

7   *Kommunisten*

*As though they possessed
not . . . . I Cor. 7:30*

STILL ANOTHER AREA OF TENSION BETWEEN THE REFORMERS
and their Stepchildren involved what was known as "community of goods." It finds its classic expression in Article 36
of the Belgic Confession, where we read: "Wherefore we
detest the Anabaptists and other seditious folk, and in general
all those who reject the higher powers and magistrates and
would subvert justice, introduce community of goods, and
confound that decency and good order which God has established among men." Here the charge that the Stepchildren
"reject the higher powers and magistrates" (which charge
we have already weighed) is followed by the charge that they
"would introduce community of goods"; and this is further
expanded in the words "and confound that decency and good
order which God has established among men."

On the face of it this sounds very much like a translation of
an ancient cliché in the German. There is in the German
language an ancient idiom, used through the centuries to
describe the "heretic"; he was said to be a person whose
ambition it was to put an end to *alle Ober- und Erbarkeit* (all
magistracy and all decency). This idiom seems to lie behind
the wording of the Belgic Confession. The lilt and the alliteration were of course lost in the translation but the idea was
preserved, namely that the "heretic" had two ambitions: (1) to
"overthrow the magistracy," and (2) to "put an end to all
decency," a feature of which was the ambition to introduce
"community of goods."

221

We have indicated that this was an ancient cliché. It was by no means invented when the Second Front was opened; for it had been bandied about for a long, long time already. Leo the Great had already said around the year 450: "Heretics overthrow all order and decency . . . . By them every care of honesty is removed, every compact of marriage dissolved, all law, divine and human alike, is subverted."[1] This accusation became standard procedure and this feature became a part of the stereotyped delineation of the "heretic." It quite automatically devolved upon the Stepchildren.

That this was so may be gathered from a memorandum which the archbishop of Cologne sent to the Emperor in 1535, a memorandum intended to alert the emperor to the dangers allegedly lurking in the Anabaptist vision. Said the archbishop: "The Anabaptists wish to redivide all properties etc. — just as the nature of the Anabaptists has always been, even as the ancient chronicles and the Imperial laws made a thousand years ago do testify."[2] Here was a well-informed man who, as he saw the Anabaptist movement coming up, recalled the ancient cliché that "heretics" have radical ideas in the area of economics; for a millennium or more, he recalls, rebaptizers have been inclined that way.

There was an element of truth in this ancient cliché. The "heretics" had indeed, from very early times, revealed certain sensitivities in the general area of "mine and thine," sensitivities that the Constantinians disliked, disliked so much that they called it a matter of "community of goods." A group of these "heretics," apprehended in the vicinity of Turin in the year 1030, had confessed that "All our possessions we have in common with all men."

So much was this a stereotype that when the attack upon Luther was first launched this too was thrown at him, that he advocated "community of goods." When people heard that there was a new "heretic," the "heretic" of Wittenberg, they automatically included this in the report.[3]

There is reason to believe that the cliché of which we speak had its roots in the Donatist rebellion. The French scholar Martroye has written:

> It is to be noted that Donatism began when the orthodox clergy became the ally and protege of the Emperors. Apparently the

Christians had seen in Christianity the promise of a new social order and they considered it tantamount to surrender to accomodate themselves to the social organizations represented by the Emperor. The orthodox priests were considered traitors . . . because they seemed to have betrayed the religion itself.[4]

Certain it is that, whatever was novel in the economic vision of early Christianity, this was again lost in and with the Constantinian change. The economic conscience, if indeed there was one in medieval society, can hardly be said to have derived from the New Testament writings; one does not have to go beyond the writings of ethnic origin to locate the sources of medieval ideas of economic justice.

Two things stand out very clearly in the Christian Scriptures in regard to mine and thine. One of these is that no man is ever in absolute possession; only God owns absolutely; and this precludes absolute ownership by men, His creatures. Human beings, according to these Scriptures, are at all times amenable to God in the matter of ownership. This makes human ownership to be always less than absolute.

A second thing that stands out clearly in the Christian Scriptures concerning "mine and thine" is that since the earth and its riches have been entrusted to mankind as a whole, no individual man may ever hold things as though he were alone on the earth. The fact that there are other human beings puts a further check upon the idea of ownership. This points to a moral problem connected with being a possessor. The moral problem of coming by one's possessions honestly is by no means the only problem which the Christian vision posits. Perhaps it may even be said that in this vision the moral problem only *begins* at the point of lawful acquisition. The Parable of the Rich Man and Lazarus does not address itself to the problem of *acquiring* honestly but to a subsequent problem, the problem of *holding* property in the context of human suffering. Dives went to hell in the Parable because he lived in luxury with not so much as a thought for the privation that lay at his doorstep.

Moreover, no sin is scored so frequently nor rebuked so

severely in the New Testament as the sin of *pleonexia,* whatever that is. The word means, literally, "much-having" or "more-having." This word has been translated, very conveniently, with the English word *avarice,* a word meaning some *inordinate* craving for wealth. So translated, it loses most of its cutting edge, for one can always persuade himself that his own desire for enlarged possession does not exceed the limits of the correct and proper. Whether "more-having" connotes the ambition to have more than one's rightful share, or, more than one's neighbor has, or whatever, it certainly lies very close to unrestrained, undisciplined, conscienceless acquisition.

The question has been raised, and the final answer is still to be given, as to whether capitalism is the legitimate offspring of Christianity. Much depends on one's use of the word "Christianity." If by Christianity one means "Christendom," then it could very well be that the product of that Christendom is that irresponsible capitalism that is now happily on the run. But if by Christianity one means the life and world view that stares at us from the pages of the New Testament then it must be said that Christianity has never supported conscienceless ownership. Irresponsible "mine and thine" is the child of sacralist "Christendom" and not of authentic Christianity.

It was felt, and said, in medieval times that when the Church "fell" the economic insights that were uniquely Christian went into eclipse. A fifteenth-century rebel put it this way: "All that is evil comes from the Latins; they posit the *jus quiritum militare,* this is mine and that is thine, with which they wreck all kindness and the love of God, for Roman law is contrary to natural and divine law, and from it all envy and hatred have taken their origin." This rebel went on to date the moment of the great innovation of evil: "the Donation of Constantine laid the foundation for the deterioration; and greed and avarice have from that time reared their heads mightily among the clergy."

It is apparent from the above quotation that it was especially the callous wealth of the clergy that irked those who rebelled against the medieval orde.. The clergy did indeed eat of the fat of the land; their standard of living was incomparably much

higher than that of the common man.* Save for the bankers
perhaps, the Church's men were the only ones who could
afford brocaded cloth and ermine. Small wonder that in the
eyes of the Restitutionists some of the outstanding sins were
the sins of pomp and pride, of avarice and exhibition, the very
sins that later re-appear as outstanding sins in the eyes of the
Stepchildren.

It goes without saying that the "heretics'" ideal priest was
the priest in homespun. "How can anyone recognize under the
regalia of the pope a disciple of Jesus Christ?" they asked
wistfully. The Poor Men of Lyons, otherwise called the Waldensians, wore undyed wool by way of contrast, and alleged
that "all who are proud are sons of the devil."

This evaluation of wealth and splendor, this rebuke of callous
wealth, passed over into the camp of the Stepchildren, as a
cursory glance at the record makes apparent. One needs only
to consider the contemporary descendants of these Stepchildren,
our Mennonites, to see the connection. Here we still find
clergymen who wear frocks with hooks and eyes rather than
buttons, who wear no ties or jewelry — and that as a matter
of principle, these being considered evidences of pretentious
living.

This high appraisal of frugal living was quite non-existent
in the camp of the Reformers and therefore did not take its
origin in the events that began in 1517. One needs to read but
little of the Anabaptist literature to discover that here the sin
of gluttony and similar excess stands at the head of the list
of deadly sins, in a unique way. Men who think that "a basic
dualism" is the key to the understanding of Anabaptism have
sought to derive this Anabaptist peculiarity from it, a sort of
neo-Platonic vilification of the flesh; but it is more likely that
this sensitivity resulted from the conviction that he who over-
eats is thereby denying to some fellow-man the very necessities

*It is said that when Pope John XXII died (in 1334), he had amassed
a fortune of 25,000,000 florins. For purposes of comparison we may
observe that at about the same time, the ransom demanded by the
ruffians who had abducted the King of France was set at 800,000 florins,
a sum which his subjects had difficulty raising. John XXII may have
been exceptional in his avarice, but it was only too true that the
Church was the outstanding possessor in those times. (For details see
Coulton, *Inquisition and Liberty*, p. 217.)

of life. It is therefore related to the sensitivity that earned the
Stepchildren the charge of "community of goods."

As the late Dr. Lydia Müller saw, with a bit of womanly
intuition perhaps (for she was, generally speaking, no friend
of the idea that Anabaptism has roots that go far back of
1517), this trait in the Anabaptists is a "Waldensian heritage."
It will be recalled that Peter Waldo began his career by
selling all that he had and giving it to the poor. It was so much
a part of this earlier eruption of protest against the Church's
fallenness that the Waldensians were commonly known as the
Poor Men of Lyons. These "heretics" were great sharers,
noted exponents of "community of goods."[b]

Another feature in the Biblical vision concerning mine and
thine is the prohibition of usury. This word, which has come
to stand for a too-high rate of interest, does not in the Christian Scriptures have to do with interest rates. It has to do with
human distress. In pre-modern times men borrowed money
only in emergencies; and the prohibitions were to prevent one
man from lining his pockets with another man's misery. What
was forbidden was the cashing-in on the distress of a man who
had been overtaken by calamity. This sensitivity was lost in
the medieval world; only a regulation as to rates of interest
remained. It is no wonder that in the Restitutionist vision the
taking of usury was likewise under fire. It was prominent in
the assaults lodged by the Stepchildren in Reformation times.
As such it is closely related to the clamor for "community of
goods." Both are integral parts of a protest against irresponsible
ownership; both are features of a desire to return to the
sensitivities that run in the Scriptures as they deal with mine
and thine.

Associated with the charge of "community of goods" we
frequently find the charge of "community of wives." The origin
of this companion accusation is not in all respects clear. In all

---

[b] It is true, one finds a similar exaltation of voluntary poverty among
certain groups that continued within the Church, the Mendicants for
example. We know that the Church sometimes took over certain features
of the "heretics" in order to take the wind out of their sails, as it were,
and fight fire with fire. It created an order of itinerant priests in an
effort to counteract the *Leufer*. It could be that in a similar way
voluntary poverty within the Church was devised in order to off-set the
effect of the voluntary poverty of the "heretics."

likelihood it is connected with the image of the "heretic" which
was constructed in pre-Constantinian times in the assaults made
upon the early Christians, an image which was then conveniently transferred in post-Constantinian times to the Restitutionist "heretic." The idea of a "love-feast," celebrated in
total darkness or in greatly subdued light as a safety measure,
was enough to stimulate the imaginations of the early Christians' pagan neighbors and so give rise to unsavory tales, the
more so since many an ancient religious cult had gone hand in
hand with sexual abandon. When we find the enemies of the
medieval "heretics" repeating these pre-Constantinian charges,
sometimes quite verbatim, we are led to say that the accusation
of "community of wives" was an ancient, extremely ancient,
cliché, one that was a millennium and a half old when it was
hurled after the Stepchildren. Such legends are extremely
long-lived.[c]

It is also possible and even likely that the slur of "wives in
common" was fed by the fact that the Restitutionists, who
avoided the Church's "sacrament of matrimony," cohabited in
a way that must have looked quite irregular. It was difficult
or even impossible for an outsider to know for sure which
woman went with which man, there being no such thing as a
civil record of marriage. This situation afforded a fine opportunity to raise the cry of "community of wives."

In all events, the charge was a cliché, part of a legend which
men repeated uncritically. How uncritically may be gathered
from the fact that the unbelievably vulgar priest, Broer Cornelis
as he was called, ascribed the same evil behavior to the
Calvinists. He had accused the Anabaptist Jacob de Keer-
segieter of "wives in common"; in an effort to show how
intolerable was this slur, his Anabaptist victim said: "We are
not the only ones who have to hear this from your lips, you
preach this likewise, so I hear, concerning the Calvinists." To
this Broer Cornelis then replied: "They do indeed also have
their wives in common. Don't you think I know what it is

[c]How persistent some of these ancient vilifications can be may be
gathered from the following. In 1950, during a stay in the Netherlands,
the present writer was told, not by some credulous fish-wife but by a
professional man, that "When the Baptists celebrate the Lord's Supper
it all ends in a frightful promiscuity."

they do when they blow out the candles after they have had
their accursed devilish Supper?" What we have here is simply
this. Broer Cornelis considered the Calvinists to be "heretics";
by that token they "have their wives in common." So stereotyped was the image of the "heretic."

All this determined the lot of the Stepchildren. They too
cohabited without the benefit of the Church's ceremony. They
too were therefore under suspicion of "repudiating marriage."
But, since children continued to be born, it was apparent that
they did cohabit. But, by having their "wives in common."

Here was a chance for their foes to apply pressures. It
was decided "to record every marriage that has ecclesiastical
status so as to know who cohabits lawfully and who not;
then all who are not honorably joined are to be driven either
to the Church or to separation."[5] Very similar steps were taken
in 1601 in the Reformed city of Groningen.[6]

Finally, it may be that the charge of "wives in common" was
fed by the fact that Anabaptist husbands travelled a great deal,
partly because of their urge to carry the Gospel to others and
partly as a safety measure. During their absence their wives
and little ones would be parcelled out with other members
of the fellowship. This could lead to the suspicion that the
woman who lived now under this roof and anon under that
was "held in common." This would also explain how that,
occasionally at least, the slur of "wives in common" went hand
in hand with the charge of "children in common."

The charge of "community of wives" was a false charge. It
did not result from observation; rather was it an ancient cliché,
which came to people's minds whenever they heard the word
"heretic." For example, no sooner had the archbishop of Mainz,
Johann Cochlaeus, been informed of the fact that there were
18,000 Anabaptists in Germany, than he reached for his pen
and in a letter of January 8, 1528, urged Erasmus of Rotterdam
to prepare a book against them, specifying that there should
be a chapter in the projected book on the Anabaptist tenet
"that all things should be held in common, wives, virgins,
temporal goods, etc."[7]

John Calvin did his bit to keep alive the ancient slur about
"wives in common." In his writings against the Anabaptists
he repeated the accusation[8] — with as much justice as when

Broer Cornelis levelled the same charge at Calvin and his followers![d]

In his Tracts against the Anabaptists, Calvin slides from the charge of "wives in common" to that of "goods in common."[e] He says, "Now in order not to leave any order at all among men they commit a similar confusion as to possessions, saying that it is part of the Communion of the saints that no one possesses anything as his own but that each ought to take what he can get." But Calvin makes this charge gingerly, puts it in the past tense, saying, "At the first there were indeed some mixed-up Anabaptists who talked that way, but after such absurdity had been rejected by all as being repugnant to human sense . . . they have become ashamed of it." What had happened is that two decades of laboratory proof had demonstrated that "community of goods" was not an integral part of the Anabaptist vision — so that Calvin refrained from putting it in the present tense. One could wish that he had pointed out who had in the earlier days repudiated "mine and thine" only then to repudiate the repudiation. He would have found it hard to document this thesis. We find him on the one hand granting in substance that contemporary Anabaptists did not advocate "community of goods," and on the

[d]Calvin's misrepresentation of the Anabaptists must have had serious consequences seeing the wide publicity his tracts received, having been translated at once into English and Dutch. These tracts, perhaps more than anything else that was put in print, turned the tide of the Reform from the Restitutionist vision in which it had run hitherto and into the channels of neo-Constantinianism. It has been said of late (by Franklin H. Littell, in his *The Anabaptist View of the Church,* p. 7) concerning Calvin, that "Among widely read authors probably none understood them [the Anabaptists] less." Certainly it is true, as the same historian asserts, Calvin's writings "lent misunderstanding to the historiography of the Anabaptists."

[e]To Calvin's credit it may be said that he was one of the first to realize that not all "Anabaptists" were birds of a feather, writing two Tracts, one against the "furious" Anabaptists and one against the milder kind. This was a step in the right direction. At the same time, as Littell has pointed out (*op. et loc. cit.*), when Calvin attacked the free-thinking Spirituals at Geneva, he thought that he was dealing with the same movement that had expressed itself at Schlatten am Rande, a regrettable confusion. Calvin "made no distinction between the Spirituals and the Biblicist wings of the movement — if, indeed, he knew there was such a distinction."

other hand assailing the idea — so whipping a dead horse, as it were.

But, at that, the dead horse had never been alive. The early Anabaptists, generally speaking, did not teach what Calvin lays to their charge. Perhaps the fact that Calvin did not read German (the language in which just about all writing that is Anabaptist was couched), so that he had to have everything at second hand, may have contributed to Calvin's unfair treatment of the Stepchildren. The saying is that if a man wants to hurl a stone at a dog he can usually find the stone; Calvin was out to get the Anabaptists, primarily because they stood in the way of his idea of reform sponsored by magistrate; in his eagerness to make a good case he gave them less than a fair deal.

Consider the example of Schlatten am Rande. In the manifesto put forward there, nothing is said about the doctrine of the incarnation — for the quite sufficient reason that in 1527 there were as yet no tensions touching this item. But when Calvin wrote his tracts against the Anabaptists the situation had changed. Menno Simons, following Melchior Hofmann, had abandoned the orthodox view concerning the incarnation. Rather than admit that in 1527 there had been no occasion to say anything about the matter, Calvin suggests that the silence of 1527 was due to bad faith, a "cunning trick" (*par cautelle*), "seeing that their doctrine is curse-worthy."[9] Surely this is less than fair.

Nor was Calvin alone in this unfair treatment; the Reformers generally were so emotionally involved in the battle that raged at the Second Front that they were unable to pass a fair judgment concerning it. It would have been quite impossible to find twelve men who would be acceptable as jury members at the trial of the Stepchildren. A man like Zwingli for instance, who said with a straight face: "The Anabaptists have their wives in common and meet at night . . . for lewd practices . . ."[10] had already disqualified himself.[f] One can only regret the

[f] How tendentious the testimony of the Reformers touching the Anabaptists was may be gathered from the fact that they said of them also that they lived exemplary lives, but that this was nothing but a device of the devil, bait put on the hook in order to catch more people. These testimonies cannot both be true. There was therefore an inner contradiction in the Reformers' testimony concerning their Stepchildren.

un-Christian charges hurled at the Stepchildren: "As often as you confess Christ you make a confession which is worse than that of the demons; for they had experienced His power, in such measure that they sincerely confessed Him to be the Son of God, but you, when you confess Him, do so hypocritically."[11] This allegation was uncalled for, no matter how one looks at it. It was the direct result of an uncritical acceptance of an ancient cliché, one that only time could wear down.

Only so can we understand how it was that when Anabaptist prisoners denied everything that even remotely resembled "community of wives and of goods," men only turned the thumbscrews tighter or drew the rack up closer. So sure were they that the "real" Anabaptist was hiding behind the empirical one, that they were unable to believe their own eyes and ears. And so, back to the rack!

When Zwingli laid the charge of "community of goods" against Hübmaier, in 1526, the man answered:

> I have always and at all places spoken about community of goods as follows: that a man must at all times be concerned for his fellow man, in order that the hungry may be fed, the thirsty given to drink, the naked clothed. For we are verily not lords over our own possessions, only administrators and dispensers. There is, believe me, no one who advocates taking another man's goods and making it common — then rather leave to him the coat as well as the mantle![12]

That should have put an end to the accusation — at least until there was empirical evidence of a contrary thrust. But to expect that would be to forget what a hold the tradition had on men. Zwingli and the rest kept making the accusation, just as he made the charge (printed above) a year after this same Hübmaier had testified:

> I am being suspected of wanting to make all things common. But this I have not done. I have the rather called that a Christian community of goods where one who has the wherewithal and who sees his neighbor suffering want then distributes his alms to him, with which the hungry, the thirsty, and the naked, and those in prison may be helped. The more a person practices such acts of compassion the closer he comes to a Christian mode of existence.[13]

When Jörg Dorsch, another Anabaptist prisoner, was instructed to inform the Court "what the Anabaptist rule, order, or intention or conspiracy may be," he replied:

> I verily know of nothing concerning any rule, order, or conspiracy which I share with other Anabaptists, save only this, that when a poor person who has received the sign^g comes to another Anabaptist he is to be given that on which he may exist. No one is required to give to another that which he himself needs . . . . I have not heard that they wish to be against the magistracy or that their intention is that all goods, wives, and children are to be held in common or be free to all comers.[14]

Heinrich Seiler, an Anabaptist from Arnau, said at his trial, in 1529, when asked to state his ideas in regard to "community of goods": "I allow that a Christian man owns property — in such a way, that when there are needy people he shares with them and deals correctly with them in the matter, for he is no more than a steward thereof."^h

Felix Manz, who was drowned in the Limmat for his Anabaptist convictions, gave as his idea touching property: "A good Christian shares with his neighbor when the latter is in need."

Concerning August Wurzlburger the Clerk of Courts wrote down:

> The thrust of his position is that the people of this sect are minded not to let any one live by begging, but the rather that they who have more than enough lay money together and

---

^gI.e., the sign of baptism, believers' baptism, as administered among the Anabaptists. The reader will observe that whatever the Anabaptists meant by "community of goods" it was intended for those who *belonged;* it did not contemplate society in general.

^hThis idea, that ownership is nothing more than stewardship and that he who possesses must answer both to God and to his fellow man, led the Anabaptists to a sort of "Christian Conservationism," the idea that a man must use the resources of the earth in such a way as not to deprive later generations of what is rightly theirs. Moreover, it was felt that the government has an assignment in this matter, must keep men from stripping the earth bare, as it were. We find the Anabaptist Jörg Schnabel saying that the civil magistrate is "van got verordenet . . . , dan wann neit oberheit were, es wur wider holz noch feld gedeien mögen, es wurden auch weinig fleische einer dem andern gleichs tun, seintemal die fleischliche art so gar verdorben ist, das sei neit weiter dan das ihr sucht und der nachkomling weinig acht hat" (*Quellen Hesse,* p. 178).

give sustenance from this. He who is able to work and fails to do so, but chooses to rely on this arrangement, him they bar from their communion and let him pass for a heathen. He says he knows nothing besides this concerning any order, rule, or community of goods.[15]

Andres auf den Stultzen, an Anabaptist pioneer (so named because he walked with crutches), outlined his ideas in matters of economics as follows:

The man who doesn't need it, be he clergy or lay person, and practices usury with his prebendary or otherwise, or lays up more goods than he needs in order the more royally to take care of his fat belly, such a man, when compared with a man with needy children who steals because of poverty, in an effort to find a way out for himself and his little ones, such a man is no better in God's sight than the man who steals out of poverty.[16]

Hans Scherer said that he had heard this Andres say that "If a man has a big income and with this drives a poor man from his homestead or field, such a man is more wicked than a thief, in God's sight.[1]

Georg Blaurock, still another Anabaptist pioneer (so named because he wore a blue coat), testified: "I do not advocate community of goods; however a man that is a Christian will

[1]Even secular jurisprudence has come to see the justice of the philosophy here set forth; in many States a creditor cannot divest a man of his shelter, that which stands between him and the elements, no matter how great is his indebtedness. This exemption was already provided in the Old Testament; one could not take and keep as security a man's coat, but had to return it before nightfall, when he would be needing it as bed under him and cover over him. (Cf. Deut. 24:10-14.) It was forbidden to take either the nether or the upper millstone in payment for debt, for that would be to "take a man's livelihood in pledge" (Deut. 24:6). The medieval world had completely forgotten these humane laws; it sold men into slavery for debt, imprisoned them for debt, without the slightest qualm. The Reformers, although quick to quote the Old Testament when it could serve them, did not recover the Biblical vision which Andres auf den Stultzen is here enunciating. It must be said that the recovery of it, when it came, did not come as the result of the pulpit; it came the rather as the result of the pamphleteer and the journalist. It was the humanizing tendency of the Renaissance rather than the Reformation that gained the victory, these, fed perhaps by the spade work done by the Anabaptists.

dispense of his goods, otherwise he is not a good Christian."

Conrad Grebel, often considered the father of Anabaptism, said that he "never taught that we must not obey the magistrate; I do not recall that any such matter was discussed as "community of goods."

Julius Leuber, also an Anabaptist, declared before the Court: "As to community of wives I would say that if anyone teaches that, his doctrine is of the devil and not of God. However, as to community of goods, I am obliged to help the brother near me, out of brotherly love and without being coerced."

To the charge of "community of goods" Menno Simons replied with: "This charge is false and without truth." He went on by quoting Scripture, as follows: "If there be among you a poor man, one of your brethren, within your gates . . . thou shalt not harden thine heart or shut thy hand from thy poor brother." Then he added, with an apparent sense of victory, that although his people had an abnormally large number of indigent ones, thanks to the persecutions and confiscations, "yet not one of the devout who have joined themselves to us,[1] nor any of their orphaned children, have been left to beg their way . . . . This mercy, this love, this community of goods we do teach . . . . If this is not Christian practice then we might as well abandon the whole Gospel of our Lord Jesus Christ, his holy sacraments and the Christian name." He then turned upon those who pressed the charge, "Shame on you . . . , you who have been unable with your Gospel and sacraments to remove your needy ones from the streets, even though the Scriptures say plainly enough: 'whosoever hath this world's goods and seeth his brother in need and shutteth up his compassion for him, how dwelleth the love of God in him?'" One would expect that such a reply would put a damper on the charge of "community of goods" as something frightfully wrong, at least until there was some tangible evidence pointing that way.

But that was not possible, it seems, to men reared on a diet

---

[1]The reader will observe again that whatever the Anabaptists had in mind in regard to "community of goods," it was something intended not for society in general but for a "brotherhood" that came by voluntary association. As we have had occasion to say before, there is nothing vicious about such an arrangement.

of sacralism. After similar protestation they took the Anabaptists to the torture chamber. We read:

> . . . he was thrice stretched; he prays God to give him grace to bear the torture. He is told to confess in plain language why he has left the pure teachings as taught by Martin Luther and others . . . . Something more must lurk behind all this, namely, that you desire to destroy all government and have all things in common. And even though you say that this community of goods is meant for you and your people only, yet your heart and ambition are far different, in actuality to have the goods of all men in common.

How could this man, with his pain-tortured body, say more? What if a man's solemn assertions, made under such duress, are thrown to the winds?

> God forbid that we should be against government or act contrary to it . . . ; we must be obedient to them, whether they be good or bad . . . . And as to community of goods, no one is forced among us to put his property in a common treasury and we have no intention of making it common by force. But he who possesses and then sees his brother or sister in need, he is duty bound in love and without constraint to help and to succor.[17]

Nothing helped. These Stepchildren posed a threat to the sacral society; and that, to a person of sacralist thought habits, made them nihilists. Only so can we understand the advice, given by a committee of clergymen in Bavaria, in 1528, touching the Anabaptists:

> That they have their goods in common and bring them together, each member voluntarily, without constraining any to bring all or even a specified portion of it, this we do not consider an intolerable thing or worthy of punishment. Nor are we able to quote Scripture that militates against it.

But these clergymen, nevertheless, were certain that there was something very sinister about the whole movement — the book said so. And so they continued:

> And yet it is to be feared that where such a small beginning is allowed to go on, permitted and tolerated, then it might with the passing of time increase and attain to greater and more inclusive evil. Therefore our opinion is that also such a

confessedly trivial and not very culpable plan should be met and obviated with suitable counter-measures, in view of what is likely to develop out of it.[18]

Against such logic it is futile to argue — as the Stepchildren found out to their dismay.

From the advice given by the Bavarian clergymen, just quoted, it is apparent that they were acquainted with that sector of the Second Front that followed Jakob Hutter and practiced communal holding of property. These people, known to us as Hutterites, continue to do so to this day, in some of our western plains states and in Canada. The story of the origin of this practice among the Hutterites is a pathetic one. It was among a band of fleeing refugees, men and women and little children, who had no roof over their heads other than the forest, having been driven from their homesteads because of their faith. The leader among them, in anguish of soul, spread out his coat on the grass, threw such coins as he himself had upon it, and bade all those who would follow Christ and His Cross to do likewise. All complied. It was here that the Hutterite practice of group ownership originated. In keeping with Acts 2 and 4 several *Diener der Notdurft* were provided to see to it that each one's needs were met as the common fund allowed. Under the leadership of Peter Ridemann and Peter Walpot this voluntarily-accepted way of life was developed and grounded confessionally, so that today it is a matter of principle still.[k]

It should be remembered that even these Hutterites did not think of foisting their views upon others nor of divesting any man of his belongings against his will. One had to agree to such communal ownership to be accepted into the fellowship;[1] but one joined it by an act of free will. There is cer-

---

[k]The Anabaptists as a whole "neither praised nor defended" the Hutterite idea, that of combining mine and thine in social holding. We read "Dass aber in Mehren gemeinschaft der güter haben, wollen sie nit loben noch verteidigen" (*Quellen IV*, p. 193).

[1]In a few instances there were people who had joined the Hutterite *Brüderschaften*, who had therefore put their assets in the common treasury, and who then decided to quit this association — these people did complain that they were unable to recover anything. This constituted a complicated problem, one that in all likelihood would not be solved to everybody's satisfaction.

tainly nothing vicious about this way of life; if there were, then the little company that followed Jesus was a vicious lot.

And there was Münster, the city in Westphalia where the Anabaptist movement resorted to measures which were later to prove a disgrace to them. Here the Anabaptist leaders did divest those who had remained in the city (long under siege by the armies of the bishop) of their possessions, ordered them to bring their stores into a central commissary, out of which supplies were then rigidly rationed. No doubt there were many in the ill-fated city who brought their goods against their will.

But it must be remembered that the Münster tragedy occurred after many years of frightful suffering, almost a decade of burnings and garrotings, banishments and incarcerations, not to mention the torturings. The leaders of the Münster rebellion were men who revealed a condition very like unto battle fatigue. In our day they would have been hustled off to an institution. Surely a man who alleges that he has been instructed by the Almighty to behead his own lawfully wedded wife, would in our more enlightened times be hauled off to a place where he could not harm himself or others. Professor Gooch has said that the outburst at Münster "must be traced to oppression which goaded men to madness," and with this one can easily agree. As is commonly the case with men deranged, there was present an apocalypticism and a messianism, with hallucinations thrown in.

Much has been made of Münster; to this day, especially with men with a sacralist hangover, it affords an easy dismissal of all that the Stepchildren lived, and died, to achieve. But Münster was far from being typical of Anabaptism as such. As that great historian Toynbee has said, Münster was "a caricature of the movement." Or, to quote Professor Gooch once more, "the tragedy of Münster drew attention to a phase of the movement that was far from typical of its real nature." Münster must be dealt with as the lunatic fringe of Anabaptism.

It was to be expected that Münster would be repudiated by the Anabaptist camp itself. A very scathing rebuke of Münster, written in 1535 (the year of Münster's capitulation), and allegedly by Menno Simons, bears the significant title "The

Blasphemy of Jan van Leiden," and is an almost fierce denunciation of Münster.

One gets the impression that among the enemies of the
Stepchildren the news from Münster was quite welcome. It
gave them an opportunity to say something that all human
beings dearly love to say, namely, "I told you so." They had
predicted that Anabaptism would lead to chaos; and now there
was laboratory proof that they had been right. They pinched
the last drop of propaganda value out of the unhappy event.
A pattern was set that continues to almost modern times, the
pattern of painting the picture of Anabaptism on the canvas
of Münster.[m]

By making Münster typical of the movement, men were
likewise able to blame Anabaptism for the Peasant Revolt. This
misconception also continues to this day. There is no need
to deny that the peasants were emboldened by the writings
of Müntzer; but the revolutionary ravings of this fanatic jarred
on the souls of the Stepchildren from the start. Did not
Grebel and his colleagues hint very plainly that cooperation
between him and them was contingent upon his abandonment
of revolutionary tactics? It so happens, however, that the
essential outlines of the story of Anabaptism can be told
without reference to either Müntzer or the Peasant Revolt.
Neither of these was cherished by the Stepchildren.

In conclusion it must be stressed that the Stepchildren's idea
in the area of economics was a much-needed thing in the
age of the Reformation. The medieval world had been rather
callous in the matter of the "haves" and the "have-nots." A
change was very much needed. And in the days of the Reformers' earliest agitations, they had shown a tendency to
suggest certain changes.[n] Luther had, in these days of the

[m]Early in this century Edward Armstrong (in his *The Emperor Charles
V, p.* 342) wrote, with specific reference to the Anabaptists: "Whenever
they momentarily gained the upperhand they applied the practical
methods of modern Anarchism and Nihilism to the professed principles
of Communism." The only excuse for that kind of writing is the fact
that the sources were not yet available then. No reputable historian
of more recent times would repeat Armstrong's words.

[n]Wilhelm Pauck thinks the early Bucer was inclined to some form of
"Christian communism." (Cf. his *"Martin Bucer's Conception of a Christian State,"* in the Princeton Theological Review, Vol. XXVI.) This

dawn, broken a lance for much-needed reform, had said that
"all begging should be made to end, in all of Christendom."
Even this statement, mild enough it would seem, was deeply
resented by his Catholic opponents, who would be sure to be
hurt by any rearrangement in the area of "mine and thine."
Jerome Emser, the "Billy-goat," as Luther affectionately called
this his archenemy in the Catholic camp, took him to task
for saying this. Emser said it was

> Picardian rather than Christian; for the Picards° have the
> practice of not letting anyone of their number go begging . . . .
> But Alexius earned heaven by begging and Martin and Eliza-
> beth as well as Hedwig and all God's servants became well-
> pleasing to God by the giving of alms . . . . Just as water
> puts out fire so do alms take away sins. It is therefore not
> a good thing that begging be discontinued; lots of good works
> will thereby be brought to their end!

But this promise of renewed social sensitivity contained in
the early Reformation was not realized. Luther became more
and more conservative in the matter of economic reform. He
was being blamed for the unrest that was manifesting itself
among the peasants. It seemed that the Stepchildren's agitation for more responsible ownership was contributing to the
unrest. It seemed that the Reformation age, far from causing
the lot of the dispossessed to improve, actually made it worse.
And this only made the Stepchildren increase their clamor for
conscience in the matter of property. One of them, Jörg
Schnabel, at any rate, said in the course of his trial:

> In the days when the papists were in the ascendancy it did
> not happen that poor people were forced to surrender their
> house and field; now however they are being dispossessed. And
> the magistrates at Wolkstorff have been heard to say that if
> they were to listen to their preachers then they [i.e., the poor]
> would not be sitting there any more, then their Excellencies
> would deal more severely with them.[19]

---

would not be surprising, seeing that the Reformers in their earliest
years were kindly disposed toward many of the items that later came
to be known as Anabaptist excesses.

°"Picard" is a synonym of "Waldensian." Luther used the two terms
interchangeably, as did many in his day.

Interest rates had gone up. When it is recalled that in those days people did not borrow money unless they were in distress, this only made a bad situation worse. Schnabel said, "The rate of usury is one florin on twenty; but now they take a *malter* of corn, which is worth two or two and a half florins. The Church used to take five percent, which is forbidden in the Bible."[20]

It was the heartless usury, practiced by the Protestant Churches, in typical medieval style, with the Church's money, that had driven this Schnabel into the arms of Anabaptism. He had left the Lutheran Church, of which he was the treasurer (so that he had firsthand knowledge of what was going on), because it put out its money on interest while many poor people who lived in the shadow of the Church lived in dire poverty. Conscience-stricken over such a policy, he had appealed to the pastor, to the mayor, to the City Council (Marburg), but to no avail. He thereupon turned in his books and joined the Anabaptists.[21] This was in 1538. In this new company Schnabel found the sensitivity toward human distress that he had missed in the established Church. In this Anabaptist congregation one of the questions put to a prospective member was, "If need should require it are you prepared to devote all your possessions to the service of the brotherhood and do you agree not to fail any member that is in need and you are able to help?"

Although the Stepchildren's idea of "community of goods" was opposed by the Reformers and their following, so much so that a Protestant clergyman was deposed for supporting it, it may be said of this item, as of so much that was an integral part of the vision of these Radicals, that it was finally accepted as a valid Christian ideal. The Reformed Churches of the Low Countries in later times established something of an enviable record in giving of their substance to alleviate human misery; fantastic sums of money were sent, for example, to the distressed Waldensians of the Piedmont, in 1698. But even after so many years it was remembered that in this practice of Christian stewardship, the Stepchildren had led the way. In those days a person, who was not an Anabaptist, wrote with them in mind: "Although the people of the Reformed Church of Holland do indeed deserve to be commended for their benev-

olence toward the poor, yet is this virtue particularly true of
these people. Moreover they are careful to dress unas-
sumingly."[22]

In our own times the children of the Stepchildren continue
in the erstwhile vision as to the duties that devolve upon him
who calls something his own. The relief programs of the
Mennonites are known throughout the world and need only
to be mentioned. Wherever there is human suffering, there
these descendants of the Stepchildren are likely to put in
their appearance to do what can be done to help.[p]

Whatever it was that men meant by "community of goods,"
it was a good thing. It is not too much to say that if the
Western world had listened to these Radicals and had taken
over their ideology and practice (which is to ask too much),
then Karl Marx would have had little with which to sustain
his economic theories, would have had little to write about.
And that would have made a vast difference in the course
of world history.

We propose a posthumous nod of approval to a band of
men and women who pioneered for a Christian view of ownership, a view that was referred to disdainfully as "community of
goods." All who respond to this proposal and who are also
bound by the Belgic Confession will want to do something
about the passage: "we detest the Anabaptists . . . who reject
the higher powers and magistrates and would subvert justice,
introduce community of goods, and confound that decency and
good order which God has established among men."[q] The

[p]When a few years ago a devastating tornado struck the city of Flint
in southeastern Michigan, several trucks carrying scores of young men
arrived on the scene; they pitched their tents on the Fairgrounds, and
proceeded to help clear away the debris and relieve the distress caused
by the disaster. They were Anabaptists (Mennonites) from a neighboring
State. After the city was back on its feet, they disappeared as unceremoniously as they had come.

[q]It would at least be a step in the right direction if the text of the
Belgic Confession as it was fixed at the Revision Synod of 1566 were
replaced with the text of the original version. Guido de Brès, the author
of this Creed, had said: "Nous detestons tous ceux qui veulent reietter
les Superioritez et Magistrats et renverser la iustice, mettans communautez
des biens et confondant l'honnestate que Dieu à [sic; a misprint for a]
mis entre les hommes." The Revision Synod replaced the verb form
mettans with introduis. The reason for the change is not given, of course;

Stepchildren were saying things which the Reformers should
not have shrugged off with some ancient clichés and the
sinister charge of *Kommunisten!*

---

but may be significant. *Mettans* is from *mettre,* a verb meaning *to bring
about by fiat* (cf. the perfect participle of this verb, *mis,* as it stands
in this same sentence, in *que Dieu a mis entre les hommes*) whereas
introduis is from *introduire,* a verb meaning to introduce in *any* fashion.
Mettre means to introduce in dictatorial fashion, to introduce as God
introduces; *introduire* means to introduce in any way, even by completely
democratic procedures. The version of 1566 is therefore much more
sweeping than the original version; for the text of 1566 condemns the
"community of goods" practiced by the Hutterites; the text of 1559
(composed in that year but first printed in 1561) does not.

8 *Rottengeister*

Fear not, little flock . . . .
Luke 12:32

IN HIS DAY LUTHER SAID THAT THERE HAD GONE FORTH FROM
his camp *Wiedertäufer, Sacramentschwärmer, und andere Rottengeister.* In earlier chapters we have busied ourselves with
the first two of these terms of reproach applied to the Stepchildren; in this chapter we take up the last.

The term *Rottengeister* was a sort of catch-all, an and-soforth, to cover the rest of an allegedly evil crew. We shall
therefore take up in this final chapter several of the remaining
features of the vision of the Stepchildren.

In a way, the name *Rottengeister* leads more directly to the
heart of the Second Front than most of the rest of the smearwords used. A *Rott* is a clique, a faction, an element; and
Rottengeister are clique-organizers, faction-makers, elementcreators. In more sophisticated language, *Rottengeister* are
people who agitate within a society to form a party. In our
present terminology, we may say that *Rottengeister* are agitators whose activity leads to a composite situation. This makes
them identical with "heretics," for, as we saw, the word "heretic" points to choice-making. In medieval times, as in any
sacral situation, *Rottengeister* were held to be the epitome of
evil because they were a threat to the monolithic society. In
language borrowed from the scene of the Crucifixion they
were said to be guilty of "rending the robe of Christ." The
term *Rottengeister* was very useful in the psychological warfare that raged at the Second Front — for what the "heretic"
had been in the eyes of medieval sacralism, that the Anabaptists were in the eyes of the neo-sacralists of Reformation
times.

Not one of the Reformers seems to have been aware of the
fact that Christians are, and in the nature of things must
be, *Rottengeister*. Christians are out to create a following, an
element, a faction. The Church of the New Testament is by
definition a sect, a following (the word *sect* is, as we have said,
from the Latin *sequor*, a word of which *follow* is the essential
idea). The very thing that sacralists want to avoid at all costs
is in the Christian vision the *sine qua non*, namely to "choose
this day whom you will serve." It may be said that if the
Reformers had been willing to be guided by the New Testament, there would never have been a Second Front; for then
the Stepchildren's ambition to organize a Church that consisted
of followers would not have seemed objectionable.

The Donatists realized in their day that to eliminate out
of the lives of men the "for or against" of Christianity was
to make an end to Christianity. The medieval "heretic" realized
it too. As did the men of the Second Front. All of these were
committed to the creation of a Church composed of Christians-
by-choice, to take the place of a Church consisting of chris-
tians-by-happenstance. The Restitutionist vision looks to the
creation of islands in the sea of humanity, continents if that
can be. It constructs a relief map, with parts below and parts
above sea-level; it has a native fear of a landscape such as
is said to have existed prior to Genesis 1:9. One must not be
surprised to hear people with such a vision called *Rottengeister*.

It was part of the Restitutionist heritage to *refuse the oath*.
We shall study this feature at this time; and we shall discover
that this refusal to swear an oath was the consequence of
the basic conviction of the "heretic."

In contemporary Western society the oath is primarily a
device intended to secure veracity; it is a device whereby
men think to get "the truth, the whole truth, and nothing
but the truth." But this is a narrowing down. Formerly the
oath was quite as much a device intended to secure loyalty,
particularly the loyalty of subjects to those who stood over
them. This was an oath of fealty.

Although the oath is referred to in the Christian Scriptures,
in the Old as well as in the New Testament, it is not an
institution broached in these Scriptures. The oath is pre-

Christian. It was in common use, for example, in the ethnic society of pre-Constantinian Rome. In this society the oath of fealty was in common use.[1] In ancient Rome the oath served especially to procure fealty to the emperor. In this capacity the oath had a decidedly religious flavor. As such it was part and parcel of a sacral situation. Back of it lay the assumption that ruler and subjects recognize and bow to one and the same Object, in the presence of which the ruler and the ruled alike place themselves as they covenant with each other. In this society the oath is a sacralism-sustaining thing. In it one's religious loyalty and one's political or civil loyalty meet, in fact, coalesce. In this society the oath is the exact opposite of "render to Caesar the things that are Caesar's and to God the things that are God's"; in fact, in this society this Biblical expression makes no sense; deity and ruler are too indistinguishable for that.

It was to be expected, *a priori,* that the early Christians would get in trouble in regard to oath-taking, the oath being what it was. Their God was not the same Object as the one that informed the emperor. They were perfectly willing and ready to promise fealty to the emperor, but not to the emperor's god. These early Christians had a problem here, a problem very similar to the one that harassed the Jews, namely, "Is it lawful to give tribute to Caesar?" Their conscience forbade them to get involved in the oath, the oath as it existed in pagan Roman society.

The early Christians were therefore more than likely to develop a dislike for the oath. It seemed to them — and in this they were quite right — that the oath had been devised to catch them. Small wonder that they began to look upon the oath as a hateful thing, a thing inspired by the powers of darkness. It is perhaps this conviction that comes to expression in the saying attributed to Gregory of Nazianzus: "What is worse than the oath? Nothing, I say."

It will be recalled that, in the days of Decius, men had been required to sign an affidavit (an instrument that may properly be called an oath-in-writing) attesting to loyalty to the imperial religion. This also was a net in which the Christians were caught, it being planned that way. And this, too, may have contributed to a dislike for the oath as a sacralism-serving thing.

It seems that this developing tradition of dislike toward the oath was not detained very much, nor very effectively, by the fact that the Old Testament not only tolerated the oath but seemed to have enjoined it. The early Christians realized that the New Testament comes with a new formula for human society, seeks to create a "people of God" that cannot be equated with any other "people." They were convinced that the "old," which had been "nigh unto vanishing away" (cf. Hebrews 8:13) had lapsed when the new regime had been launched. They were prepared for the idea that the oath might well be a part of the now obsolete; the fact that it had been an implement for the creation and preservation of a non-composite society made them the more ready to take the oath to the attic. In all events, the down-grading of the Old Testament and the disallowing of the oath have long been companions in travel.

The promoters of the Constantinian change were quick to appropriate the already-existing institution of the oath and to bend it to their purpose. The Constantinians were as much the friends of the oath as the "heretics" were its enemies. One's attitude toward the oath consequently became an index to one's position in regard to "Christian sacralism." Therefore we read, in the jurisprudence of medieval times, that "If any man by a damnable religious superstition rejects the religion of the oath, so that he refuses to swear, he shall because of this behavior be denominated a heretic." It became standard procedure among the inquisitors to try their victims by confronting them with the oath; if they refused to swear, this was *prima facie* proof of addiction to "heresy." One of the notorious inquisitors of medieval times, Bernard Gui, summarized the procedure in these words: "all who repudiate the oath and refuse to swear, these are *ipso facto* to be condemned as heretics."[2] Such policies only made the "heretics" the more convinced that the oath was demonic, invented by the devil in an effort to get the faithful in trouble.

So much was the oath a sacralism-serving thing that the medieval Church employed it freely in its expansion program. The oath helped create the kind of world the advocates of "Christian sacralism" wanted and it served to find and mark for destruction those who stood in the way of this objective. It was ordered, at Toulouse in 1229, as follows:

> In order that . . . heretics may be the more readily exterminated and the Roman faith the more speedily planted in this land, we decree, that you shall . . . make all males above fourteen and all females above twelve to abjure all heresy and besides promise with an oath that they will defend the Catholic Church and persecute the heretics. All those who after such abjuration shall be found to have apostatized . . . shall be punished as apostates deserve.[3]

Whenever there was an epidemic of "heresy," the medieval Church looked to the oath as the device wherewith to solve this problem. For example, the Council of Verona, held in 1184, which had as one of the main items on its agenda the problem of the rapidly-spreading "heresy," decided that in every community there were to be named three or more men who were to "bind themselves under oath to divulge the names of any who are heretical, who hold *Winckelpredigten* or err in any other way."[4] It is no wonder that the "heretics" deprecated the oath as an institution.

In the early years of the thirteenth century the same policies were employed in the Netherlands. In order to locate and then liquidate the "heretics" in those parts, the following oath was extracted from the populace:

> I, N.N., swear by God Almighty, to the magistrate or to his lieutenant, that I will tell the sincere truth, without fear, touching all matters known to me and concerning which I am interrogated, not only in regard to myself but also in regard to others. So help me God and His holy mother.

A somewhat expanded form read as follows:

> I, N.N., swear an oath by God Almighty, to my lord, bishop N.N., without dissimulation, that henceforth I will go no more to people that call themselves . . . , . . . , . . . , etc., and that I will have no fellowship with them nor with their leaders, teachers, etc., as long as they remain heretics. Moreover I forswear all manner of unbelief that is contrary to the open faith taught and maintained everywhere in the holy Roman church and Christendom . . . . So help me God and his mother.[5]

In view of the fact that the oath was constantly used as a weapon with which "Christian sacralism" was sustained, and

which the "heretic" opposed, it is no wonder that hostility to
the oath became a distinguishing feature of the "heretic." We
find it listed as such:

> The wicked blasphemies of this heresy are: the denial that
> in baptism sins are forgiven; the assertion that the sacrament
> of the body and blood of Christ is a folly; that by the im-
> position of pontifical hands nothing is conferred; that no one
> receives the Holy Spirit unless good works go before; that
> marriage is condemned; that the whole Church is found with
> them only; that all oath-taking is a crime.[6]

Anyone who hesitated in regard to the oath was at once
under suspicion of "heresy," so indicative of heresy was it said
to be. We find a well-informed man and a loyal son of the
prevailing Church, Peter Cantor, the precentor of Notre Dame
in Paris, asking the question, somewhat carpingly be it said
to his credit: "Why do we forthwith proclaim that man who
keeps this command [of Christ; i.e., 'Swear not at all'] to
be a Cathar?"[7]

There was then a long tradition concerning the oath when
in the sixteenth century reform was undertaken; for many
centuries it had been a mark of orthodoxy to swear the oath,
and a mark of unorthodoxy to have an aversion to it.

As was the case with respect to so much of the ancient
Restitutionist heritage, the Reformers at the first were quite
sympathetic toward the position which the earlier "heretics"
had taken in regard to the oath. As one investigator has
put it: "Certain ideas that were later called Anabaptist ideas
had a great appeal for some of the early reformers in the Low
Countries; consider for example, the aversion to the oath which
Willem of Utrecht revealed in 1525."[8] This Willem of Utrecht
was not an Anabaptist — although he could easily have become
one. In those early days, an admirer of Hendrik Voes and
Johannes Esch (the first men to die for the "Lutheran" cause),
a man by the name of Reckenhofer wrote that "The customary
oath which the civil rulers require of their subjects is illicit and
goes counter to the commands of Christ."[9] This Reckenhofer
had in all probability derived this conviction from the pre-
Reformation "heretic" — where else had these things been

said? As late as the year 1546 there were still some people, not Anabaptists, who had no use for the oath — one Pierre Alexander, for example.

With the Reformers' swing to the right, which swing had landed them in neo-sacralism, any hesitation in regard to the oath came to be looked upon as a grievous fault. Calvin did not hesitate to say that this sensitivity in Pierre Alexander, whom we have just mentioned, was a "lourde fault," a serious error.[10] Calvin had become sufficiently sacralist to make him look askance at any man who frowned on the instrument that had so long served the sacralist cause — the oath.

By the time the Heidelberg Catechism was being written, neo-sacralism had become firmly entrenched. In the meantime the Stepchildren had opened the Second Front and all the ancient dislike for the oath-refusers had devolved upon them. With them in mind, Question 101 in said Catechism was inserted: "But may we not swear by the Name of God in a godly manner?" The Palatinate, for which the Heidelberg Catechism was primarily intended, was a sacral State — not without challenge by the Stepchildren — and here was a good chance to put in a good word for the sacralism-serving oath; and so the answer in the Catechism was "Yes, ..."

The Stepchildren were as disinclined to the oath as the Reformers were inclined to it. They had inherited this negative attitude to it because they had inherited the Restitutionist vision that had long ago engendered this negative attitude. And now that the two camps had formed, the Reformers began to prod their magistrates, precisely as the medieval sacralists had prodded theirs. They pressured the magistrates to stretch the net across the path of men, so as to catch every dissenter, the same net that Decius had used in the days of the ancient pagan sacralism and that the Constantinians had used in the days of "Christian sacralism." The Reformers whispered in the ears of the civil ruler, with specific reference to the Stepchildren: "If they refuse to swear the oath then let them be banished and told never to return . . . . Then if they thereupon re-enter the domains of my lord, then let my lord deal with them in such a way that they don't do it again."[11] (The last phrase is a euphemistic way of saying that they should be put to death.)

At Zürich the civil authorities, spurred on by the Reformers there, published an Edict, in 1539, intended to liquidate the Stepchildren by providing:

> We strictly command all inhabitants of our domains . . . that if they hear of any Anabaptists they are to inform us concerning them by virtue of the oath with which they are bound . . . . We shall punish without mercy, as having violated the faith and the oath which they have sworn . . . , all who assist, and do not drive away or report, or bring to us as prisoners, all such persons.[12]

It is easily understood that such tactics did not increase the Stepchildren's love of the oath.

At nearby Basel new and special oaths were devised, looking to the elimination of every last Anabaptist with his threat to the homogeneous society.

In the Reformed Netherlands the policy was the same. As late as the year 1574, at the Synod held in that year at Dordtrecht, the question was asked, "How can the Anabaptists be eliminated or made to go on the right path?" The answer given by this ecclesiastical body was, "Admonish and petition the magistrates not to receive or tolerate any in the land save only those who take the lawful oath." A few years later, in 1601, the Edict of Groningen, mentioned earlier in these studies, proposed likewise to screen out the Anabaptists by means of the oath.[*] Such use of the oath only made the Stepchildren the more sure that oaths are of the devil.

In their policy of severity toward the Stepchildren, the Reformers were not evil-intentioned men; they were simply mistaken men. They honestly thought that society can hang together only if it is bound together by a common religious commitment; the oath was both a symbol of such common commitment and a device for securing it. If this their premise is granted, then their rigor toward the Stepchildren is explicable, and even justifiable. As a recent writer puts it: "Since

---

[*]The Edict read: "Oock sal niemandt tot eenighe Administratie bedieninge publicke ofte Privatie, noch oock tot cunschap ofte ghetuighenisse toeghelaten worden hij doe dan de solemnelen daer toestaenden Eedt, alsulcken Eedt weygerende sullen ghestraft worden, als nae recht behoort" (printed in No. 1172 of the Knuttel Collection of Dutch Historical Tracts).

the ancient loyalties and traditions of the community found
their symbolic center in the civic oath, this rejection of the
oath was deeply disturbing." To the man who had not rejected
the sacral premise, the repudiation of the oath was the beginning of the end of all order and decency. As Zwingli put it:

> You seek to destroy the magistracy and the power vested in
> it. Take away the oath and you have dissolved all order . . . .
> You see, dear reader, all order is overthrown when the oath
> is abrogated . . . . Give up the oath in any State and at once,
> and in keeping with the Anabaptists' desire, the magistracy is
> removed and all things follow as they would have them. Good
> God, what confusion and up-turning of everything![13]

In this matter both sides were honest with themselves and
with others; but one side was *mistaken*. Every Protestant can
only deplore the fruitage of this mistakenness. To think that
they "stretched" as large-hearted a man as was Georg Blaurock
in order to force him to repeat the words of the customary oath!
This was undiluted devilry. And then when the tortured wretch,
faltering at the prospect of even grosser torture, went through
the motions of oath-taking, a "sin" for which his people did
not censure him, then to hear Zwingli say to them, "You follow
neither Christ nor your own ordinances" — this is devilry multi-
plied.

All told, one must surely rejoice that men have come to see
that the sacral premise in not tenable, have come to realize that
it is not a prerequisite for civic peace that all citizens worship
at the same shrine. One can point to Switzerland, the very land
that made life well-nigh impossible for the oath-refusing Stepchildren, to demonstrate the fact that the sacralist premise is
wrong. Here we have a land in which there are pronounced
religious diversities (going hand in hand with racial and lin-
guistic difference, moreover) but which for a long time now has
been a classic example of peace and quiet. Manifestly it is not
the repudiation of the sacralist premise, but rather the retention
of it, that occasions turmoil and tension.

With sacralism's basic premise discredited, most of the noise
and the tumult about oath-taking has subsided. We no longer
feel the need for an oath of fealty; we no longer feel that men
must be bound by oaths to inform on their fellow men; we have
only the oath of veracity left. And even here "I solemnly

swear" may be replaced with "I solemnly affirm" — an alternative intended for the man who feels that the oath is not quite permissible. And we are none the worse for it. The frightful dissolution of all order and decency, which was predicted so surely by the Reformers and by all the rest who were caught up in the pre-Christian view of human society, has not materialized. We have taken up our station where the Stepchildren stood in this matter and bedlam has not overtaken us.[b]

✵   ✵   ✵   ✵   ✵

One does not have to listen very long at the Second Front to hear something said about the *incarnation;* the Stepchildren were accused of entertaining grossly incorrect ideas in this matter. This accusation finds its classical expression in Article 18 of the Belgic Confession, which speaks of "the heresy of the Anabaptists, who deny that Christ assumed human flesh of His mother." This heresy was sometimes put this way, a bit too graphically: that Jesus Christ did not take His human nature from His mother, Mary, but brought it with Him, from heaven, and simply carried it through Mary, very much as water is carried through a tube. This representation was considered highly objectionable because it would make Christ's humanity like unto, but not identical with, the humanity of those He came to save.

This aberration from traditional Christology was never an integral part of the Anabaptist vision. If this fact were commonly known and accepted, we could properly omit a discussion of it here. But since the Belgic Confession speaks of it as if it were common to Anabaptism as such we must give some attention to it, the more so since the unwarranted generalization of the Belgic Confession continues to be made.[c]

[b]In lands where the influence of Restitutionism was not strong, the oath was used until quite recent times, to prevent "revisionism." Less than a century ago one could not attain to the rank of Professor in the University of Vienna unless he was prepared to swear to be loyal to the Roman Catholic ideology. (Cf. Herzog, *Realencyclopaedie für Prot. Theol. und Kirche,* IX, S. 204.)

[c]Professor Berkouwer continues to speak of this error as an integral part of Anabaptism, deriving from a basic item in the Anabaptist vision, namely a "false dualism" of "nature" vs. "grace." Allegedly, it was this "dualism" that made the Anabaptists balk at the idea that Christ actually

It was Melchior Hofmann, it seems, who injected this deviating view of Christ's humanity into the stream of Anabaptism; why he was drawn to it is not altogether apparent. He did not invent this docetic[d] notion, however. It had been entertained earlier; in fact, it was already on the scene when the New Testament Scriptures were being laid down. It was from Hofmann that Menno Simons, perhaps the most influential writer in the camp of the Stepchildren, appropriated this docetic strain. Principally by way of Menno, it entered the stream of Anabaptist thought more or less widely. Menno had been an Anabaptist leader for some time before becoming entangled in docetic Christology; he had preached and taught the orthodox view, a fact that goes far to prove that docetism is not inherent in the Anabaptist vision. Moreover, docetism was never accepted in large areas of the Second Front, remaining confined quite consistently to those areas that were under Dutch influence. Even in these areas it was dislodged again in the course of time, so that for a very long time now the descendants of the Stepchildren have held the orthodox view. All this goes to show that the docetic Christology was a "sport," an *accidens*, a more or less foreign body in the tissues of Anabaptism.

It is evident from the record that Menno was driven to adopt the docetic view, driven to it in the heat of battle. It was principally John à Lasco, the Polish nobleman who played a leading role in the Reformation in the northern Low Countries, that led Menno to take to the docetic road. This à Lasco had expressed himself in a way that left him wide open to the charge that he taught that Christ was clothed with the same fallen nature that characterizes those whom He came to save;[e] as one

---

identified Himself with human nature. We think there are two errors implied in Berkouwer's views; one (in which Berkouwer has the Belgic Confession on his side) is that this deviating view of the incarnation was an integral part of the Anabaptist vision; the other is that it was the outworking of "een uitgesproken dualisme."

[d]The word *docetic* is derived from a Greek verb meaning *to appear* or *to seem;* in the docetic view, Christ's humanity was only a *seeming* humanity, not really real. Docetism was one of the first errors to plague the Christian Church; we find it rebuked already in 2 John: 7.

[e]For reasons that have never been adequately explained, there was present in the Polish Reformation a pronounced tendency toward unitarianism. This tendency manifested itself from the earliest times, and

reads à Lasco one gets the impression that he held that Christ
shared in original sin, both as to its guilt and as to its pollution.
This was more than Menno could take; and to find a way around
the position espoused by à Lasco Menno backed into the docetic
corner.

The matter à Lasco had undertaken to theologize about is in
the nature of things a theologizer's happy hunting grounds and
a theologian's headache. How Christ could identify himself with
the human race without thereby falling heir to the fallenness
of that race is a major theological puzzle, one which in Catholic
theology is "solved" by the invention of the idea of the "im-
maculate conception" of Christ's mother, a device whereby
men seek to secure the sinlessness of Christ by providing
Him with a sinless mother. (Actually this is not a solution
of the problem; it merely moves the problem back one generation, for it leaves unexplained how Mary came to be that way.)

Menno entered the fray reluctantly. He was not at all a
speculative theologian. He refused to carry the matter into his
sermons, it being too speculative for the common man. But à
Lasco's theologizing left him no choice, especially when à Lasco's
associates, notably Gellius Faber and Martin Micron, gave evidence that they stood with à Lasco. When Menno objected to
à Lasco's views, saying that they robbed him of the Sinless One,
à Lasco and his followers ganged up on Menno. They filled
tedious reams of paper to show up another of the "errors of
Anabaptism," and Menno filled equally many and equally
tedious reams of paper with a defence of his position. It would
have been better if à Lasco had not tried to deal with the
mystery of the incarnation as though it were subject to exact
science, better if he had realized that whatever he could do
it would remain the *"groote verholentheyt"* (the great mystery)
that Menno said it was. One thing is unmistakably clear; it is
that Menno did not relish theological speculation and that he
entered into the argument only because he was honestly convinced that the dignity of the Christ was being jeopardized.

Now that the noise of the battle had died down, now that

---

it soon became dominant. It could be that à Lasco's startling assertions
concerning the Christ's relation to original sin were in themselves symptomatic of this tendency toward unitariansim.

those gracious forces that keep the atmosphere of this planet
from getting too polluted by the dust men stir up, as we look
back at those turbulent times it is refreshing to discover that there
was at least one clergyman who kept the poise that becomes
every man who handles the mysteries of the Christian Faith. We
are thinking of that freckle-faced preacher, Adrian van
Haemstede, a native son of the Flemish soil, who said, as he
beheld the theologians tearing at each other, that it reminded
him of the coarse persons who played at dice at the foot of the
Cross, fought with each other as to who was to have the robe,
without great concern about Him whose robe it was. He asserted that the whole contention turned not about the incarnation as such but around the details, the *circumstantiae*. He
said that when Anabaptists died for their convictions they died
for the Gospel; he referred to the Stepchildren as "weaker
brethren in Christ." He was ready to grant that Menno had
made some mistakes — but he added, in the same breath, that
this was true of others also, Calvin included. He tried to persuade the magistrates of the England to which he and his
countrymen had fled, not to act on the advice of his countrymen
but to leave the Anabaptists alone, since they did not disturb the
peace. It was four centuries too early to say such things. The
leaders of the Refugee Churches persuaded the authorities to
depose van Haemstede and to expel him from the realm. He died
a demoted man.

We have said that docetism is not constitutive of the Anabaptist vision. But it is possible that the drift toward the
deviating view was somehow related to the Anabaptist vision
nevertheless. The Stepchildren's quarrel with "Christian sacralism" may have conditioned them in that direction. They were
pitted against a theology that slurs over the distinction of "regenerate" and "not regenerate," a theology that identifies the
Volk Gottes with the *Volk,* a theology that equated the *Corpus
Christi* with the *Corpus Christianum,* a theology in which there
runs a continuity that cannot be harmonized with the authentic
Christian vision. And, as Menno saw it, now à Lasco was continuing this line of continuity onward still, was extending it
until it included the Christ also. This was too much for Menno.
The Anabaptist theology had sought to recover the discontinuity
that is inseparable from the New Testament vision, a discon-

tinuity whereby "Church" and "World" are disjunct and not coextensive. Small wonder that Menno could not resist the opportunity to introduce discontinuity in the area of Christology. In the Anabaptist theology there is a marked awareness of a heterogeneity between the Church and society as such; when Menno saw a chance, and a need, to posit a similar heterogeneity between the Head of the Church and human society, he was constrained to seize the opportunity. In the words of a contemporary investigator, "In Menno's view of the incarnation of Christ we see his customary sharp antithesis between regenerate and unregenerate, between Church and society, extended to the Source and Head of the Church."[14] If this is so, then Menno's excursion into the field of the ancient docetic error becomes at least relatable to the basic thrusts of the Anabaptist vision, an explicable if unwarranted working-out of its basic thrust, that of a radical break with "Christian sacralism."

✿   ✿   ✿   ✿   ✿

The Stepchildren fell heir to the concept of the "Cross" which one encounters also in the medieval "heretic." Because they were rebuked for this, the matter deserves a place in this study.

In authentic Christianity the Cross is God's most emphatic *no* to man's *yes,* His most emphatic *yes* to man's *no.* A clear example is to be found in Galatians 6:12, where St. Paul pits a religion of human achievement and merit (of which circumcision was the symbol among the people whom the Apostle was opposing) against a religion of grace. He brings the issue into sharpest focus by saying "they constrain you to be circumcised; only lest they should suffer persecution for the cross of Christ." The Cross is a sweeping declaration of man's inability to save himself from his predicament; this is bad news for every man who has not as yet capitulated to the speech from the beyond; hence it entails persecution against those who have so capitulated. When one experiences the hostility which the Gospel of grace is certain to encounter as it collides with unhumbled man, then one experiences the Cross. This is the one and only meaning Cross-bearing has in the New Testament writings. To bear the Cross is to experience the dislike which confirmed unbelief is wont to heap upon the Christ and upon those that have aligned themselves with Him.

It goes without saying that when Christianity is thrust into the sacral pattern Cross-bearing becomes obsolete, there being no further occasion or opportunity for it. Who would vent his spleen, and on whom, and what for? The erstwhile tensions subside in the climate of "Christendom"; the controverting speech from the beyond is no longer heard; autosoterism is again enthroned.[r] What further Cross-bearing will there, can there, be?

If the Constantinian change made Cross-bearing obsolete, the word Cross was of course retained; it was too much a part of the erstwhile Christian vocabulary, too much a part of the heritage, to be simply excinded. It was therefore transvaluated. The old and only authentic meaning was dropped and a new meaning was infused into the word. On the one hand the Cross was carried into the liturgy of the Church; it became an object that henceforth occupied a prominent place in the Church's furniture. Moreover, the custom of "striking a cross" arose, a piece of pantomime that to this day marks the man who stands in the tradition of medieval "Christian sacralism." On the other hand a new content was poured into the expression "bearing the Cross." Whereas the New Testament reserves the expression for the unpleasant experiences that are wont to follow upon being a *Christian,* the expression was now made to connote the sufferings that dog our footsteps because we are *men.* Here is a man with a sightless eye, a palsied hand, a cloven palate — what a "cross" for such a man! This spurious connotation, however, finds not the faintest support in the New Testament. It is part of the perversion which the "heretics" called the "fall of the Church."

Rebellion against the Constantinian change, whereby Cross-bearing was precluded, was instantaneous. With the Donatist rebellion begins a long tradition of "heresy" in which one finds a studied attempt to conserve and preserve Cross-bearing, that experience which in authentic Christianity is the hall-mark of

---

[r]Autosoterism is, of course, the theology in which man is his own savior. The most subtle autosoterism comes to expression in the place assigned to Mary in the Catholic theology, the "Mother of God." In this theology humanity has itself provided what was needed, by a sort of "miracle-of-Mary." The "heretics" refused a theology in which Mary becomes in any sense *"co-redemptrix."*

genuineness. When the coming of "Christian sacralism" had made martyrdom a thing of the past, the Restitutionists went to great lengths to preserve it. The followers of Donatus said expressly that to "bear the reproach of Christ" was as necessary and as definitive of the believer as it had been heretofore; the only thing that had changed was that, whereas in earlier times the Christians had been molested by the pagan world, they were now being molested by "christians," who were another variety of pagans. This implied for them that not the Catholics but they, the Donatists, were the true continuation of the authentic Church. They said that "the true Christian must expect a life of continuous hardship, his fate is that of all just men, from Abel on down."[15]

Since Donatism was reactionary, it was a matter of course that something of fanaticism entered the picture. So sure were the Donatists that the hall-mark of the true Christian is that he experiences hardship because of the Faith that they began almost — and sometimes even without the almost — to seek martyrdom. Especially was this true of the *Circumcelliones*, that lunatic fringe of the Donatist movement, among whom men sometimes leaped from bridges and cliffs in order to accompany to their reward some who were being put to death for the Faith. These extremists were simply taking steps to make sure that they were *not* members of the now "fallen" Church, in which there was no longer any Cross-bearing. Although the mainline Donatists did not go to such extremes, they did exalt the martyr to great height. There was a tendency to glory in martyrdom. This is, of course, not far removed from the attitude of the earliest disciples of the Christ; had not they rejoiced "that they had been counted worthy to suffer shame for His name"? (Acts 5:41).

In medieval times the Restitutionist camp kept alive the Donatist appraisal of Cross-bearing, sometimes even carrying it to the same extremes to which the *Circumcelliones* went. We read for instance in the official report of the slaughter of a large pocket of "heretics" in the vicinity of Béziers, that "There was no need for our men to cast them in [i.e., into the fire]; nay, all were so obstinate that they cast themselves in, of their own accord."[16] Possibly this is an exaggerated report of the martyrdom-seeking of these "heretics"; it may also be that the "fallen" Church recalled that it had once had to do with people who volunteered for martyrdom, so that this became part of the stereotyped image of the "heretic." But there can be no doubt that at times such fanatic willingness to die for the Faith did come to expression.

Nor must we be greatly surprised at this frame of mind. Life did not hold forth much promise in the case of a "heretic" who remained behind, when all that mattered was going to the fire! Better to enter at once into glory than to drag out an existence of almost total bereavement on earth!

This also explains the light-heartedness that often marked the "heretic" as he went to the flames. We read of a colony of such "heretics," apprehended in the vicinity of Cologne in 1163. They were called "Cathars" — a designation with which we have become acquainted — and they had lay-folk who preached; they were "well versed in the Scriptures"; they considered themselves to be "the true Church" and all the rest to be outside it; they disdained the Church's clergy and sacraments, etc. Of this group, we read, eight men and three women were going to the fire "cum exaltione" (in high spirits) when an unusually beautiful young woman stepped forward, "touching whom the judges and the by-standers were moved to compassion, so that they tried to spare her. . . . But she, suddenly eluding the hands of them that held her, jumped into the fire and perished with the rest."[17]

To quote but one more example. In 1414 when some forty-four "heretics" were about to be burned at Winckel, near Langensalza, in Thuringia, a man came riding up just as they were going to the stake. He, crying "I too am one of them!" leaped into the inferno and so died with his comrades.

Although the earliest rustlings of the Reformation occurred *sub crucis*, that is, "under the cross," the swing to the right put an end to the Cross-bearing. When the Reformers accepted the hand of the local rulers the sacralist climate returned;*

*There is a long and persistent custom on the part of historians to begin the story of the Reformation in any given area at the point when civil rulers appear on the scene ready and willing to support the Reform; this means that these historians begin at the point where some new and now Protestant version of "Christian sacralism" has become feasible. This makes them begin the story of the Reformation in Germany at the point where the Princes give evidence that they will support the Reform;

the Cross no longer awaited the person who walked the way
of the Reform.

For men who had Restitutionism in their blood this looked like
a betrayal, a betrayal very like to the one against which the
Donatists had fought. To them a Cross-less discipleship was
a contradiction in terms. As a recent scholar has put it: "The
Anabaptists accepted suffering not as an incidental but as an
essential to discipleship. Baptism is a baptism into death. When
the Church is true to its calling, it is a suffering Church. With
the conversion of Constantine, however, it exchanged its status
as a suffering Church for that of a persecuting Church and
therefore lost its status as the true Church."[18] Of, as another
modern investigator has put it:

> . . . a 'theology of martyrdom' developed among the Brethren,
> an understanding that the citizen of the Kingdom of God
> will necessarily meet suffering in this world . . . . The Ana-
> baptist accepted the idea of the suffering Church in an almost
> matter of fact fashion, and every member of this group under-
> stood it without much explanation. In fact, we often discover
> even a kind of longing for martyrdom, a desire to be allowed
> to testify for the new spiritual world through suffering and
> supreme sacrifice.[19]

It is apparent that in the Second Front baptism was looked
upon as the rite in which one lays bare his back, as it were, in
anticipation of the Cross. As Conrad Grebel put it:

> He that is baptized has been planted into the death of Christ . . . .
> True Christians are sheep among wolves, ready for the slaugh-
> ter. They must be baptized into anguish and affliction, tribu-

---

it makes them begin the story of the Reformation in England with
Henry VIII; in France with the coming of the Conde's, etc. In this
school of thought, the Reform in the Low Countries begins at 1566,
with the *Compromis* of the Nobles. Now it is quite true that the Reform
that saw things through to victory in the Low Countries did begin with
the *Compromis*. But this school of history must of necessity make light
of all that went before 1566. This is to make light of a very important
chapter in the story, the first chapter. After all, the Reformation was
already fifty years old when the *Compromis* was drawn up. The *Compromis*
did indeed start a new chapter; but it quite as certainly brought a chapter to its close, the chapter in which Restitutionism, and not neo-
Constantinianism, calls the signals.

lation, persecution, suffering, and death.[h] They must be tried in the fire and must reap the fatherland of rest, not by killing their bodily enemies but by mortifying their spiritual ones.

What the Stepchildren had against the Reformers was that they had "welded the Cross to the sword," an operation whereby in the Stepchildren's eyes they lost the right to the name of Christian. As Leonard Schiemer put it, in words written from the prison where he was incarcerated for being an Anabaptist: "If the Cross is not experienced then we have the proof that we are false Christians, not yet adopted into the sonship of God." Schiemer was burned for writing that way, on January 14, 1528.

A simple peasant woman who had joined the Anabaptist movement said, "We want to attend preaching services where Christ is preached; your Christ brings you no suffering." Another plain person put it this way, "Wherever you hear about the Cross, there the true Church is in evidence."

Baptism was not only the prelude to suffering in the Anabaptist system of thought; it was also part of the symbolism of the Lord's Supper. Christ had drained a bitter cup, to the dregs, and they who follow Him will have a similar experience. As Hans Cluber, an Anabaptist on trial in Hesse in 1535, put it, "What men take to themselves in the sacrament is neither blood nor flesh, but trouble and anguish; He who would drink the sweet cup in the hereafter must empty the sour one here."[20]

The readiness with which the Stepchildren shouldered this Cross and the singular constancy with which they bore it, had tremendous propaganda value. In a way that reminded of the medieval "heretics" and of the early Christians, the ashes of the martyrs became the seed of the Church. For every Anabaptist that was burned, a whole handful rose up to take his place. Menno Simons himself was sent on the way toward Anabaptism by the spectacle of Sicke Snijder being put to death. So effective was this Cross-bearing that it became the custom to tie a piece of wood crosswise in the mouth of a person about to be executed,

[h]The identification of Cross-bearing and baptism is of course well grounded in the New Testament. In Mark 10:38f., Jesus, speaking of his passion, refers to it as a baptism, a baptism, moreover, to which His disciples would also be treated. The "baptism" mentioned in Luke 12:50 is also, so it seems, synonymous with the Cross.

so that he would be unable to testify and so draw men and women after himself.

The neo-Constantinians were at their wits' end to neutralize the effectiveness of the Stepchildren's Cross-bearing. Luther spoke with some disdain of "people who fashion for themselves a willingness to suffer and leave all behind; and then they boast of being martyrs, so seeking their own honor." He saw an exact parallel with that which had happened in the days of the Donatists; for he said, "We see many die with a smile on their lips, facing death without blanching, just as people possessed have no fear of death. This sort of thing we had occasion to see previously in the Donatists, and we see it in our own times in the Anabaptists."[21]

At another time Luther wrote:

> St. Augustine in earlier times had much to do with the Donatists; they were the same kind of customers and seducers in that they too begged men to put them to death, asking executioners to slay them, in their passion for martyrdom. And then when no one complied by taking them in hand they hurled themselves from bridges or tumbled from housetops, or broke their necks, the while quoting the saying about "whoso loves his own life more than me," etc.[22]

The enemies of the Stepchildren exploited Augustine's saying, coined in that man's rounds with the Donatists, "Martyrem fecit causa, non poena" (it is the cause that makes the martyr, not the punishment). They also informed the Anabaptists that Christ did not say "Blessed are they that suffer" but "Blessed are they that suffer for righteousness' sake" — which was, of course, to beg the question.

Luther's hint that it was demon-possession that inspired the Stepchildren's fortitude in the face of death was enlarged upon by Adam Krafft, who had this to say:

> That they are possessed and blinded by the devil becomes apparent . . . when they go willingly into death, into fire and into water. The devil is wont to do such things. In the Gospel we read of him casting a young man into the fire (Matthew 17) . . . as also he drove Judas into the noose. It is apparent that in our times he continues to drive people so that they end themselves, just as in earlier times the Donatists went of themselves into the water and into the fire. The devil tried

also to get the Christ to make a martyr of himself when he
suggested that the Christ should leap from the temple tower.[23]

For a long time this explanation of the Stepchildren's willingness to bear the Cross continued in vogue. We find it still employed at the Disputation held at Emden in 1578, where the
spokesman for the Reformed position cautioned his Anabaptist
opponents that "a man may fool himself with the Cross and with
persecution. . . . The Donatists sought similarly to prove by their
Cross-bearing that they were the Church of God. . . ."

One thing that Augustine left unexplained was left unexplained by the Reformers also. It is this. If one withholds from
the people whom they called "Donatists" the passages in the
New Testament that speak of Cross-bearing as the mark of the
believer, to whom then are they applicable? Least of all can they
appropriate them who sit snug and smug behind the arm
of flesh, the sword of the civil ruler, in a situation of "Christian
sacralism,"[1] in a situation in which there was nothing even remotely resembling the Cross-experience of the early Christians.

✧   ✧   ✧   ✧   ✧

Another term of reproach employed to stigmatize the Stepchildren was the word *Leufer*, a word meaning "one who walks,
or, runs." As such it calls attention to the practice of traveling
about in missionary fashion.

The original Christian Church was a missionary society.
Its members were constantly drawing into its fellowship those
who were "outside." The method was that of witnessing. At life's
more intimate junctures the early Christians witnessed con-

---

[1]The New Testament plainly teaches that the true follower of the
Christ will experience something of the Cross. Whether the very preaching
of the Cross will be able to humanize men to such an extent that this
Cross becomes less heavy is of course a question by itself. Menno Simons
had his ideas about this question, alleging that to the end of time the
faithful would have to bear the Cross. He wrote, in his most influential
tract, his *Fundamentboek*: "Do not comfort one another with senseless
comfort and unfounded hope, as do those who think that the Word will
yet be taught and practiced without the cross . . . . Tear from your
heart the harmful thought of hoping for different times, lest you be
deceived in your false hope. I have known some who waited for a
day of freedom; but they did not live long enough to see their hope
realized."

cerning the Faith that was in them. What was true of the apostolic Church was true for the pre-Constantinian Church generally: "The Lord added to her daily such as should be saved."

In the account given in the Book of Acts the witness to the Resurrected One did not elicit much ill will, if any, at the hands of the people confronted. (The only significant exception in Acts is the case of Ephesus, recorded in Chapter 19; and here the motive is economic rather than religious.) Such ill-will as came to expression issued from the apostate Jews rather than from the gentiles. This less than hostile reception of the messengers of Christ and their message, characterized the entire post-apostolic period.

This was a period of almost incredible expansion. Men from every walk of life came into the Church in large numbers, from one end of the empire to the other, and from the regions beyond. Christians insinuated themselves into every activity of the society of the day. They were in the army, in politics, in the courts and palaces. It is hard to visualize what might have been if this method had been continued.[1]

But the Constantinian change put an end to this epoch. In the climate of "Christian sacralism," missions in the erstwhile sense are unthinkable. To whom can an individual witness if all men already "belong"? Such expansion programs as there were became just an aspect of military annexation, the kind we witness for example in the late medieval times when the New World was discovered and a *conquistador* and a *padre* stepped ashore simultaneously, the former to plant a flag and the latter a cross. Then the conquerors moved on to further

---

[1] In far less than a century the Christian Faith had found adherents in virtually every place. As early as the year 112, Pliny the Younger, in a letter to the emperor Trajan said of the Christianity of his day: "The disease of this superstition has spread itself over the cities not only but also across villages and towns." So great was the number of adherents of the new faith that this pagan Roman expressed the fear that the resulting reduction in the volume of sacrifice would incur the wrath of the gods and so bring calamity upon the State. For, as an emperor put it early in the 4th century, "All the calamities have come to pass because of the destructive notions of the folly of these reckless men, since this folly has seized them and has placed virtually the whole world under their ridiculous behavior."

"conquests for Christ." Sometimes a token baptism of some key men in the area passed for the "christening" of the whole tribe. Needless to say, men so "converted" were changed not at all. Commonly the only effect was the laying of a painfully thin veneer upon the existing heathenism. One can see the out-workings of this kind of "missions" in many a land today; the same old superstitions, the same poverty and squalor that existed before, with nothing but a shrine and a steeple and a crucifix to tell us that this is a region that has been "evangelized."

Missions in the New Testament sense the medieval world did not know. The prevailing view was that the Great Com-mission, the command to preach the Gospel to all nations, had been executed, finished, in and with the "larger fulfillment" of which Augustine had spoken so oracularly. As a consequence, the eschatological hope that had lived so fervently in the early Church came to a halt; that far-off event to which the New Testament Church had cast its eyes had been realized; all promises had been fulfilled. So thought and lived the medieval Church. The "Maranatha!" of the erstwhile Church died on her lips. Save for a stray voice, such as that of Joachim of Fiore (who was himself a "heretic," albeit within the "fallen" Church), now and then, the recovery of the eschatological hope had to wait until Constantinianism had eroded away.

A sense of mission and a practice of mission did continue to manifest itself — in the camp of the "heretics." Here we find men going on missionary journeys, usually two by two, so emulating the pattern of Luke 10. A striking thing about these missionaries was that they were oblivious to *borders*, the kind surveyors establish. They traveled across such "borders" with the nonchalance that marks the meadow-lark that flies singingly from Montana into Alberta. The mobility of these medieval missionaries is apparent from the fact that, although Waldensianism was originally based in the Piedmont, there were converts to it in every area of the empire, and beyond it, from the Baltic to the Mediterranean.

Naturally, it was frightfully dangerous to engage in such activity. It was therefore done as secretly as possible. Its dimensions must have been infinitely more extensive than the *recorded* facts would indicate; for when things went as planned there was no record made; written accounts were occasioned only if and when things did not go as planned. Then, since the liquidation procedures were recorded, we do have a record. It is safe to say that this missionary activity was like an iceberg — by far the largest part of it was invisible. We get only glimpses.

One such glimpse reveals something of the courage and the conviction, the sense of mission, of these "heretical" missionaries. We read of one of them swimming across the Ibs River, full of floating ice at the time, in the deep of night, in order to reach a person on the other side who had given evidence of being receptive to the gospel.[24]

The Church was frantic over these activities. It invented several damning words, in its fight against this threat. We read of *Schwärmer* (a word that is distantly related to our English word "swarm"); of *Schleicher* (a word meaning one who crawls in); of *Truands* (a word related to our "truant," one who is not in the expected place); of *gyrovagi* (i.e., wanderers in circles); of *Gartenbrüder* (a word meaning wandering ones; it is related to the expression *gardende Knechte,* i.e., mobile soldiers); also of *Leufer.*

Strong testimony to the Church's concern (and therefore to the effectiveness of the missions of the "heretics") may be seen in the steps it took to stop the *Leufer*; it bound every cleric to a parish, so that men might know in all situations who were the authorized clerics and who the not-authorized. By this device the "heretic," unattached as he was, was at a severe disadvantage. The "fallen" Church seems not to have given a thought, and, if she did, then she did not care a fig, for the fact that the New Testament knows nothing about such parishes and such delimitations, whereby a man is told where he may witness and where not.

Strongest testimony of all to the effectiveness of this missionary activity of the "heretics" is the fact that the Church copied it. The Order of the Dominicans was actually created as a response to the "heretic." This Order was to fight fire with fire, simulate the "heretics" in all respects — save one. The Dominicans also were to go out two by two; they too were to go in austere attire; they too were to roam about at will; they too were to preach outside hallowed precincts. The one point of difference was that while the "heretics" spoke evil of the "fallen" Church the

Dominicans were to speak well of her. Save for this point of difference, the two varieties of itinerant preacher looked very much alike — up to such details as the wearing of a beard.ᵏ

Needless to say, the creation of this Order (notorious from the outset for its *ketterjacht*, its inquisitorial tactics in connection with "heretics") made the lot of the "heretic" much more difficult. Henceforth it would be hard to know friend from foe.

It seems that in some instances these measures against the "heretics" boomeranged. So well had the Church instructed her obedient children to shun the roving missionary, run him out of town, stone him, that when the new variety put in its appearance in outlying districts, where the news of the creation of the new Order had not yet penetrated so it seems, they were received gruffly with "Are you heretics and did you come to infect Germany as you have Lombardy?" Not being too well at home in the language, they answered in the affirmative. Upon this they were stoned and only with some difficulty got out of town unhurt.[1]

Since missions cannot thrive in the climate of sacralism and since the Reformers turned to a new version of "Christian sacralism," it is not at all surprising that the Reformation did not develop a theology of missions nor a practice of missions.ᵐ

ᵏIt was a common feature of the medieval "heretic" to wear a full beard, so much so that "heretics" were commonly called *Bartmänner*, men with beards. This throws an interesting, and probably significant, light upon the fact that among the more conservative descendants of the Anabaptists there still is a religious sensitivity that prescribes a beard for the adult male.

[1]It seems that a similarly ludicrous occurrence took place in Cologne as well as in Paris (related by Mens in his *Oorsprong en Beteekenis van de Nederlandsche Begijnen en Begarden Beweging*, p. 31ff.). One can hardly believe that the news of the newly-created Order had not yet reached these important *centra* when the events occurred. We must therefore seek for an other explanation for the hostilities there. In view of fact that in a great many instances the populace was on the side of the "heretics," as were in many instances even the local governors, the less than friendly reception of the Dominicans may find its explanation in popular disapproval of the increased inquisitorial activity provided by the creation of the new Order of heresy-hunters.

ᵐTo this day it is customary among the Reformed people of the Netherlands to reserve the word *Zending* (missions) to the foreign scene. Missions within the homeland are usually referred to as *Evangelisatie*. Back of this usage there lies, of course, the assumption that people who

The swing toward the right prevented that. It has been said that

> The prevailing view with regard to foreign missions at the
> beginning of the Protestant era was that the command to
> preach the Gospel to all nations was given only to the original
> apostles and expired with them. This view was to persist
> within Protestantism for three centuries and more.[25]

The people of Reformation times looked upon all those whom
they met in daily contact as in some genuine sense *Christian;*
and this precludes a missionary outreach. The recovery of the
missionary insight dates from the moment when the sacralism
of Reformation times had eroded away sufficiently. Not until
the concept of the Church as "including all in a given locality"
was overcome was it possible for missions in the New Testament
sense to be resumed.[n] And then it was discovered that there was
a big dike of resentment to be overcome — men in areas that
had had bad experiences with "Christendom" looked upon the
missionary with understandable distrust. As Emil Brunner has
put it:

> The main obstacle in our day to Christian advance is obviously
> the guilt of the past centuries, namely the Christian mission
> having been a part of western imperialism, or to put it more
> mildly, the Christian mission letting itself be protected by the
> western powers. It will take a long time until the memory of
> this fact is extinguished.[26]

One of the first things that had to be done in the drive to
recover the mission of the New Testament was to convince men
that the Great Commission was still in force. William Carey, per-

---

are part of *Christendom* can hardly be objects of *missionary* activity,
that the "heathen" who lives, let us say, in a suburb of Amsterdam is
less a "heathen," or at least a significantly different kind of "heathen,"
than is the native of Borneo.

[n]Little by little European Churchmen are beginning to recover the
New Testament dimension of *mission,* and this recovery is contingent
upon the awareness that the Constantinian experiment is a thing of the
past. Recently, so it is reported, a young Swiss pastor accepted his
office only on condition that it be clearly understood that the role and
mission of the Church in Switzerland is "precisely the same as in pre-
totalitarian China." (Cf. Franklin H. Littell, *The Free Church,* p. 4.)

haps the pioneer in this recovery, was obliged to argue at great length "whether the commission given by our Lord to His disciples be not still binding on us." His book entitled *An Inquiry into the Obligations of Christians to Use Means for the Conversion of the Heathen*, written in 1792, marks the beginning of a new era, the Era of Missions — three centuries after 1517!

These three centuries would not have been lost if the Stepchildren had had their way. For with them, missions in the New Testament sense were in vogue from the outset. In fact, this lay evangelism, this witness of man to man, not only played a large part in the rapid spread of Anabaptism but appeared to the Reformers to be one of its most objectionable and dangerous features. To obstruct it, they revived the ancient Catholic weapon against the *Leufer*, insisting again that every man who presumes to handle the Word of God must be "called" by the magistrate and then restricted to a parish. To this the Stepchildren, as early as 1525, said, with Zwingli and Leo Jüd in mind: "If you were as evangelical as you think you are, you would obey the Gospel and go out as emissaries of God, to preach the Word of God and return the erring to the right way."

The Stepchildren had re-discovered that there is such a thing as the "world" and that it lies right at every man's doorstep. It was by this rediscovery that, as a modern student has put it: "Evangelism, which for the Constantinian reformers was by definition inconceivable, became a real possibility; alone of the churches of the Reformation, the Anabaptists considered evangelism as belonging to the essential being of the church."[27]

Among the Stepchildren the distinction of pastor and missionary was unknown; every pastor was a missionary, and every missionary was a pastor. For the Stepchildren the world was populated with two kinds of people, those who witness and those who are witnessed to. There was for them no third category.

Nor does the distinction, so proper enough in the framework of "Christian sacralism," of Home Missions and Foreign Missions, make sense in the thought-world of the Stepchildren. It makes sense only to men who operate with the concept of "Christendom." It is an interesting and significant fact, but not a surprising one, that the Reformed Churches in the New World are embarrassed by this ancient terminology.° It rests upon the mistaken notion that the world is populated with three kinds of people, Christians, christians, and non-Christians; wherever men return to the New Testament teaching that the world is populated with but two kinds of people, believers and not-yet-believers, the distinction of Home Missions and Foreign Missions is certain to lose its meaning. Whether a man lives in the jungles of the Amazon or in the jungles of Omaha makes no essential difference; both are objects of the missionary outreach, and in the same way. For, as Lesslie Newbigin has said, so very correctly:

> The precise differentiation which entitles an activity to be called "missionary" . . . does not lie in the crossing of a geographical frontier . . . . It lies in the crossing of the frontier between faith in Christ . . . and unbelief.

Newbigin spoke from a situation in which there is no Constantinian heritage, and it is this fact that led him to say what we have just quoted. In so speaking, he was but appropriating an idiom of the Stepchildren, who four centuries earlier knew that "Christendom" is and always was a myth, only a myth, and who said so, come what may, and who for saying this were belabored with the spiteful name of *Rottengeister*.

✿   ✿   ✿   ✿   ✿

°The Christian Reformed Church, for example, is presently toying with the possibility of bringing its total missionary activity under one head. This Church, which began as a transplant from European soil, had inherited the concept of *inwendige zending* (which it rendered "Home Missions") and *heiden zending* (which it rendered "Foreign Missions"). From the original names of these two it is apparent that the distinction intended was not that of mission-within and mission-without (as men conveniently try to believe). The terms stand for mission to people who are a part of "Christendom" and mission to people who are not. Home Missions hope to make Christians out of christians, whereas Foreign Missions hope to make Christians out of non-Christians. It is significant that this Church, early in its career on this continent, when it discovered that there were Indian tribes in the great Southwest which were in no sense a part of "Christendom," began mission work among them, placing this work under the heading of "Heathen Missions," even though the terrain was within the boundaries of the United States, so setting up a Foreign Mission that was not foreign. Needless to say, now that the Constantinian past is a thing of the past, this terminology is no longer tolerable.

The Stepchildren of the Reformers were frequently known as "*weerloze Christenen*," that is, defenseless Christians, people who believed in non-resistence. To this day the typical descendant of these Stepchildren will be classified as a "C.O.," a conscientious objector. The conviction that to bear arms is incongruous for a Christian has perhaps been the greatest single factor contributing to the frequent and distressingly difficult migrations in which the descendants of the Stepchildren have been involved. Throughout their history, right up to modern times, have they preferred to leave all behind, pull up stakes, and migrate to a far-away place, rather than participate in the business of war. It may be said that this refusal for reasons of conscience to don a soldier's uniform is the one feature of these people with which the man in the street is familar.

In this feature of the Anabaptists' vision they were not indebted to the Reformers, were not even of a piece with them. They were also in this aspect not "Left-wing." For the Reformers one and all made their peace with the institution of war. (Zwingli himself died on the battlefield.) No, in this matter, as in so many others, the Stepchildren were a resurgence of an ancient insight, heirs to an ancient legacy, the legacy of the "heretic."

In a sacral society, warfare is not only in honor but is blessed. The god of ethnic religion is a god of *battle,* and the priest gives blessing to the expedition of war. In fact, in a sacral society religion has as much, if not more, to do with war as with any other thing that involves society.

Original Christianity struck a new note in regard to all this. The Christ came "meek and lowly" and the rôle of the conqueror was utterly foreign to Him. "My kingdom," said He, "is not of this world; if it were then would my servants fight . . ., but now is my kingdom not from hence." And when one of His disciples sliced the air with a well-aimed sword, so cutting off the ear of a man in uniform, Jesus said majestically, "Enough of that, put it back; all that take the sword will perish at its edge." And, stooping down, He forthwith repaired the damage — lest His cause be misconstrued from the beginning.

The early Church remembered. It had an army and an arsenal — but its weapons, though "mighty . . . to the pulling down of strongholds" were strictly "not carnal," nor, it may be added, carnage-creating.

It is true, the New Testament Church still had the Old Testament; and in it warfare had the status that it regularly has in a sacral society. But so sure was the primitive Church that it was heir to a new and better covenant, so sure was it that the Old had been superseded by the New, that it looked upon the Old Testament's attitude toward war as little more than a curious relic of the past. It would, if there had been no other alternative, have repudiated the Old Testament rather than lose the novelty of Christ's attitude toward war: "Better [as Adolf von Harnack has it] to let go of the Old Testament than to let the image of the Father of Jesus Christ be clouded by a warlike shadow." The rise of Marcionism proves the point we are making. Marcion saw no chance of harmonizing the regime of Jesus Christ with the dispensation of the Old Testament; and in desperation He abandoned the Old Testament, relegating it to some lesser deity.[P]

The Constantinian change put an end to all of this. When it had come full circle "the meek and peaceful Jesus had become the God of battle, and the cross, the holy sign of Christian redemption, a banner of bloody strife."[28] "The God of the Christians had changed into a God of war and of conquest." And "the sign of the cross, to which Jesus had been led by his refusal to sanction or to lead a patriotic war and on which he had died for the salvation of men, was now an imperial military emblem, one bringing good fortune and victory." Be it remembered that Constantine introduced the monogram in which the first two letters of the name of Christ are combined, on the shields of his soldiers! And bits of iron, which the emperor's mother persuaded herself were relics of the nails of the Cross of Christ and which she had sent to her son, were by him made into parts of a bridlebit of his champion war steed, and a helmet, which he used in his military expedition.[29] Pagan that he was at heart,

---

[P]Of Marcion and his followers Harnack has said, "Marcion hat ungezweifelt den christlichen Gottesbegrif wesentlich richtig erfasst . . . . Es wird stets ein Ruhm der marcionitische Kirche . . . bleiben, dasz sie lieber das Alte Testament verwerfen, als das Bild des Vaters Jesu Christi durch Einmengung von Zügen eines kriegerischen Gottes truben wollte" (*Militia Christi*, p. 25). The adherents of "Christian sacralism," who had no trouble in the matter, poured out vials of vitriol on the Marcionists, more than they deserved.

and remained, he thought that he had found a new God of battle, one mightier than the Mars of old had ever been![q]

And ever since Constantine, when the Church at last got to the place where it could win wars and gain political advantages from them, it has supported war in the name of the Prince of Peace. War became a Christian enterprise, perhaps the noblest of them all. By the year 416 the tables had been so completely turned that non-Christians were no longer wanted in the army.[30]

Small wonder that there was rebellion against this deformation. There were those who kept in contact with the New Testament and who were therefore in position to know from what heights the Church had fallen. It became a feature of medieval dissent to frown on war and the tumult thereof.

At times this dissent took the form of rejecting not only warfare but also capital punishment. It was a feature of Waldensianism to acknowledge that the sword of the magistrate is "of God," to obviate social chaos, but must not go the full length, must stop short of taking human life.[31]

Although it can be argued that the Reformers, notably Zwingli, at the first held a position approaching that of pacifism,[32]

---

[q]In our own times, during the second World War, the world witnessed a very similar role assigned to religion. What Shintoism was to the Japanese war-lords, that the religion of the Christians was to Constantinians, a thing with which to bind together a total people in a concerted war effort. With Constantine begins a martialization of the Christian religion that changed its nature very radically, so radically that it became quite unrecognizable. Is this to say too much? Who can recognize anything of the Man of Galilee in the brutal boasting of pope Innocent III, who after the fearful carnage wreaked upon the Albigensians, gloated: "God has mercifully purged His people's lands; and the pest of heretical wickedness which had grown like a cancer and had infected the whole of Provence is being deadened and driven away. His mighty hand has taken many towns and cities wherein the devil dwelt in the persons of those whom he possessed; and a holy habitation is being prepared for the Holy Ghost in the persons of those whom He hath filled, to take the place of the expelled heretics. Wherefore we give praise to Almighty God because in one and the same cause of His mercy He has deigned to work two works of justice, by bringing these faithless folk their merited destruction, in such fashion that as many as possible of the faithful should gain their well-earned reward by the extermination of these folk . . . . He hath deigned by their destruction to grant a means of wealth, nay more, of salvation, by the armies . . . that have lately triumphed over them . . . ."

it is beyond cavil that in their final edition they were ready to give their blessing to warfare — even to warfare waged for the faith. Their espousal of neo-Constantinianism left them no choice but to return to the medieval theology, in which "the Son of God goes forth to war, a kingdom to subdue." The many and frightful "religious wars" were the direct outcome of the Reformers' return to that mongrel version of the Christian faith that began in the days of Constantine. If kings must support the "true religion" with the weapons of war, then there will be no end of bloodshed and carnage, seeing that men, and nations, will not agree as to what the "true religion" is.[r]

Upon the heels of the Reformers' re-espousal of war as a Christian undertaking, especially upon the heels of their drift toward war as a proper instrument for the propagation and preservation of the faith, came the Stepchildren's assault upon war, as a device for the promotion of the cause of Christ at the outset; but soon against war as such. With them "Christian warfare" was a warfare waged not with clanging engines of destruction but with weapons "mighty to the pulling down of the strongholds of sin." "True Christians," said one of them, "are sheep in the midst of wolves, sheep for the slaughter, to be baptized in anguish and distress, trouble and persecution, suffering and death, tried in the fire; they attain to the fatherland of everlasting peace not by killing foes of flesh, but foes of spirit."[33]

In their haste to come clear of the Constantinian distortion, a distortion whereby the very Christ took on the features of the Mars of ancient ethnicism, they presently found themselves in a quandary as to whether a man can be both a Christian and a magistrate, seeing that a magistrate must be prepared to pick up the sword, and, if need be slay men with it. This was the same hard question over which Tertullian had mulled long ago, "aut si Christiani potuissent esse Caesares," whether Christians can also be emperors. They came to no unanimity touching this question. The prevailing opinion was that it is better for the Christian to stay away from an assignment that may take him

---

[r]It was one of the bitter ironies of history that Huldreich Zwingli, the man who had served as midwife at the birth of Protestantism, had had a hand in welding the sword once more to the Cross of Christ, himself died on the battlefield, caught in the traffic between two "Christian magistrates," each doing his duty in regard to religion.

to the place of bloodshed. Better to leave that assignment to
once-born men, with whom "an eye for an eye" is the standard
of dealing with infractions. They would then themselves be free
to practice the stipulations laid down in the Sermon on the
Mount. Since no policeman can live by the command to "turn
the other cheek," the job of the policeman was not for them.
We may smile at the *naïveté* of this philosophy; we may frown
at this solution; but he who has been with the New Testament
will have even greater trouble with the person who has no
problem here, no problem because he has allowed the unique
message of Jesus Christ to be cast into the mold of pre-Christian
systems. Only that man is "fit for the kingdom" who encounters
a real problem here. And that man will find himself drawn to
the sensitivity, if not to the practical solutions, that marked the
vision of the *Rottengeister*.

Postscript

In this book we have dealt with the rift that developed between the Reformers of the sixteenth century and the men of the Second Front. This rift was the result of a problem that perennially besets the Church of Christ, the problem of how to relate that Church to its environment. It is the problem that is posed by the formula "in the world but not of the world." The history of the Church is, to a large extent, the story of a tension between two extreme tendencies: the one extreme makes so much of the principle "in the world" that the Church loses her identity; the other extreme makes so much of the principle "not of the world" that the Church becomes irrelevant. There is a frighteningly large element of truth in a sentiment expressed by Roland H. Bainton: "If there is no accommodation [to culture] Christianity is unintelligible and cannot spread; if there is too much accommodation it will spread, but will no longer be Christianity."[1] The way of orthodoxy is often the way of recovering equilibrium.

In this volume the Radicals of Reformation times receive more sympathetic treatment than they are wont to get, especially in the Reformed tradition. There are two reasons for this sympathetic treatment. One is that the time seems to have come to reverse the derogatory treatment to which these Stepchildren of the Reformation have been traditionally subjected. One can speak very well of them indeed before he becomes guilty of a bias as pronounced as that of those who have so long spoken evil of them; one can let these Stepchildren play the rôle of the hero and he will be at least as near to historic truth as is the tradition that has so long assigned to them the rôle of the rogue.

A second reason for the sympathetic treatment given these Radicals of the Reformation is that history has to a large extent demonstrated that they were in a large way right. Little by little, step by step, item by item, Protestantism has, at least in

276

the New World, come to endorse the very emphases for which these men pioneered. The free Church, the Church by voluntary association, the missionary Church, and a host of other features for which the Stepchildren agonized, have become part and parcel of the Protestant vision — so much so that men are often surprised to learn that it was not always thus. It is not too much to say that in the New World, as well as among the so-called Younger Churches, the vision of the men of the Second Front has, to a large extent, fought through to victory. The First Amendment of the Federal Constitution of these United States, has, as has been intimated in this volume, carved out the kind of pluralistic situation for which the Stepchildren toiled; it has secured, by the highest law of the land, the kind of cultural and societal compositism for which they labored; it has laid low the sacralism against which they fought. And it has done so with apparent blessing. At the end of the New World experimentation with Old World sacralism, on the eve of the ratification of the Federal Constitution with its First Amendment, but six percent of the citizenry was Church-related; from that moment, the moment of the official repudiation of the sacral formula, dates the return to the Church, in a gradual increase, which without a single setback, has continued to this day, so that now the percentage of Church-relatedness stands in excess of sixty percent. When it is remembered that this is all strictly on a voluntary basis, with complete absence of the compulsions that go with the sacral formula, then it may be said that the American people have become the most religious people on earth. There are voices even in the Catholic Church* in the New World asserting that the Catholic Church is nowhere else in possession of the state of health in which it finds itself here. The heritage of the "heretic" seems therefore to be salubrious. For that reason also have we dealt kindly with it.

All this is not to say that the Stepchildren's solution of the Church's knottiest problem solves all her difficulties. No indeed. In fact, it raises some new ones. The problem with which they dealt, the problem of the *mode d'integration* of Church and

---

*We say "even in the Catholic Church" because of the fact that the Roman Catholic Church has not to this day rejected the sacral formula, nor officially espoused societal compositism.

society, is in the very nature of things ultimately and finally insoluble; that which derives from the resources supplied by the *paliggenesia* (the new birth) cannot be intergrated smoothly with that which has no other resources than those that are present in the unregenerate heart. Perhaps a *modus vivendi* (a way of getting along as best we may) is the best we can hope for, a being "in the world" without being "of the world."

This problem remains, even if and when the Stepchildren have their way. The Christian, in the New Testament sense of that word, is a sojourner. But to play well the part of a sojourner is no easy task. For a sojourner stands halfway between a native and a migrant; he must walk the thin line that separates total engagement from total disengagement. This can never become easy.

There are straws in the wind which indicate that the battle that raged at the Second Front is not ancient history and a thing of the past. We shall mention a few.

There are, to begin with, certain overtones of the so-called ecumenical movement that leave the impression that sacralism is not quite dead, not even in the areas in which the First Amendment is in force.

Although it is indisputably true to say that whatever may be good and great in the American tradition developed in the climate of religious pluralism and denominational multiformity, one detects in the temper of some of the advocates of Church union a decidedly negative attitude toward America's past in this matter. We are asked to go in sackcloth because of the "sin of denominationalism" — whatever that "sin" may be. What is this but to look askance upon a feature of the American landscape, a feature concerning which we have laboratory proof that it is a blessing, even if not an unmixed one?

Under the tutelage of such ecumenicalism, an "American religion" could be developing, a religiosity to which every right-thinking American would be expected to rally. This would be the "Common Faith" of which John Dewey spoke so oracularly. This could usher in a new sacralism; it could herald the coming of a new "right" religion. And that would call for the creation of a new Second Front; it would make needful again the creation of a Protest such as that of the Stepchildren in their day, against the everybody-embracing Church. Such a development would bring back into the parlance of men once again the expression "the fallen Church," or "the false Church:"[b]

Closely related to the foregoing, and perhaps likewise indicative of an emerging neo-sacralism, is the revival on the contemporary scene of the medieval word "sectarian." Need it be pointed out that in the climate of authentic Americanism there can be no such thing as "sectarian"? This word is a correlative, a word that derives its meaning from a companion concept. Just as the word "wife" requires the concept "husband," just as the word "employer" requires the concept "employee," so does the word "sectarian" require the concept "sacral." A thing can be sectarian only in the climate of establishment. A sectary is, historically, etymologically, by definition, a person who deviates from the "right" religion. But as long as in America there is no "right" religion, that is, as long as the First Amendment stands unrepudiated, there can be no "sectarian" position. He who labels a thing "sectarian," or a man a "sectary," has already in substance embraced the idea of establishment, has already abandoned the postulate that in the American vision all religiosities are equally right in the eyes of the law. Such a man is already operating with the concept of a "right" religion; he has already embraced a new sacralism. And he is but one step short, and it is a short step, from the inevitable concomitant of all sacralism, namely, persecution for him who dissents from the "right" religion. He has done his bit to bring back the world against which the Stepchildren inveighed. He has already approximated the days of the Stepchildren, in which it was held that he who declares that the pope is the vicegerent of Christ is fully entitled to the floor but that he who denies it must sit down and hold his peace. Theism is a "sectarian doctrine" only if and when atheism has been called the "right" position.

This brings us to the educational front in the contemporary American scene. Here the First Amendment, which was written in order to provide and secure a climate in which all religious persuasions would have equal rights before the law, which was

---

[b] It is an alarming fact that in the literature advocating the amalgamation of all churches into a single church the concept of "the false Church" is virtually unknown; all that calls itself the Church is, so it seems, by that token entitled to the name.

intended to provide religious multiformity, is being quoted as though its intention had been to provide religious vacuity. The First Amendment, which was intended to preclude a too favorable position for one religious tradition (and the consequent handicap for the rest), has become a handicap for all religious orientations. This piece of legislation, intended to preclude the rise of sacralism in the United States, is being quoted in support of a new sacralism, the sacralism of secularism. The upshot of all this is that, in the classroom, he who believes that the universe is "running" talks at the top of his voice while he who believes that the universe is "run" must prudently lower his voice. This handicap for the person of the latter conviction is an intolerable violation of the First Amendment, which forbids the highest law of the land to prevent the free exercise of religion no less than it forbids the "establishment" thereof.[e]

Although the First Amendment officially repudiates sacralism, and so endorses the views for which the men of the Second Front fought, the repudiation of sacralism has not as yet become the heritage of every individual American. That this is so, and the extent to which it is so, became apparent during the campaign of the late and much lamented President Kennedy. There were many Americans who were against Kennedy because he was a Roman Catholic in his religious loyalties. Their tacit assumption was that the "right" religion in America is some version of Protestantism. These people were blissfully unaware of the decidedly un-American nature of this stance in the matter; they were blissfully ignorant of the fact that their pose is a direct rejection of the highest law of the land; they were blissfully un-

---

[e] How a member of the Supreme Court can argue that the First Amendment restrains the government of the land from "promoting a religion, all religion . . ." is indeed difficult to understand. The First Amendment actually sets no limit to the extent to which the government can support "all religion" — save the limit imposed by a policy of impartiality. As far as the first Amendment is concerned, laws could be passed whereby the salaries of clergymen and all other practitioners of religion would be paid in whole or in part with public funds — just so there be no partiality shown. This would merely be to extend to the civilian area certain policies that are already in vogue in the military; the First Amendment is not being violated when the salary of an army chaplain is paid; violation would occur if and when a partiality toward the Protestant (or Catholic) chaplain is evinced.

mindful of the fact that theirs is an essentially medieval position, one that has bathed the world in blood and tears.[a]

In all events, the battle that raged at the Second Front is a battle that did not end with those who fought there. It is part of an Eighty Years' War, a contest in which generations succeeding each other will be involved. For this reason the story that we have sought to tell in this volume will be useful reading for all who come after them and who seek to fight the good fight of faith.

---

[a] It is of course an altogether different question whether a Roman Catholic can with good conscience take the oath of office. The Roman Catholic Church has not openly, much less officially, repudiated the sacral formula — which he who promises to support the Constitution must repudiate. In situations where she can get away with it, the Catholic Church leaves no stone unturned to impose serious civil handicap upon all who dissent from her position. And she does this with the full knowledge and approval of those who govern her affairs. In view of these incontestable facts it is not incorrect to hold that in order to take the oath of office as President of the United States one must be either an off-color American or an off-color Catholic. When John F. Kennedy made it unequivocally clear that he was the latter, declared in very clear terms that he shared heartily in the American rejection of sacralism, then there was no further reason to oppose his candidacy on this score. (How he could do this without thereby coming under the rebuke of the Catholic Church leaders is a question by itself.) His career in office, from the very beginning to the hour of infamy on the streets of Dallas, left little to be wished for in the matter of fidelity to the American principle of a-sacralism.

Bibliographical Footnotes

INTRODUCTION

1. Cf. Luther's Commentary on Genesis 41:45 (*Werke*, St. Louis Edition, Vol. II., col. 417).

CHAPTER I (DONATISTEN)

1. *Epistle to Diognetus*, V, 1-5.
2. Cf. Leo Pfeffer, *Church, State, and Freedom* (Boston, 1953), p. 11. (The University of Michigan has among its papyri holdings an executed exemplar of this formulary. See Inv. 263.)
3. Cf. Origen, *Contra Celsum*, VIII, 69.
4. We are dependent here upon Leo Pfeffer, *op. cit.*
5. Details in this paragraph are derived from W. H. C. Frend, *The Donatist Church* (Oxford, 1952).
6. Cf. *Codex Thedosianus*, XVI, 1:2.
7. *Quellen Hesse*, p. 381.*
8. Cf. Adolf Harnack, "Die Didache und die Waldenser," in *Texte und Untersuchungen zur Geschichte der Altchristliche Literatur* (Leipzig, 1886), S. 269.
9. Gordon Rupp, in *Archiv für Reformationsgeschichte*, Vol. IV (1958), p. 14.
10. A. J. F. Zieglschmidt, ed., *Die Aelteste Chronik der Hutterischen Brüder* (Ithaca, N. Y., 1943), p. 42.
11. John C. Wenger in *M. Q. R.*, October, 1946, p. 253.
12. *Quellen* V, p. 65.
13. *Cornelius*, II, 18.
14. John H. Yoder in *Recovery*, p. 97.
15. Obbe Philips' *Bekenntnisse*, printed in *B. R. N.*, Vol. VII, pp. 12ff.
16. Walter Hobhouse, *The Church and the World in Idea and in History* (London, 1910), p. IX.
17. *Corpus*, cf. Vol. I, p. 143.
18. *Quellen Hesse*, pp. 111f.
19. *Ibid.*, pp. 112f.
20. The Schleitheim Confession has been printed often, *inter alia*, in *M. Q. R.*, Vol. XIX, pp. 243-253. Calvin's refutation of it may be consulted in *C. R.*, Vol. XXXV.
21. The University of Michigan has a microfilm copy of this translation.
22. Abraham Kuyper, *Pro Rege* (Kampen, 1911, 1912), Vol. III, pp. 166f.

* For abbreviations used in these notes, see List of Abbreviations, p. 10.

CHAPTER II (STABLER)

1. *Quellen IV*, p. 381.
2. This and the following two quotations are from Augustine's *Letter to Donatus*, No. 173, as printed in *Select Library of Nicene and Post-Nicene Fathers*, ed. Philip Schaff, Vol. 1.
3. George Gordon Coulton, *Inquisition and Liberty* (London & Toronto, 1938), p. 189, and quoting Sacconi, a Dominican Inquisitor who was himself an ex-heretic.
4. *Quellen Hesse*, p. 108.
5. John Horsch, *Mennonites in Europe* (Scottdale, 1950), p. 325, quoting.
6. The correspondence from which we quote may be consulted in *Fontes Rerum Austriacarum, Band 19*. Cf. also *Revue d'Histoire et de Religieuses* for 1951, No. 1.
7. *Quellen Hesse*, pp. 102f.
8. *Ibid.*, p. 110.
9. *Ibid.*, p. 231.
10. *Archiv für Reformationsgeschichte*, 1959, *Heft 1*, p. 49.
11. This and the following two indented quotations are from *C. R.*, Vol. XXXV, pp. 87ff.
12. *Institutes*, IV, 20:4.
13. This and surrounding quotations are from the Dutch translation of Beza mentioned earlier.
14. *Embder Protocol*, fol. 316, 332.
15. For data see H. Q., *De Kerkhervorming in Vlaanderen* (Arnhem, 1868), Part II, pp. 149, 154, 166, 170, 186, 209.
16. Franklin Hamlin Littell, *The Free Church* (Boston, 1957), p. 18.
17. Quoted in No. 1172 of the *Knuttel Collection of Dutch Historical Tracts* (Copy in General Library of the University of Michigan).
18. Roland H. Bainton in *Recovery*, p. 317.
19. Ernst Troeltsch, *"Die Bedeutung des Protestantismus für die Entstehung der Moderne Welt,"* in *Historisch Zeitschrift*, 1924, 63.
20. Friedrich Lezius, *Der Toleranzbegriff Lockes und Pufendorfs* (Leipzig, 1900).
21. *Quellen IV*, p. 217.

CHAPTER III (CATHARER)

1. Herbert Grundmann, *Religiöse Bewegungen im Mittelalter* (Hildesheim, 1961).
2. *Quellen IX*, p. 119.
3. *Complete Writings of Menno Simons*, translated by Leonard Verduin (Scottdale, 1956). p. 506.
4. Schmidt, *Justus Menius* I, 165.
5. *Quellen IX*, p. 340.
6. *Quellen VI*, pp. 120f.
7. *Acta des Gespraechs zwueschenn predicantenn Uund Tauffbrueden Ergangen Inn der Statt Bernn. . .* (In Vol. 80 of certain *Unnütze Papiere* reposing in the *Staatsarchiv des Kantons Bern;* the Mennonite

Historical Library at Goshen College, Goshen Indiana, has a copy of this manuscript.)

8. *Quellen* VII, p. 403.
9. *Werke,* St. Louis edition, Vol. VII, p. 200.
10. *Ibid.,* Vol. I, p. 296.
11. *Quellen* IV, p. 379.
12. William Joseph McGlothlin, *Die Berner Täufer bis 1532* (Berlin, 1902), p. 36.
13. *Cornelius,* Vol. II, p. 45.
14. Cf. Bullinger's *Der Widertäufferen Ursprung,* fol. 15 verso.
15. Cf. Bullinger's *Unverschämte Frevel,* etc., B, iv.
16. *Quellen Hesse,* pp. 238f.
17. *Ibid.,* p. 270.
18. *Ibid.,* p. 224.
19. This passage occurs in Rhegius' *Widderlegung der Münsterischen newen Valentianer und Donatisten* (1535), near the end.
20. *Quellen Hesse,* pp. 238f.
21. *Ibid.,* pp. 202f.
22. *Ibid.,* p. 444.
23. *Quellen* VI, p. 17.
24. This and surrounding quotations are from Calvin's refutation of Schlatten am Rande, printed in *C. R.,* Vol. XXXV.
25. *Werke,* St. Louis edition, Vol. V, col. 747.
26. *Ibid.,* Vol. X, col. 229.
27. *Quellen Hesse,* p. 178.
28. De Wette, *Luthers Briefwechsel,* Vol. IV, p. 180.
29. Cf. Schwenkfeld's letter to Friedrich von Walden, in *Epistolar* (1570).
30. Schmidt, *Justus Menius* I, 159.
31. *Embder Protocol,* fol. 300 verso.
32. Alfred Mervyn Davies, *Foundation of American Freedom* (Nashville, 1955), p. 16.

CHAPTER IV (SACRAMENTSCHWARMER)

1. *Corpus,* I, 9.
2. *Ibid.,* 19.
3. For these details concerning Tanchelm see *Corpus,* the indexes.
4. *Corpus,* I, 41.
5. *Cornelius,* II, 7.
6. Cf. Zwingli's *Freundliche Auslegung* of 1527.
7. For these and further details concerning the *Flagellantes* see *Corpus,* the indexes.
8. *Corpus,* II, 41.
9. George Gordon Coulton, *op. cit.,* p. 63.
10. *Corpus,* III, 42.
11. *Ibid.,* I, 142.
12. *Ibid.,* I, 54.
13. George Gordon Coulton, *op. cit.,* p. 184.
14. *Recovery,* p. 219.

15. *Quellen Hesse,* p. 299.
16. *Cornelius,* p. I, 228.

CHAPTER V (WINCKLER)

1. Minuscius Felix' *Octavius,* VIII, 4; X, 2.
2. *Corpus Juris, lex codicis* (Justinian), Book I, sec. 6:2.
3. *Quellen* III, p. 147.
4. A French translation of Innocent's letter is in Montet, *Histoire Littéraire des Vaudois du Piedmont* (Paris, 1885), pp. 36f.
5. *Corpus,* I, 54.
6. *Ibid.,* 39.
7. For details concerning the Flagellantes see *Corpus,* the indexes, under *Kruisbroeders* and *Geeselaars.*
8. *Corpus,* I, 32.
9. Cf. Sermon LXV in Migne, Vol. 195.
10. *Corpus,* I, 352.
11. George Gordon Coulton, *op. cit.,* p. 198.
12. *Corpus,* I, pp. 353f.
13. *C. R.,* Vol. XXXV, pp. 592, 613.
14. Herminjard, *Correspondence des Reformateurs* (Geneva & Paris, 1868), II, No. 384.
15. *Quellen* IV, p. 150.
16. *Quellen* VI, p. 394.
17. *Quellen Hesse,* p. 3.
18. *Ibid.,* p. 42.
19. *Ibid.,* p. 150.
20. *Ibid.,* p. 40.
21. *Ibid.,* p. 38.
22. *Ibid.,* p. 63.
23. *Ibid.,* p. 178.
24. *Werke,* St. Louis edition, Vol. V, cols. 720f.
25. *B. R. N.,* Vol. VII, p. 18.
26. Cf. *Complete Writings of Menno Simons* (Scottdale, 1956), p. 1021.
27. James H. Rigg, *The Churchmanship of John Wesley* (London, 1886), p. 25.
28. John Robinson, *A Justification of Separation,* p. 221.
29. Cf. *Commonweal* of September 6, 1957.

CHAPTER VI (WIEDERTAUFER)

1. Josef Beck, *Die Geschichts-Bücher der Wiedertäufer in Osterreich-Ungarn,* being Vol. XLIII of *Fontes Rerum Austriacarum* (Vienna, 1883), p. IX.
2. *Codex Theodosianus,* XVI, 6:1.
3. Charles Gachard, *Correspondence de Philip II,* I, 550.
4. *Corpus,* I, 9.
5. *Ibid.,* 54.
6. George Gordon Coulton, *op. cit.,* p. 234.

7. *Corpus*, II, 41.
8. Cf. Luther's *Postille* on Matthew 8:1 (*Werke*, Weimar edition, Vol. XVII, Abth. 2, pp. 81f.).
9. *Cornelius*, I, 228.
10. *Quellen* VI, pp. 184f.
11. *C. R.*, Vol. 91, p. 241.
12. *Quellen* IX, p. 186.
13. *C. R.*, Vol. 91, p. 228.
14. *Werke*, St. Louis edition, Vol. VII, p. 990.
15. *Quellen* VII, p. 29.
16. *Werke*, Weimar edition, Vol. XXVI, p. 167.
17. *M. Q. R.*, January 1931, pp. 12f.
18. *Ibid.*, Vol. XXI (1947), p. 283.
19. *Quellen* VI, p. 51.
20. *Ibid.*, p. 123.
21. *Ibid.*, p. 214.
22. *Quellen* II, p. 91.
23. *Quellen Hesse*, p. 278.
24. *Ibid.*, p. 291, n. 2.
25. *Ibid.*, p. 382.
26. *Ibid.*, p. 363.
27. *Recovery*, p. 204.
28. *C. R.*, Vol. 91, p. 246.
29. *Werke*, St. Louis edition, Vol. XX, col. 1718.
30. *M. Q. R.*, January 1950, p. 25.
31. John Horsch, *Mennonites in Europe* (Scottdale, 1942), p. 356.
32. *Quellen Hess*, pp. 226f.
33. *C. R.*, Vol. 91, p. 635.
34. *Ibid.*, p. 284.
35. *Ibid.*, p. 246.
36. *Quellen Hesse*, pp. 247f.

CHAPTER VII (KOMMUNISTEN)

1. George Gordon Coulton, *op. cit.*, p. 20.
2. Ludwig Keller, *Die Anfänge der Reformation und die Aeltere Reform-parteien*, p. 396.
3. *Corpus*, IV, pp. 338f.
4. In *Revue des Questions Historiques*, Vol. LXXVI (1904), p. 399.
5. *Quellen* VI, p. 117.
6. The Groninger Edict is printed in No. 1172 of the Knuttel Collection of Dutch Historical Tracts.
7. *Quellen* IV, p. 117.
8. *C. R.*, Vol. XXXV, col. 214.
9. *Ibid.*, col. 103.
10. Samuel Macauley Jackson, *Selected Works of Huldreich Zwingli* (Philadelphia, 1901), p. 191.
11. *Ibid.*, p. 150.
12. *Quellen* IX, p. 178.

13. *Quellen* VI, p. 148.
14. *Quellen* II, pp. 125f.
15. *Quellen* V, p. 34.
16. Emil Egli, *Aktensammlung* No. 623.
17. *Quellen* II, p. 238.
18. *Quellen* V, p. 259.
19. *Quellen Hesse*, p. 221.
20. *Ibid.*, p. 223.
21. *M. Q. R.*, July 1931, p. 167.
22. *Ibid.*, July 1934, p. 133.

CHAPTER VIII (ROTTENGEISTER)

1. Cf. James Endell Tyler, *Oaths, Their Origin, Nature and History*, p. 30.
2. George Gordon Coulton, *op. cit.*, p. 188.
3. Quoted in Van Bragt, *Martyrs Mirror* (Scottdale, 1951), p. 316a.
4. *Corpus*, I, p. 55.
5. Quoted in Van Bragt, *op. cit.*, p. 312b.
6. *Corpus*, I, p. 32.
7. George Gordon Coulton, *op cit.*, p. 186.
8. De Hullu, *Bescheiden Betreffende de Hervorming in Overyssel*, Vol. I, p. 132.
9. *B. R. N.*, VIII, p. 76.
10. Cf. Calvin's letter to de Falais, dated March, 1546.
11. *Quellen* VI, p. 75.
12. Quoted in Van Bragt, *op. cit.*, p. 438b.
13. Samuel Macauley Jackson, *op. cit.*, p. 209.
14. Cornelius Krahn, *Menno Simons* (Karlshruhe, 1936), p. 161.
15. W. H. C. Frend, *The Donatist Church* (Oxford, 1952), p. 196.
16. George Gordon Coulton, *Death Penalty for Heresy* (London, 1924), p. 8.
17. *Corpus*, I, p. 42.
18. *Recovery*, p. 146.
19. *Ibid.*, p. 114.
20. *Quellen Hesse*, p. 87.
21. *Werke*, St. Louis edition, Vol. VI, col. 461.
22. *Ibid.*, Vol. VIII, col. 4.
23. *Quellen Hesse*, p. 102.
24. George Gordon Coulton, *op. cit.*, p. 175.
25. Charles W. Ransom, *That the World May Know* (1953), p. 67.
26. Cf. *Christianity Today* of October 12, 1962, p. 33.
27. *Recovery*, pp. 97f.
28. Henry Hart Milman, *The History of Christianity, from the Birth of Christ to the Abolition of Paganism in the Roman Empire*, in three volumes (London, 1867-1875), Vol. II, p. 287.
29. Cecil John Cadoux, *The Early Church and the World* (Edinburgh, 1925), p. 558.
30. *Ibid.*, p. 589
31. Herbert Grundmann, *Die Religiöse Bewegungen im Mittelalter* (Hildesheim, 1961), p. 96, n. 48.

32. Ernst Corell, *Das Schweizerische Täufermennonitentum* (Tübingen, 1925), p. 23.
33. *Quellen* VI, p. 17.

POSTSCRIPT

1. Quoted by Paul Peachey in *Recovery*, p. 334.

Index

Agape, 136ff.
Alanus of Lille, 150
A Lasco, John, 253f.
Albigensians, 99
Alexander III (pope), 169
Alexander, Pierre, 249
Alting, Hendrik, 91
Alting, Menso, 86
Amandus, 69
Amish, 219
Andres auf den Stultzen, 233
Anselm of Laon, 165n.
Anti-Revolutionair, 87n.
Apostles' Creed, 34
Apostolic succession, 142
Aquinas, Thomas, 43, 119n.
Armstrong, Edward, 238n.
Augustine, 33n., 37, 65ff., 112n., 262

Barbes, 178n., 179
Bartmänner, 267n.
Barth, Karl, 213n., 214n.
Beck, Josef, 14n., 189
Belgic Confession, 48, 57, 70, 79f., 104, 120n., 221, 241, 252
Bellius, Martin, 53f.
Bender, Harold, 209
Berengarius, 143
Berkouwer, G. C., 99n., 214n., 252n.
Berne, 109
Beza, Theodor, 54ff., 83ff., 90, 92
Blaurock, Georg, 74, 233, 251
Black Death, 146, 170
Bogerman, Johannes, 56ff., 60, 84ff.
Bohemian Brethren, 64, 124n., 158, 197
Bougres, 99f.
Bouwens, Leendert, 118n.
Breskens (Classis), 88
Broer Cornelis, 227

"Brother Michael," 194
Brownists, 193n.
Brunner, Emil, 24n., 33n., 93n., 268
Bucer, Martin, 76, 107n., 111, 154, 203, 213
Bullinger, Henry, 60, 75f., 109, 110, 208

Calvin, John, 50ff., 57ff., 80ff., 102n., 120n., 123, 174n., 177, 179f., 228f.
Cantor, Peter 248
Canterbury Tales, The, 170
Capito, 108
Carey, William, 268
Castellio, 92
Cat-cult, 195n.
Catharer, 95ff.
Cathedrals, 165
Celsus, 161n.
Chanteries, 178n.
Charlemagne, 69, 191
Chelcicky, Peter, 70
Chianforan (Synod), 178
Christening, 190
Christian Reformed Church, 215n., 270n.
"Church visible," 82f.
Circumcelliones, 37, 258
Circumcision, 211
Clement VI (pope), 171
Cochlaeus, Johann, 228
Codes of Theodoslus, 190
Codes of Justinian, 52n., 169
Cogley, John, 187
Common grace, 24, 62n.
Community of wives, 226f.
Conscientious objectors, 271
Constantine (the Great), 31, 70, 83, 91
Constantinianism, 33
Cornelius, C. A., 39, 145
Council of Verona, 247

Cross-bearing, 256ff.
Cumulus lapidum, 167

Damian, Peter, 87, 101
De Beaumanoir, Philippe, 44
De Brès, Guido, 52n., 118n.
De Bruys, Pierre, 194
Decius, 29, 137
De Hiellin, Jehan, 150
Denck, Hans, 75
Deutsche Messe, 127, 183
Dewey, John, 25n., 278
Discipline, 118ff., 122ff.
Docetism, 253
Dominicans, 266f.
Donatism, 32ff., 39, 48f., 64f., 96f.,
    104, 113, 120n., 126, 164, 192,
    222, 258, 262
Donatisten, 21ff.
Dordt, Synod of, 60, 88
Dorsch, Jörg, 231f.
Dostoevsky, 33
Dualism, 98, 209, 252n.

Ebrard, 99
Eckebertus of Schonau, 98, 166, 173
Emden Disputation, 86, 130, 181n.,
    211, 263
Emser, Jerome, 239
Episcopalian, 157
Epistle to Diognetus, The, 26
Etienne de Bourbon, 152
Ex opere operato, 140, 157n.

Farel, William, 178
Farner, Alfred, 18n., 39n., 120n.,
    125n., 136n., 213n.
First Amendment, 61, 187, 277, 280
Flagellantes, 146, 170, 171n.
Frend, W. H. C., 32
Friedmann, Robert, 217

Gooch, George P., 193n., 237
"Good Christians," 150
Great Commission, 66, 268
Grebel, Conrad, 106, 120, 205, 260
Gregory of Nazianzus, 245
Gronginger Edict, 85f., 161n., 228,
    250n.

Grundmann Herbert, 98, 150, 165
Gui, Bernard, 246

Hadorn, Wilhelm, 154n.
Hagepreken, 160, 178n., 180
Harnack, Adolf von, 35, 272
Hausmann, Nicolas, 127
Hedge-priest, 160
Hedio, Caspar, 46n.
"Heretic," 72
Heidelberg Catechism, 92, 249
Hilary of Poitiers, 71, 164, 167
Hobhouse, Walter, 41f.
"Hocus pocus," 141n.
Hübmaier, Balthasar, 103n., 105n.,
    155n., 157n., 167n., 200, 203n.,
    231
Hus, John, 72
Hussite Churches, 149
Hut, Hans, 105
Hutter, Jakob, 236

Idolothyta, 27
Innocent III (pope), 168, 273n.
Institutes (of Calvin), 102n., 120n.,
    125n., 139n.

Janssen, H. Q., 88n., 89n.
John XXII (pope), 225n.
Jurgens, Diederich, 156

Keller, Ludwig, 152, 197n.
Knipperdollinck, Bernhard, 113
Kommunisten, 221ff.
Krafft, Adam, 77, 262
Krahn, Cornelius, 131n., 155
Kuchenbacker, Hans, 114
Kuyper, Abraham, 61, 62, 79n.

Landeskirche, 212
"Larger fulfillment," 67, 130n., 265
Leo the Great (pope), 222
Leufer, 151n., 174, 182, 226n.,
    263ff.
Leurle, Georg, 148n.
Liebesmahle, 166
Littell, Franklin H., 229n., 268n.
Lollards, 170
Los, Peter, 115

Lucius III (pope), 169
Luther, 17ff., 37, 48f., 72ff., 107f., 126f., 140n., 157n., 183f., 196, 201, 262

Manz, Felix, 74, 121, 205, 217
Mapes, Walter, 143n., 168n.
Marcion, 272n.
Margaret of Parma, 52n., 191
Marpeck, Pilgram, 74f., 110
McGiffert, Arthur Cushman, 126n.
"Means of grace," 136n.
Melanchthon, 52, 209
"Meister Hans," 185
Menius, Justus, 104, 129
Monism, 62n., 209
Müller, Lydia, 226
Müntzer, Thomas, 120, 238
Münster, 100, 237
Mysterion, 137f.

Nazism, 82n.
Newbigin, Lesslie, 270
Nicodemitism, 172f.
Noll, Tilemann, 49
Noordmans, 82n.
Norbertus, 145
Nordlingen, 198n.

Oath, 244ff.
Octavius, 95n.
Oecolampadius, 204
Old Testament, 209
Olivianus, Caspar, 92
Origen, 30

Pallor, 100
Parable of the Tares, 116n.
Patrimonium, 66n.
Payne, Ernest A., 112n.
Peasant Revolt, 238
Pelagius (pope), 71
Penn, William, 91
Perfectionism, 103
Peter the Venerable, 195
Philip of Hesse, 108, 182, 206
Philips, Dirck, 210
Pijper, 154
Plato, 135, 162n.

Pleonexia, 224
Potion, 110f.
Purgatory, 134n.

Reckenhofer, 248
Reformed Journal, 66n.
Restitutionists, 40
Rhegius, Urbanus, 50, 73f., 78, 113
Rhode Island, 93n.
Rieker, Karl, 58n.
Rinck, Melchior, 181
Robinson, John, 186
Röhrich, T. W., 185
Rottengeister, 243ff.

Sacramentarian, 142n.
Sacramentschwärmer, 132ff.
Sacramentum, 137ff.
Saint Louis, 168n.
Sattler, Michael, 105, 197
Sauberment, 156
Sauermilch, 156
Schleicher, 184
Schlatten am Rande, 50, 57ff., 122f., 230
Schnabel, Jörg, 112, 232n., 239f.
Schwartzhaus, 206
Schwenkfeld, 108f., 128
Seckler, Hans, 205
"Sect," 200n.
Servetus, Michael, 50ff.
Seu, Johannes, 90
Shintoism, 273
Simons, Menno, 103, 140, 234, 237, 253f., 263f.
Sonderkirche, 209
Stäbler, 63ff.
Stephen (king of Poland), 89n.
Strasbourg, 46, 196, 202n., 203
Sweet, William W., 89n.
Sylvester (pope), 70
Synod of Dordt, 60, 88

Tanchelm, 144
Tertullian, 28f., 30, 73, 274
Tesch, Peter, 218
Theodosius, 33n., 34
Thulin, Chillebert, 150
Tibbe, 195n.

Toynbee, Arnold, 237
Transubstantiation, 141
Troeltsch, Ernst, 91
Truand, 174
Turlupins, 100
"Two swords," 42, 46, 57

Unam Sanctam, 43
Usury, 226

Van Arkel, Jan, 146
Van Bingen, Hildegarde, 166
Van der Zijpp, 155n.
Van Haemstede, Adrian, 255
Van Maastricht, Leonhard, 111
Veluanus, Anastasius, 157n.
Verona (Council of), 151
Von Usingen, Bartholomäus, 197n.

Waldensians, 44, 64, 131n., 143n.,
    147, 152f., 173, 175f., 178, 195f.
Wassenberg, 156, 196f.

Wazo, 71
Weavers, 165ff.
Wesley, John, 186
Wiedertäufer, 189ff.
Wiek, Bernard, 122
Wieland, Philips, 44
Willem of Utrecht, 248
William of Newburgh, 149
Williams, George H., 15f., 134n.,
    149n.
Williams, Roger, 185
Winckelehe, 161
Winckler, 160ff.
Winfrid (Boniface), 69
Wurzlburger, August, 232

Zachers, Casper, 109
Zaunring, Georg, 167
Zwangtaufe, 69n., 192, 206
Zwingli, Huldreich, 11, 38, 106,
    145f., 154n., 166, 198ff., 203,
    213n., 214f., 230, 251, 274